Teaching

Social Studies

in the

Elementary School

Alpha Gama Delta
Sue Bettestelli
21st Feb
5:30 (Tue.)

Teaching
Social Studies
in the
Elementary School

JOHN R. LEE

THE FREE PRESS
A Division of Macmillan Publishing Co., Inc.
NEW YORK

Collier Macmillan Publishers
LONDON

The Free Press
A Division of Macmillan Publishing Co., Inc.
866 Third Avenue, New York, N.Y. 10022

Collier–Macmillan Canada Ltd.

Library of Congress Catalog Card Number: 73–14017

Printed in the United States of America

printing number
1 2 3 4 5 6 7 8 9 10

Library of Congress Cataloging in Publication Data (Revised)

Lee, John R
    Teaching social studies in the elementary school.

    Includes bibliographies.
    1. Social sciences--Study and teaching (Elementary)
I. Title.
LB1584.L42   372.8·3·044   73-14017
ISBN 0-02-918370-7

Contents

669-3834

Dedicated to my mentors . . .

Paul Hanna and Norton Pearl.

Editor's Introduction

A distinguished professor who reviewed the manuscript for John R. Lee's *Teaching Social Studies in the Elementary School* wrote in his extensive critique that the content and author's writing style will "motivate the student to want to read this book." In summary the reviewer said of the book, "It is unpretentious, well-written, has a conversational writing style, amusing, yet highly relevant anecdotes and lucid, carefully developed prescriptions for teaching." Superlatives are appropriate for describing both the content and style of this book.

The book is written in clear and concise language with a specific and understandable focus. Unlike many textbooks that purport to be comprehensive but in fact are panoramically superficial, this one concentrates on carefully selected topics and deals with each one thoroughly. The author does what few textbook writers do and that is "practice what he preaches." By precept and example, by theory and illustration, through content and methodology, John Lee teaches through this book.

It is not possible for me to write about this book without writing about the author as well. John R. Lee is a gifted teacher-scholar. His teaching is esteemed by both prospective and experienced teachers as well as his colleagues. Evidence of his effectiveness as a teacher is the tribute paid by Northwestern University students on Honors Day last year when the Outstanding Teacher Award was bestowed upon him. Experienced teachers for whom frequently he does demonstration teaching accord him the status of master teacher.

Professor Lee's versatility and stature as a scholar can be documented extensively. His bibliography is distinguished. It includes books for children, texts for social studies teachers, invited papers in scholarly journals, more than a hundred films and film strips, and much of the material in the law-focused education program of the Law in American Society Foundation. A previously published book in the *Introduction to Teaching* series is highly regarded by professors, high school teachers, and students.

Is this book appropriate as a text for elementary social studies methods courses? For continuing education of experienced teachers? For professors who give methods courses? The answer is yes to all three questions, in my judgment. John Lee points out in the first chapter that no single book can cover everything. He encourages the study of supplementary books and parsimoniously suggests additional readings.

It is the author's judgment, and mine, that teachers of social studies in elementary schools want understandable, sensible, concrete illustrations that can be used in real classrooms. John Lee has provided useful concepts, basic content, and applied illustrations in this book. It therefore is characteristic of the teaching methods books in the Free Press *Introduction to Teaching* series.

My own prognosis is that *Teaching Social Studies in the Elementary School* will be enjoyable and useful for both prospective and experienced teachers as well as for professors who work in this field.

B. J. Chandler, Dean
School of Education
Northwestern University

Preface

*Above all else, making wise choices
is the first quality of a teacher.*

Good teachers are practical professionals. They know there are a few things worth teaching well, and they have decided which of these they will stress. They develop the use of materials and activities to a high point of common sense. They expect results and know they get them when the behavior of pupils changes.

Good teachers are professionals, because they think about their beliefs and their behaviors. They abandon old theories before their thoughts about education stagnate. They avoid the new shibboleths that others substitute for thoughts about education. They learn from the writings and examples of others by judging them against standards of logic, humaneness, and predictable consequences. Professionals operate from a theoretical base because they believe that, if they do specific things with specific students under specific conditions, then specific results will occur.

Good teachers are practical, because they test their ideas about education in the crucibles of reflective thought and classroom results. They abandon beliefs that do not produce desirable results. They avoid practices and materials that bore children or produce trivial results. They learn by judging the results of their performance against the standard of valued changes in pupil behaviors.

This book will not tell you how to teach, but it will describe how others have taught social studies. When you have read it, you will know there are many ways children learn social studies. When you have read it, you will still need to decide if any of these ideas and procedures will be of use to you.

Note 1: In this book, any similarities to teachers, living or dead, is intentional, and I hope they are pleased.

Note 2: For my convenience, throughout this book I have usually used the pronoun *she* to refer to a teacher and the pronoun *he* to refer to a pupil. The choice was made by flipping a coin. I explain this because I don't want to be accused, for unimportant reasons, of being a sexist.

Note 3: I want especially to thank B. J. Chandler, Joe Park, Bill Joyce, John Wick, Lisa Polakoff, and Susan Dye Lee for their nagging encouragement.

John Lee
Evanston, Illinois
and Woodruff, Wisconsin

Social Studies and Learning

Grace Jessup was my fourth-grade teacher. I don't remember anything specific in reading or science or arithmetic learned from her classes, but social studies was another story.

"What are the three greatest nations in the world today?" she would ask.

"England, France, and the United States!" we would chorus.

"How do you know?"

"It was in our book!"

"Which do you think will be the three greatest nations when you grow up?" When Mrs. Jessup asked that question, the funniest little smile came over her face.

"England, France, and the U.S. of A.!"

"I don't think so," she would say. "Why do *you* think I don't think you are right?"

Thus began the hunt for an answer to Mrs. Jessup's question. We had a mystery to solve. What did Mrs. Jessup think, and why did she think what she did?

We tried guessing, and she let us guess. But she would always ask why we guessed what we did and that would stump us.

"The U.S.A. will still be a great nation when we grow up," we said.

"Why do you think that?" she would ask.

"Because it's our nation!"

"That's an answer, but it's not a reason," she would say. "Your answer tells me what your attitude is. You like the idea of the United States being great. So no matter what question I ask about nations, if I use words like good or strong or rich, then you will say 'the United States.' Now, *why* do you think the United States will be a great nation when you grow up?"

In time we settled on an answer for that question. We found what we called *evidence*. Size, population, resources, industrial capacity, location, respect for learning, the ability to apply knowledge in solving problems—we cited all these in favor of the United States. Then Mrs. Jessup said she agreed with us. But what were the other two nations?

How we worked to discover those two mystery nations. We read our textbooks. We pored over the atlas. We dug into the encyclopedias. We poked around the library. We spun the globe. Then it hit us: If the United States would remain great because of certain characteristics, what other nations would have most or all of the same characteristics?

We tested France and England against those characteristics and found they didn't measure up. What nations did? Russia? China? That was the answer we said, Russia and China were the other two!

"Why Russia and China?" asked Mrs. Jessup.

"Because of the evidence!" we said. And we could cite our evidence.

Mrs. Jessup agreed with us and with our evidence, but she wasn't done asking questions. "Do we know this will be true? Or do we believe it will become true?"

LEARNING FROM BOOKS AND QUESTIONS

We learned a number of things from Mrs. Jessup. We learned something about the differences among attitudes, beliefs, and knowledge. We learned all the good questions were not at the end of the chapter and all the answers were not printed out for us in the book. We learned to believe in the likelihood of change, and we learned to predict changes that might occur. We learned to use reference books, and we learned to combine facts from several sources into an organized statement. We learned to draw conclusions and to recognize the difference between an applicable and a tentative conclusion. We also learned to get along with each other in a classroom where there was more freedom of movement and speech than we had had in other classes.

Social studies to Mrs. Jessup was the study of five major topics: man, ideas, environment, time, and space. The content for study was drawn from the social sciences and adapted by authors for use with elementary-school pupils. The method was inquiry into questions that could only be answered by thinking about information drawn from a number of sources.

We learned facts, but we learned them in their relationships to one another. We didn't learn our facts merely by reading and memorizing and reciting. We learned our facts because we *needed* them, because we *found* them, because we *used* them.

Quite frankly, Mrs. Jessup believed we learned social studies because we would need our knowledge and skills to be good citizens when we grew up. Someday, we would have to earn a living, influence our government, get along with each other. She wanted us to be able to sustain and improve the society we would inherit.

LEARNING FROM CLASS ACTIVITIES

Miss Shepherd was another teacher I remember. She taught fifth grade and she also taught my Sunday-school class. I remember her partly because she was one of the two Sunday-school teachers who did *not* tell me I would automatically go to hell if I smoked or took a drink when I grew up.

I also remember her because she was always asking questions about right and wrong. "Was it right for one man to have another man as a slave?" How I looked in books for the answer to that question. But the books never answered the question. They just stated that some men were slaves. I found one book that said slaves in the South were happy. I shared my discovery about the happiness of slaves with two of my young buddies. We announced our finding to the class and defended it by claiming that if it was in a book, it must be true.

Our "fact" led to one activity and our "defense" led to another. The class was asked to search through books for statements that might not be true. And Miss Shepherd made the three of us slaves for a week.

What a week! We were put in the hall during social studies so we couldn't learn with the class. We were given boring jobs to do as we sat in the hall. We couldn't just goof off, because if the job wasn't done, we worked right into recess. But even recess was no longer great fun, for no one would play with us. We had to serve the other kids. "Fetch that ball!" "Bring me a drink of water!" (No one before had ever had a drink of water *brought* to them on the playground.)

We had to say "Sir" and "Mam" to our classmates, but they could make up names for us. Nothing during the week quite bothered me as much as losing my name. I was called Snotnose; this outraged me because my nose was kept as clean as any kid's. Miss Shepherd really didn't like the word, but she used it with a vengeance.

We were given the worst seats and the oldest books. We had to write on the back of used paper, and we had to beg pencil stubs from other pupils. We had to rise to speak, although no one else did.

Miss Shepherd talked to our parents and certain arrangements were made with them. We got no allowance for that week, we had to wear our shabbiest clothes, and our shoes and socks were taken from us when we got to school. We couldn't take lunches with us (in those days we all carried our lunch) and for lunch we were given what looked like scraps from some-one else's lunch. Years later Miss Shepherd told me she had made sand-wiches, cut the centers out, and torn the crusts up. We had actually eaten clean food, but at the time we thought the scraps came from the lunches of other pupils.

There was more, of course. We were ignored most of the time, and when we were noticed it was in a derogatory way. By the second day, we were plotting to beat up certain kids, but that had been anticipated. Miss Van Avery, the principal, had a chilling chat with us. If we even touched one classmate, she promised she would take care of us. Her threat was enough; we lived with frustration.

By the end of the week, we were becoming paranoid. We were mean, resentful, frustrated. We were losing confidence in ourselves. For the first time since I had begun school, I had cried; they were tears of rage, to be sure, but they were real tears. After I cried, a few classmates began to act a little differently toward me. Some began to ask rather than demand. A few stopped having anything to do with me. One girl gave me her new pencil one day—a whole, new, yellow pencil, the eraser hadn't even been chewed. I kept it hidden so no one would take it from me.

The last hour of that week was spent talking about happiness in slavery. Miss Shepherd kept asking questions about what was right and what was wrong.

Not long after the three of us had been liberated, a new boy joined our class. Today, all I really remember about him was that he wasn't really good at anything, and he was so poor he didn't have shoes; he just wore overshoes over his socks. The three of us hadn't fully recovered from slavery, and I remember being torn between two courses of action toward the new boy. To an extent, I wanted to pick on him; I seemed to need someone to look down upon. To an extent, I felt sympathetic; it wasn't *his* fault his parents were too poor to buy shoes.

Miss Shepherd knew what was going on. She didn't raise any questions with the class, but I remember her talking with some of us about what might be the right thing to do with the new boy. We talked about how he must feel in a strange group. We talked about how there were no "rules" for dealing with newcomers. We talked about what a person might do when there were no rules.

Social studies to Miss Shepherd was the study of human behavior in group situations. The content for study was drawn from life in the classroom and the school. The method was inquiry into the reasons people did what they did and into the question of differences between what was done and what ought to have been done.

We learned to set standards and to judge behavior and the products of behavior by those standards. I don't suppose our standards were always the best possible standards, but we were at least thinking before we acted on some important issues. We learned that there were legal reasons for saying something was right. We learned there were moral reasons. We learned there were practical reasons. And we learned that sometimes there were conflicts among legal, moral, and pragmatic reasons.

Miss Shepherd believed we studied social studies because what we learned made a difference in our youthful lives. She wanted fairly immediate results, but she must have felt that what we were in the present would be reflected in what we became in the future.

LEARNING FROM "OUR VILLAGE"

When I was eleven, we moved to a very small village. There were two rooms in the school. The first five grades were taught on the first floor by a woman. Grades six through ten were taught on the second floor. My teacher was a man, and I'll leave him unnamed because I didn't really like him. I'm not sure why I didn't like him, but at the time I thought it was because he used to take the desserts out of our lunchpails, which he made us leave in the hallway by the stairs.

The village was too poor to buy many books. We had old arithmetics and readers and spellers. We had no books for science or social studies. The teacher didn't know what to do about social studies. He knew some Greek and Roman myths, so he told us myths during the coldest of winter months.

In the fall and spring we went for walks. We identified trees and birds and animals—it was quite clear that we knew more than he did so we taught each other. The teacher just walked along looking at the ground.

For some reason, we began to draw maps. We mapped every foot of that village. And then we got interested in why things were where they were. We began to ask questions of people in the village. "Why was this store built here?" "Who named the streets?" (There were four of them.) "Who numbered the houses?" "Who owned the school grounds?" Who? Why? Where? When? What if? We were curious kids.

The people in the village turned out to be great resources. One old lady knew the history of everything and everybody. She sat in a rocking chair on her porch sucking a cud of snuff tucked under her lower lip. We learned about not spitting to windward from her. We also learned who built what and who had lived in it and why they moved.

A businessman named Mr. Oliver sold Chevrolets (more pickups than passenger cars). He told us what it took to run a business. He told us about costs and about making a profit (I had thought everyone was paid a salary). He explained taxes, which he disliked because his were the highest in the village. He told us about the electric company and one day loaded all of us in a new Chevy truck and took us to the electric plant by the dam. The teacher agreed to the trip because he got to ride in front with Mr. Oliver.

The local surveyor lived in the village, and with his help, we redrew all our maps. We learned to use a transit and chain. We learned more math from that man than we did from books. The surveyor was also the mayor. The village really wasn't incorporated, but that didn't stop the people from having a local government. They had a town hall and town meetings. Anyone could attend town hall, and most did. Anyone could have his say, and most did. They passed ordinances by voice vote (only the election of the mayor and the marshal was by secret ballot). There was a justice of the peace who lived in town (he was elected by the township voters). There was no jail, but drunks were locked in a coal shed until they sobered up. It wasn't until later that I realized that these rudiments of government were all extralegal (except for the justice of peace). But legal or not, the "ord-nunsuhs" were effective because people agreed they were "right."

We learned something from almost everyone in town. We learned local history and local geography. We learned some economics and some politics and some sociology. And the boys learned about anthropology from looking at *National Geographics*. For a long time I thought anthropology was the photographic study of "half-nekked" women in hot and distant lands.

In this last case, what the teacher thought was social studies was not important. What was important was what we thought. Social studies was the study of everybody and everything in our village. The content was life as it was lived in a particular place, with some attention given to the influence of past events on the future. The methods were observing and questioning; the motives were curiosity about what made things tick and the sneaking suspicion that we needed to know because someday we would make things tick.

The teacher wasn't important to our study of life in our village, but it is to his credit that he didn't kill our curiosity. He didn't directly encourage curiosity, but he didn't dampen it either. As long as we were no trouble to him, we were free to learn.

THE MEANING OF SOCIAL STUDIES

Quite obviously, I chose these three examples because I remember them with fondness and because they illustrate my beliefs about social studies. (If I had drawn my examples from the life of a child today, I would have added a fourth type of experience. Today's child uses television, and his experiences with TV provide him with information about life outside his own immediate community.)

Social studies deals with mankind's social, economic, and political behavior, at any place where people live or have lived, now or in the past. I use the term *behavior* to mean what people have thought, felt, said, or done. By implication, behavior also refers to causes and reasons, and to results and consequences. My definition also implies that the social studies are related to the subject matters of history, geography, philosophy, and the various social sciences. Those academic disciplines focus on human behavior, whether it be people in relation to other people, people in relation to their environment, or people in relation to ideas; the focus may vary in time, space, or value, but one element always remains in the picture— people.

The content of social studies can be drawn from four sources: the academic disciplines dealing with human behavior, the lives of children, the lives of those in the immediate community, and the lives of people in other communities as they are reported to us in the communications media. The social-studies textbook and other commercially prepared materials generally represent subject matter drawn from the academic disciplines and adapted for use with children of certain ages and certain reading abilities. When teachers, as many do, tend to draw content exclusively from textbooks, they prevent the child from participating intellectually in classroom affairs, and they cut him off from a guided interpretation of events in his local community and in other, more distant communities. In my experience, the thoughtful teacher blends content from each of these sources and thus creates a wider body of content with greater potential for learning than could be gained from the exclusive use of any one source.

Among the major reasons for studying social studies are the acquisition of knowledge, the refinement of standards, and the development of reasoned thought. Each of these—knowledge, standards, and reasoning—is a product of thinking about experiences one has had. It is not enough to read about knowledge, hear about standards, and be told about reasoning. One has to think about them, apply them, and think again about the results of applying them.

Every society is concerned with the behavior of its members. Man is a social being; he must belong to a group or groups so that his needs may be met. If his needs are to be met, man must act, and as acts have consequences, each man has some vested interest in those acts of others that may affect him. There is no society without its social organization, without its economic system, without its political structure. Our society believes it needs members who can act wisely in social, economic, and political affairs. Knowledge is acquired, standards are refined, and reasoning is developed so that an individual can act in personally satisfying and socially acceptable ways.

Ours is an urban, technological, and industrial society. Ours is a changing society. Our stated ideals have not been fulfilled; all of us have not yet achieved what we mean by life, liberty, and the pursuit of happiness. Each generation has its own problems to solve; some are persisting problems, some are unique. Some men will have to cry out against injustice in every generation. Some will have to shout that we aren't moving fast enough; some will have to insist society is changing too quickly. Each generation moves us toward or away from our ideals, and thus our institutions, arrangements and systems must constantly be reexamined so some may be discarded, some may be repaired, and some may be replaced. Discarding, repairing, replacing are operations involving change. And change occurs because men act.

The basic justification for teaching social studies is the contribution it can make to an individual's potential for acting wisely in human affairs.

The subject matters of social studies deal with past, present, and future human events. These subject matters provide examples of men and women, by themselves and in groups, who have acted wisely or unwisely in the past and in the present. The key term in my definition of social studies is *acting wisely*. By acting wisely, I mean actions based on knowledge and judged as humane. Such acts are based on reliable information and sound reasoning. Such acts are free of the passions known as cruelty or brutality. Such acts are seen as desirable to the individual and to society. We teach social studies, in part, because the social studies deal with topics from which pupils may create their own criteria for acting wisely and then test those criteria against the events of the past and the issues of the present.

In today's troubled world, teachers worry about intervening in the beliefs and values of children. If by "intervening," the teacher means telling children what to believe and value, then she should worry. The teacher who feels she can safely avoid being an influence is silly. The teacher's very presence is an intervention; her smile, her tone of voice, her choice of words, her stance, her gestures—these are all intervening variables in an atmosphere of learning. "I don't want to talk about that, Mary." "Bill, that's the stupidest idea I've heard in years." "How do you think, Jennifer, that your idea will make a difference in your life?" All three comments intervene somehow in what pupils believe or value. The real question is: *how* will you intervene? Will you intervene in a manner calculated to increase a pupil's dependence on authority or habit or tradition? Or will you intervene in a manner intended to aid a child in retesting his beliefs and reexamining his values?

As you think about what you read in this book, I hope you will challenge much of what I have written. Naturally, I'd like you to become my kind of teacher, but I'd not like it if you did so without developing for yourself the capacity for acting wisely in your interactions with children.

PREVIEWS

The remainder of this book breaks into four parts. *Basic Definitions,* the part following this chapter, deals with the meanings of terms important to social studies today. In each case, I deal with the characteristics of the idea, its uses, and I try to use the idea in some easily recognizable situation. Although some of these terms are used in everyday language—fact, attitude, problem—they do have fairly specialized meanings. Time after time, I hear teachers say, "I gave him a good talking to, but his attitude didn't change a bit." Of course it didn't, for attitudes characteristically are marked by persistence; further, it's an unusual teacher who is seen as a *favorable* authority figure able to influence an attitude by merely passing judgment. You may believe you had all this "stuff" before—you did take Ed Psych 101—but experience has taught me that most prospective teachers never get enough concrete examples in ed psych to understand what "developing a concept" means in the hurly-burly of classroom give-and-take.

The second part, *Decisions, Decisions,* focuses on that difficult business of deciding upon goals and tests, on knowing where you want to go and realizing when you get there. Are all your goals oriented to subject matter? Or are you concerned about research skills, human relations and valuing? What issues in our nation and the world might influence your choices? And what about your pupils—do their backgrounds influence your choices? Does it matter if they are black or white, lower class or middle class, central city or suburban? Do you have a professional right to alter a proscribed social-studies program for their benefit? This section deals with such questions and some answers to them.

The third part, *The Squares,* treats some of the more conventional practices of social studies. Some of you, of course, have vowed never to teach the way you were taught. Textbooks are out! Love is in! But are textbooks always bad? Is using a textbook always always foolish? I don't think so. These four chapters should provide you with a number of ideas about how to use textbooks to achieve what you and your pupils want. In a way, these chapters deal with how to use conventional materials to gain unconventional ends.

The fourth part, *The Swingers,* is my favorite part of this book. It provides a basis for introducing action, variety, fun, and thinking into a classroom. If I liked long titles, this part would have been called "Learning Social Studies without Emphasizing Reading." These activities tend to trigger pupil interests and to generate pupil inquiry. They lead to reading. In fact, they demand reading be undertaken if pupils are to find answers to their own questions. The point, however, is that, when you use these highly active procedures, reading becomes subordinated to thinking.

The closing chapter, "Potpourri," makes my pitch for the future of social studies. It won't tell you much about how to teach; I just hope it leaves you with a pleasant memory of the book I wanted to call *My Kind of Teacher.*

SUGGESTED READINGS

A decade ago a methods text needed a long list of books and articles at the end of every chapter. These lists were impressive and sometimes useful. Along with an inch or two of footnotes on every other page, they gave an appearance of scholarship. The lists provided the author an opportunity to name his friends and to mention other authors who had earlier mentioned his articles or books. The lists helped the reader who wanted more information or who wanted to consult original sources. They helped the college instructor by providing him with ready-made lists. They also helped the book salesman by showing his book had more entries than his competitor's books.

Today, there are a number of good books of readings on elementary social studies on the market. Most libraries contain copies of these books of readings, and thus additional readings on every topic in social studies are readily available to the student of social studies. For that reason, I believe it a waste of my time, your time, and your professor's time to include a long list of readings at the end of each of my chapters.

If you are a serious student of the social sciences, you should continue to keep up with these academic disciplines as you study methods. I believe you should read some of the articles in the books of readings, and I believe you should at least skim the methods books written by my competitors. Some of them have strengths my book lacks; some of them have ideas and approaches I haven't mentioned; some of them will appeal to your biases. None of us writing on social studies could possibly cover everything in a single book. Some of us wouldn't if we could. You need more than my book, even if you should agree with my ideas about teaching social studies. This sort of outside reading will provide the basis for comparison and contrast we all need if we are to act wisely in teaching children.

Now that I have expressed my distaste for long lists and my reasons for believing they are no longer necessary, let me say that I sometimes find a book or an article so significant that I can't resist suggesting it to you. Some of my suggestions will be recent publications; some will be "oldies but goodies." In most cases they will meet two of these three criteria: they gave me a new idea, they made me rethink some idea, and they were fun to read. For Chapter 1, I recommend—

Baier, Kurt, and Nicholas Rescher (eds.), *Values and the Future*. Paperback ed. New York: Free Press, 1971. (A sound look into the future of values that is applicable to education. Difficult in places, but of high interest.)

Boulding, Kenneth E., *The Meaning of the Twentieth Century*. New York: Harper & Row, 1965. (In my view, one of the significant books of the last decade. You have to make your own applications, but this book is worth every minute you spend on it.)

Dahl, Robert, *After the Revolution*. New Haven: Yale University Press, 1970. (A reasonable, conservative view of the future; especially good for the student who wants change but hates to burn the library as a symbol of change.)

Orwell, George, *Nineteen Eighty-Four*. New York: Harcourt, Brace & Co., 1949. (A socialist in a capitalistic world the author would probably have been a capitalist in a socialist world; a fine piece of literature, well ahead of its time.)

Skinner, B. F., *Beyond Freedom and Dignity*. New York: Bantam/Vintage, 1972. (Read him and believe or read him and weep; you can't be neutral about this book; he predicts a world we daren't ignore.)

Toffler, Alvin, *Future Shock*. New York: Bantam Books, 1971. (Wham, bam, wow, and golly gee—look at the mess we're in! Great masses of descriptive, provocative information, but his prescriptions for salvation are weak tea.)

EXERCISES

1. Pick any book you have read from the list above. What relationships do you see between acting wisely or unwisely and what the author sees in your future?

2. Reminisce about your elementary-school teachers. Who stands out in your memory? For good reasons or poor ones? What do you remember about incidents or methods or materials that made a difference in the ways you want to teach?

3. Spend a few minutes writing out your reasons for teaching social studies. Compare your reasons with those of others in the class (this is really a value-clarification exercise). After reading this book, again write out your reasons. Compare your two written statements.

PART ONE

Basic Definitions

IN 1941, I enrolled in forestry in a cow college in Michigan. In 1942, the army put me in an engineering program at a Texas university. In 1948, I graduated from a non-cow college in Michigan with majors in history and English.

In 1949, I began building an addition to a school for a construction company in the Far West. There was a special class of special students in this school. These children were the sons and daughters of migrant farm workers. Their teacher thought they were stupid, and the principal acted as if he believed that stupidity was catching.

This group was isolated in their own room for all classes. They enjoyed recess only when no one else was on the playground. They couldn't play or sing or square dance with other students. They couldn't eat lunch in the lunchroom and they couldn't mix on the playground at noontime.

Quite naturally, they drifted onto our construction site at noon. They watched us eat our sandwiches and listened to us talk. They asked us questions: How did we know how thick to make the walls? How did we always get the corners of a room square? How did we get the floors flat? How did we make the holes in the walls fit the windows? How did we make plaster stick to the ceiling? On and on they went. Questions about carpentry, electricity, plumbing, equipment, tools, machines. Question after question after question.

Some of us helped them find answers. We drew pictures in the desert sand. We worked out problems by writing on pieces of lumber. We used blueprints to teach them to read. We used a cup of water to show them what level *meant. We hung a lead sinker on a string and they discovered what* plumb *meant. We used a tape and the Pythagorean theorem to make* square corners.

These children were not stupid, disinterested, or incapable of learning. They just needed a richer environment and a chance to reflect on their experiences. Nine months after I started building schools, I sold my tools and began looking for an elementary school that needed a male teacher.

Moral: *Never, never be useful to "stupid" kids*
        unless you want to end up a teacher.

Experience and Learning

All teachers of all subjects seek to help their pupils develop the potential for acting wisely. When you teach reading, you are teaching interpretation, as well as phonetic and structural analysis. When you teach art, you are teaching appreciation of form and color, as well as the ability to shape lines to represent reality.

With each subject, you try to teach something more than motor skills, or multiplying, or spelling, or hitting the right notes. That "something else" usually combines substantive and procedural knowledge. For example, a student claims there is a tundra line on all high mountains. You tell him you can't accept his assertion unless he can produce some evidence to support his claim. He checks an encyclopedia and returns to tell you that he meant "tree line" rather than tundra line.

Substantively, he probably has learned several associated facts about mountains, elevation, temperature, moisture, soil, and trees. Procedurally, he probably has learned to check the evidence when he is challenged about a statement he makes, to use the encyclopedia as a source of general information, and to state a relationship among associated facts. If, in the next situation where he must take a position on a topic open to question, he makes sure of his evidence before he makes an authoritative statement, then he has begun to act wisely.

Most teachers accept the notion that pupils "learn from experience." By this they mean that whatever happens to a person is an experience, that anything or everything you perceive, do, or live through is an experience.

And they mean the person gains skill, knowledge, and attitudes from his or her experience.

If teachers accept such obvious truths, why bother to include a chapter on experience in this book? Simple—because "accepting" does not necessarily mean understanding; nor does "accepting" mean teachers give much thought to the *quality* of the experiences their pupils have in school.

Most of us know the old saw about progress resulting from the ability to stand on the shoulders of others. When I first began to teach, I was the worst kind of trial-and-error performer. I had little experience with children, little knowledge of classroom activities, and no adequate theory of learning. Over my first three years with youngsters, as I gained experience, I began to realize theory was more useful than a bagful of trials and a pocketful of gimmicks.

I had read John Dewey in a philosophy class, and I thought him to be a dull fellow at best. His syntax was painful, he repeated himself, and he wasn't addressing himself to problems I was aware I had. And yet, from my work in construction I knew theory was related to practice in a very fundamental way. A carpenter operates with trial-and-error methods and certain rules of thumb, but a master carpenter also knows theory. A master carpenter not only knew a 12-point saw could cut hardwood molding cleaner than a 6-point saw, he knew how and why it could cut cleaner; the master carpenter never had to patch an inside corner with putty and then hope the foreman wouldn't see his patchwork. With this dim awareness of the value of theory as a spur, I went back to Dewey again and again. And as I began to pile up hours and weeks with children, I began to see what Dewey could mean to me.

The rest of this chapter really belongs to Dewey. Every idea in it is his. I don't think I've stolen his sentences, but I gratefully acknowledge that without him I'd have quit teaching years ago to sell insurance or pour cement or run for office.

THE FORM AND FUNCTION OF EXPERIENCE

Experience is a combination of the active and the passive, of trying and undergoing, of overt and covert behavior.

Two years ago, I decided to try my hand at organic gardening. I raked up my oak leaves, collected grass clippings, begged some manure from a farmer, and put together a neat compost pile. Last spring I spaded up a garden plot and mixed the compost with the soil. I put in my tomatoes and broccoli plants and planted peas and carrots. The tomatoes grew into enormous plants with exactly one huge tomato each; the broccoli was all stalk and leaf; I got one-inch carrots; but the peas grew like magic.

Anyone who has planted a garden knows I was overtly active. I planted, cultivated, weeded, watered, and sweated. I acted on my environment, but my activity didn't pay off. The consequences of my actions, except for the sweet peas, were plainly pitiful.

As for the covert element, I underwent mental agonies. I thought over what I had read in books. I recalled the instructions on the seed packets. I knew I had planted at the right times, at the proper depths, at the proper distances. I remembered and I reasoned, but I still didn't know how or why I had failed.

One day a neighbor dropped by. He looked at my garden and he looked at me. "Used a lot of compost did you?"

"Yup," I said. "Lots."

"Make your compost from oak leaves?"

"That's the kind of tree I've got," I said.

"Put any lime in the compost?"

"Nope."

"Put any on the garden?"

"Nope."

"You know oak leaves make an acid compost?"

"Nope."

"That's your problem."

According to the theory of experience, I had acted on something, and I had suffered the consequences. I recognized that there was a connection between what I had done and the way my garden turned out. What I didn't have was any meaning for that connection. My neighbor provided me with the key to the mistake I had made. In other words, my experience initially consisted of *an experiment* and *a failure to make a connection between the experiment and its consequences*. The difficulty was that although I saw a connection, the connection didn't mean anything until my neighbor helped me recognize the meaning of what had happened.

If my neighbor hadn't happened by, I would have gone on in my trial-and-error method, summer after summer, until I had stumbled onto the answer. Because he did come by and talk, I believe I can predict what will happen to my garden next summer, I have a little better control of the future than I had before. My extended experience consisted of *experiment-*

ing on my environment and *seeing the meaning in the connection between the experiment and its consequences.*

To summarize, an experience involves action and consequences, connections and meanings; it provides for a reorganization of what was known to accommodate what has been learned; it provides the power to predict and partly control the future.

THINKING AS AN ELEMENT IN EXPERIENCE

Much of what we do is done on a trial-and-error basis. We try this, we try that, we try another way, and we keep at it until we hit on something that works. Then we adopt the way that worked as a "key" to acting in similar, future situations.

After I did a bit more research on gardening, I confirmed two hypotheses: oak leaves do make an acidic compost, and lime added to the compost will neutralize the acid. I now considered the two hypotheses to be statements of fact; at least I believed they were facts, because my books on gardening were written by recognized authorities. I also thought out another hypothesis: if I added a slightly alkaline (lime is an alkali) compost to most of my garden and an acidic compost where I would grow peas, I would have a good crop, provided such other considerations as frost, sunshine, and rain were the same as they had been the year before. That is a testable hypothesis and I am ready for a new experience this summer.

Thinking, then, is part of what Dewey meant by the passive, or undergoing, element in an experience; thinking may not be overt, but unless it takes place, the experience won't produce meanings or understandings.

Suppose you are teaching kindergarteners. After an art class, a boy says to you, "Where do I put these scissors?"

"Where did you get them?"

"From the blue drawer," he says.

"Where do you think you should put them?"

"In the blue drawer?" he half asks and half states.

"Why do you think that?"

"So I will know where they are," he says.

"And?"

"So will everyone else," he says.

"How will they know?"

" 'Cause that's where the scissors go when you aren't using them."

"Why do they go there?"

"So we will know where to get them when we want them."

Instead of asking all these questions, you could say, "Put them in the blue drawer" enough times to enough children, that they would learn to put the scissors in the blue drawer. They would absorb this knowledge directly, but only a few of them would ever think, "Why?"

You could say, "If you put them in the blue drawer where they belong, then the next person who wants them will be able to find them." Some children would absorb this knowledge directly. And some would think about the connection between putting the scissors away and knowing where to find them later.

Sounds like a lot of trouble to do it the first way, doesn't it? It would be easier to tell the child what to do. "Obey the rule, kid, don't ask why!" But if you want to stimulate thinking, then you have to take the extra time and trouble. The child who gets seven lazy elementary teachers in a row gets seven years of drill, drudgery, and damnation. Even worse, every one of those lazy teachers will say, "Well, someone certainly killed his curiosity and imagination before he got to me."

Dewey says, "Thinking . . . is the intentional endeavor to discover specific connections between something we do and the consequences which result, so that the two become continuous. . . ." [1]

When we recognize a relationship between acts and consequences, we make an *inference;* we take one event or situation as evidence that something else occurs. There are those who maintain that only adults are capable of inference. Nonsense! A child who sees his mother with a bottle takes that bottle as evidence of something. The child can't say "inference," and he can't read the word, but he can make the inference. If you say, "This is sour milk; sour milk makes babies sick; so, baby, what is your inference?" the baby will only go "coo." For several reasons, you are setting that baby an impossible task—the inference you ask for lies beyond his vocabulary and meanings.

FACTS, ASSUMPTIONS, AND MEANINGS

Journalism students learn to work details of who, where, what, why, and when into the first sentence of the news stories they write.

On April Fool's Day, a Key Isle, Florida postman, angry at having been bitten by six small alligators in one block, picked up a seventh alligator and bit it on the tail. "I've got five more years on this route before retirement," commented Mr. Gnash, "and I hope this tale spreads!"

The item opens with a when-where-who-why-what sentence. Assuming it is true, it is packed with factual information. When you read it, you came to know about the event because you can read, because what you read had meaning for you, and because you have learned to absorb knowledge directly from reading.

To extend the example a bit, suppose you ran across this table in your newspaper.

The Five Great Lakes	Surface Area (Sq. Mi.)	Depth (in Feet)	Elevation (in Feet)
Superior	31,820	1,333	602
Huron	23,010	750	581
Michigan	22,400	923	581
Erie	9,930	210	572
Ontario	7,520	778	246

What can you say about this table? There is a group of lakes called the Great Lakes. Lake Superior is the largest, by surface area, of the Great Lakes. Lake Superior is higher in elevation than any other of the Great Lakes. Those are factual statements, aren't they?

Let's examine the first one—"There is a group of five lakes called the Great Lakes." You begin by making an assumption (which can be checked in other reference books)—the data in the table are true; there is no hoax or error involved. If you accept this assumption, then you count the lakes and say it is a fact that there are five Great Lakes.

Again, if you accept the assumption of true data, you can state that Lake Superior is both the largest in surface area and the highest in elevation. Your statements are factual. That is, the statements are known to be true to someone who measured, as closely as possible, the surface areas and elevations of these lakes.

In this example, opposed to the news item about the postman, you had to examine and compare data, and then draw a conclusion about comparative characteristics (area and volume) before you could make your statements.

Suppose you run across this hand-printed sign by the shores of Lake Superior.

> THERE IS MORE WATER IN
>
> LAKE SUPERIOR
>
> THAN IN ANY OTHER GREAT
>
> LAKE!

Is that a fact? Actually, it is factually true, but you can't know that just by reading the sign. If you remember the data in the table about the Great Lakes, then you might feel safe about the statement. After all, Lake Superior has by far the greatest area and greatest depth of the lakes, so it probably has the greatest volume. You may believe the statement is warranted but you may also recognize that your reasoning about area, depth, and volume might be erroneous.

It should be obvious from these examples that you are dealing with knowing, assuming, comparing, reasoning, and concluding. It should also be obvious that you won't be engaging in any of those processes unless you can read and unless the words you read have meanings.

Somewhere, sometime, you had certain experiences from which you developed meanings for *lake, five, largest, surface area, depth,* and *volume.* You also had certain experiences from which you learned

—to group items (The five lakes are called the Great Lakes.)

—to compare data (1,333 is deeper than 750 feet.)

—to separate relevant from irrelevant facts (Area and depth are related to volume of water, but elevation isn't.)

—to reason from facts to conclusions (Area and depth determine volume; Lake Superior has the largest area and greatest depth; thus, Lake Superior has the largest volume of water of the Great Lakes.)

—to recognize assumptions (The source is probably reliable; the figures are probably accurate; the underwater areas of the lakes are probably comparable.)

—to admit possible error (As you are not certain of the contours of each lake bottom, the depths are not wholly reliable indicators of volume.)

There were both substantive and procedural consequences flowing from your earlier experiences and influencing your present behavior. You have learned facts, and you have learned how to use facts. You know the role of assumptions in considering facts, and you have sufficient meanings so your facts are more than a sequence of words. All of these—facts, assumptions, and meanings—are both products of thinking and necessary elements for thinking.

REMEMBERING AND THINKING

If you had read the news item about the Florida postman biting the seventh alligator, you might have laughed and remembered the item because it was humorous. If you had attempted to see what the outcome of the story would be, then you would have been thinking. If you said to yourself, "That story is a hoax, I bet we find that out in a day or two," then you were also engaged in thought.

When you are indifferent to the news, you don't bother to think about the relationship between what happened and what will happen. If you are concerned with the news, then you hope to see a particular outcome. You look for a follow-up news item; indeed, you expect to find the initial report was a hoax. One of the problems about thinking is that thought is usually born in partiality. When we think we hope things come out the way we want them to. Remember the boy who made the claim about the tundra line on mountains? He wanted *his* answer to be confirmed. To meet the criterion of truth, however, thinking requires a detached impartiality. The tundra-line boy had to be impartial in his consideration of the evidence—he may not have liked the right answer, but he had to accept it. The same is true of all of us when we think. We invest our thoughts with value; after all, *we* thought those thoughts, so of course they must be right. This is a natural phenomenon, and apparently a universal one. It affects even the most highly trained intellects, particularly when a person thinks about a topic outside his or her own field of expertness. We have to fight constantly against viewing evidence only in terms of our desired outcomes. We have to detach ourselves enough from our desires to be impartial when we think.

If to think is to attempt to predict outcomes, then it seems fair to say thinking occurs when we become concerned with things or events that are uncertain, doubtful, or puzzling to us. What we are seeking is a conclusion that will meet the tests of logic or evidence. The person who saw the sign about Lake Superior had three obvious choices. He could ignore the sign's message. He could accept and remember the message. He could wonder about the accuracy of the message and think his way through his doubts to a conclusion about the message.

In each of our examples there have been two possibilities: the person would learn by direct absorption and might remember what was learned, or the person would learn by thinking and would likely remember what was learned. The difference between the two is a difference of kind rather than of degree. Thinking is considerably more than absorbing.

Suppose you ask this question of third graders: "Which is larger, the United States or the state of California?" Assuming no one has dealt with the question before, and you are just introducing the topics of state and nation, what happens in the minds of your pupils? Each of them is probably perplexed for a moment; next, each makes a guess; then, each acts by holding up a hand or calling out an answer. We see this three-step sequence often in elementary classrooms—perplexity, conjecture, action—and then the teacher says yes or no. The youngsters learn by absorption, through trial and error, from the teacher's response.

Now, suppose the teacher asks, "Why do you believe that is the right answer?" To respond, a pupil has to add two more elements to the sequence. The pupil must survey what he knows—what are the facts that apply to this question—and he must reason through to a conclusion—how do these facts fit together to answer the question?

As the topic is being introduced rather than reviewed, the answer may not come easily. All of a sudden one girl shouts, "My dad said California was part of the U.S., so the U.S. must be larger. That's what 'part of' means, part of something bigger." Her answer is correct and she has learned by reasoning.

If the teacher says, "Right!" and goes on to another question, what happens to the rest of the class? Again, we have our three possibilities: they can ignore the question and the answer; they can absorb the answer; or they can test the girl's answer by reviewing her reasoning and most likely arriving at her conclusion.

The bitter truths of the situation are that most teachers fail to ask the "why" question, and thus many children are restricted to learning by absorption. The teacher who fails to ask the perplexing "why" question cannot truthfully claim to be "teaching thinking." That claim can be made only if the confusion-conjecture-action sequence is expanded into a confusion-conjecture-survey of facts-reasoning to a conclusion-action sequence.

Before going on, I should make it clear that I don't believe all thinking consists of this orderly five-step sequence. Sometimes there is very little perplexity or conjecture, and often the survey of facts and reasoning to a conclusion are interwoven so closely they can't be separated. Sometimes action is limited to imaginary action, as in proposals to end wars or eliminate poverty. The business of specifying five steps is useful mainly to aid us in seeing what is involved, however mysteriously, when thinking does occur.

By now it should be reasonably clear that I believe a teacher *may* affect the nature and quality of thinking engaged in by her pupils. How she affects their thinking, of course, depends on what she believes about the nature of experience and about the role of thinking in experiences. Her effect depends on her choices regarding a learning environment. What kinds of questions does she ask? What sort of psychological climate does she create by her responses to answers? What does she do with their interests and concerns?

GRADGRIND AND GIRL NUMBER TWENTY

At the risk of beating a dead horse, I offer one last example from which you can draw conclusions.

In *Hard Times,* Dickens has Mr. Gradgrind ask girl number twenty to define a horse. Girl number twenty's father is a veterinary surgeon, a farrier, a horse-breaker. We can assume she knows something about horses, but she has never given any thought to defining a horse in any formal way. She is "thrown into the greatest alarm by this demand."

> "Girl number twenty unable to define a horse!" said Mr. Gradgrind, for the general behoof of all the little pitchers. "Girl number twenty possessed of no facts in reference to one of the commonest of animals! Some boy's definition of a horse, Bitzer, yours."

And Bitzer answers:

> "Quadruped. Graminivorous. Forty teeth, namely twenty-four grinders, four eye-teeth, and twelve incisive. Sheds coat in the spring; in marshy countries, sheds hoofs, too. Hoofs hard, but requiring to be shod with iron. Age known by marks in mouth."

> "Now girl number twenty," said Mr. Gradgrind, "You know what a horse is." [2]

Like hell she does, Mr. Gradgrind! Not unless we are willing to say that being able to repeat a memorized definition is knowing what a horse is. From this experience, would girl number twenty know the meaning of graminivorous? Would she be able to tell a grinder from an incisive? Would she know where to find the marks in the mouth and how to interpret them? Would she recognize a horse if she saw one?

A sad fact of school life rests on this example: verbal superficiality passes for the development of meanings. There is a world of difference between remembering a verbal description and developing meanings.

Girl number twenty has been around her father when he worked with horses. She has ridden and fed and curried horses. She has squared up the manure pile and has spread hay in the stalls. From her experiences with horses, she has learned about horses by thinking about her experiences with them. She has come to a number of conclusions about horses. She knows their nature and handling and uses. She has noted details about horses that depended on her observing, touching, hearing, and smelling them. The product of her experiences with horses is a rich cluster of meanings, in the form of knowledge, beliefs, and feelings about horses.

Mr. Gradgrind likely would claim that he was teaching by experience. His pupils had the "experience" of listening to him, of memorizing from their book, of reciting in class, and of being reprimanded or praised. Something is learned, of course, from the Gradgrinds of the world. Children learn to stifle their curiosity and imagination and reasoning in a Gradgrind's classroom. They learn to hate school and dislike experience, they learn to avoid creativity and to accept oppression. Unfortunately, some of these pupils grow up to become teachers who inflict their idiocy on the next generation of innocents.

The choice is yours, Gradgrind's primrose path or Dewey's hard road. What kind of person do you want to help shape for a world in which you must grow old?

SUMMARY

Experience combines acting and undergoing. By acting, we conduct an experiment on some part of our environment. That action produces results of some sort, which we suffer or enjoy. By undergoing, we engage in self-instruction about the nature of the relationship between action and consequences. We recognize the meaning of the connection between doing something and the products of having done that something. These meanings are factual and emotional. They accumulate and grow with additional experiences. They provide the knowledge for future self-instruction, and they provide the ability to predict future results.

In trial-and-error learning we try this and that until we hit on something that seems to work. Then we adopt that behavior as a rule of thumb for directing our actions in similar situations. We also learn by absorbing knowledge directly. We are told to read and memorize, we are told to listen to the teacher and remember what she says. Without doubt, we do learn by trial and by absorption, and we do remember some of what we learn by those means.

Learning by thinking, however, requires something beyond memorizing. Thinking involves intent and concern. Thinking requires analysis of what binds consequence to activity. Thinking deals with reasoning, with inference and conclusion. Thinking requires the translation of conjecture into testable hypotheses, into patterns demonstrating relationships. Thinking means being aware of assumptions and being able to make judgments. Thinking as part of experience means systematic inquiry into an area of doubt by forming conjectures to guide exploration of factual relationships to produce a hypothesis leading to an activity whose consequences permit us to accept, reject, or modify our hypothesis.

Thinking is born in doubt and perplexity, it spawns conjecture, it thrives on trustworthy evidence, it transforms details into testable inferences, and it produces tested conclusions. Inquiring leads to acquiring, and what is acquired are the meanings and emotions that prepare and predispose us to act wisely in future experiences.

The teacher constantly makes choices that influence learning and remembering. The teacher who asks who and what and where and when about textbook material affects learning in one way. The teacher who asks *how* and *why* and *so what* affects learning in quite another way.

NOTES

1.   John Dewey, *Democracy and Education,* Macmillan Paperbacks no. 38, New York: Macmillan Company, 1961, p. 145.

2.   Charles Dickens, *Hard Times,* London: Bradbury & Evans, 1854, pp. 6, 7.

SUGGESTED READINGS

Dewey, John, *Democracy and Education.* Macmillan Paperbacks no. 38. New York: Macmillan Co., 1961. (Read it, please. If you do, you will know where a great many current, unfootnoted ideas originated.)

Dewey, John, *Experience and Education.* New York: Collier Books, 1970, 12th printing. (This slim volume combines a criticism of progressive education with a restatement of his ideas after years of viewing others apply them. The sections on interaction and continuity are worth the price of even more expensive books.)

Ennis, Robert H., *Ordinary Logic.* Englewood Cliffs, N.J.: Prentice-Hall, 1969. (A skinny paperback for the student who knows logic is important, but who never took a course in it.)

Ennis, Robert H., *Logic in Teaching.* Englewood Cliffs, N.J.: Prentice-Hall, 1969. (A thorough treatment of logic in the context of teaching. A bit advanced for elementary application, but you will find much of use in it.)

Franklin, Benjamin, *The Autobiography of Benjamin Franklin.* New Haven: Yale University Press, 1964. (An old favorite, with brief gems on argumentation and learning to write.)

Vygotsky, Lev Semenovich, *Thought and Language.* Cambridge, Mass.: M.I.T. Press, 1962. (Required reading if you believe that your language and the language of children have any effect on learning. And if you don't believe, transfer to social work or nursing.)

EXERCISES

1. If an experience consists of making an experiment and making a connection between the experiment and its consequences, what is wrong with these examples of learning from experience?
   a. A child asks where to put the globe after he is done with it, and the teacher points to a table.
   b. A child asks a teacher how we know rivers run from high places to low places, and the teacher says, "Your book says water does that, so the book is good enough for me!"
   c. A child says, "These tables are interesting. The states that grow the most corn are the same states that raise the most hogs." The teacher replies, "Some religions don't permit the eating of pork."

2. Read Chapter 3, "Criteria of Experience," in Dewey's *Experience and Education.* What criteria does he set forth? What do you see as the

implications of his comments on continuity and interaction for you as a teacher of social studies? (Note: His chapter called "Social Control" is one of the best discussions available on what most of us call discipline.)

3. Read Chapter 1 of Franklin's *Autobiography*. Take the section on Franklin's method for improving his writing by using the *Spectator* as a model or the following section on his use of the Socratic method, and discuss either in terms of experience and the role of thinking in experience.

4. If you have not had a course in logic, read either of the books by Ennis. Then write a short paper, for yourself, discussing the role of logic in thinking and experiencing.

5. Vygotsky is not easy reading, but he is both easier and better in some ways than Piaget for teachers of social studies. It's a tough exercise, but offer to read *Language and Thought,* and report to your class on his ideas and their application to social studies.

Three Kinds of Facts

The products of experience may be grouped into three rough categories —thinking, facts, and attitudes. Thinking is procedural in nature, but thinking requires facts for substance and attitudes for initiating actions. Facts are substantive, the subject matter of thought and the conterbalance to attitudes. Attitudes are predispositions to act in particular ways; thought and facts serve as brakes on pure passion. The last chapter dealt with thinking, the next deals with attitudes, this one with facts.

THE COMMON-SENSE NOTION OF FACTS

As we said earlier, the common meaning of fact is something known to be true or to have occurred. The various academic disciplines sometimes sharpen the definition, but none of them vary much from the essence of the common-sense meaning. For example:

—Water is composed of one molecule of oxygen and two of hydrogen.

—In 1945, Easter Sunday fell on April Fool's Day.

—Illinois is one of 50 states in the United States.

—Most of the major cities in the United States are located by navigable bodies of water.

—The North Central States include Ohio, Indiana, Illinois, Michigan,

Wisconsin, Minnesota, Iowa, Missouri, South Dakota, North Dakota, Nebraska, and Kansas.

Most of us would accept these statements as facts, which they are. The problem is that we also accept them as absolutes, which they are not. Water, for example, might contain a minute quantity of some unknown substance, which will be discovered only when some scientist invents some new tool for chemical analysis. When we talk about Easter Sunday, April Fool's Day, and 1945, we assume all people agree with at least two events in Christian history. The statement about Illinois is true today, but it was not true when I was a boy. History has a way of changing the nature of facts.

It is also true that we don't always understand everything about a fact. How many of us know the precise meaning of "navigable" in the statement about major cities? How many of us know who put those states into the North Central Region; who had the authority to make that decision? Are we certain about the Colorado being 1,450 miles long; how can we be sure it isn't 1,450½? Thus, some statements we call facts may include ghost terms, may spring from some unknown authority, or may be approximations.

In looking up "calendar" in an almanac, I ran across this statement: "The Norsemen, before becoming Christians, are said to have had a calendar consisting of ten months of 30 days each; for the remainder of the year they stayed indoors." [1] A number of people would likely accept that as a statement of fact. There is, however, a clue in the sentence for the wary—"are said to have had" indicates that the writers could not pin down a source for their statement. As for staying indoors the rest of the year, that might be the source of the notion that blonds have more fun. The use of "it seems," "I imagine," "perhaps," and the like are signals that a writer is not certain of his facts.

The elementary teacher faces two other particular dangers in regard to facts. The first is that children tend to perceive the teacher as an authority (and teachers do little to disabuse children of this falsehood). The second is that children, like adults, tend to accept the printed word as authoritative. I can remember taking a branch of pink cherry blossoms into a sixth-grade class and talking about the "pretty, white apple blossoms" for five or six minutes before someone dared correct me. I also remember my class discovering that two encyclopedias had quite different pictures of the state capitol for some midwestern state. From that year on, I consciously taught children to challenge, civilly, any authoritative statement that instinct, perception, or faint memory warned them might be false.

Much of what the elementary-school child reads in his text or his resource books is fact, but teachers do have an obligation to guide children to challenge statements of fact and to research any fact they consider suspect.

INFORMATION AS FACT

Over the past seven or eight years, during the rising concern over the development of concepts, I have heard a great many teachers say, "I teach facts, so I don't have time to teach concepts." What they really mean is that they teach one kind of facts—information.

I hate to say it, but many teachers dearly love isolated, discrete bits of information. "Alaska is the biggest state." "The equator runs east and west." "The dollar is based on the decimal system." "Jefferson was born on the frontier." "Poor Richard was really Ben Franklin." "California grows many oranges." "South Dakota is north of North Carolina." "Each state can send two senators to congress." "The first state to let women vote in presidential elections was Wyoming." These are facts, but facts taking the form of bits of information, each dealing with a single event or condition.

There is no question about information being factual; if it isn't factual, it is misinformation. Most teachers accept this idea—information is factual and should be taught. The problem is that no one can learn all the factual information that exists. In most classrooms a sort of natural selection of information occurs: the course of study, the textbook available, the teacher's attitudes, and the pupils' interests tend to eliminate multitudes of facts and concentrate attention on certain factual information.

There are good reasons for learning information, particularly when information grows out of reflection on experience. Some information is needed for survival. Some information is needed to learn other important things. Some information is needed for cultural reasons, to keep the gang or group we want to belong to from thinking we are stupid, square, or out of touch. Some information is needed simply because we want to know it. The teacher who judges the need to learn factual information by these standards can be fairly certain that she and her class are working on something important.

There are, however, two other classes of facts that many teachers do not understand as well as they understand informational facts. Those two classes are *concepts* and *generalizations*. Of these two, concepts give us the most difficulty.

CONCEPTS AS FACTS

Misconceptions are a source of humor. All of us remember such boners as "My country Tizathe," "Round John Virgin," "A dense population is a dumb group," and "I don't like Jesus 'cause he sat on God's right hand." Misconceptions are not factual, but concepts are.

In thinking about concepts for this chapter, I remembered an incident when a friend of mine from southern California saw his first snow. Hatless, barefoot, clad only in chinos and teeshirt, he rushed out into the snow to enjoy himself. Before long, he stopped his antics and headed for the house. "Damn," he said, "that stuff's cold!"

Back inside we talked about snow. He had noted a number of details about snow—the shape of the flakes, the way they floated in the air, the way they covered the earth, their coldness, and their lack of color, smell, and taste. Without going into detail about sensory stimuli and responses, or into the role of the conscious and unconscious in sensory data, it is enough to say that my friend got some *meaning* from the details of his experience. He noted that the flakes were some form of water, and that snow is cold. He had added to his knowledge of what snow is by thinking about certain details of his experience. He probably wasn't aware he was thinking about these details, although if I had asked how he knew snow was some form of water, he could have said, "because the flakes melted and left a drop of water on my hand." What is important is that my friend now knew more than he had before about snow as an object.

My friend also developed some feelings about snow. He noted the intricate shapes of the flakes and the appearance of a landscape covered with snow. "It's beautiful." He had fun sliding on the snowy sidewalk and throwing snowballs. "It's fun." This combination of new knowledge and new attitudes combined to add new meanings to whatever snow had meant to him before. He had enriched his concept of snow.

My friend's capacity to reason permitted him to form a conclusion about what he did and the consequences of acting as he did in a particular environment. Now, I don't mean to imply that my friend spent much time reasoning formally about his experience. He didn't say to himself, "Let's see now, these are my premises, and this is the conclusion I infer from them." Nonetheless, he did understand the relationship between going barefoot into the snow and his feet getting cold: standing barefoot in the snow leads to cold feet. Discovering the relationship between bare feet and snow was a product of learning from an experience.

My friend was now in a position to use what he had learned. He could use his revised concept of snow and his conclusions about snow to make predictions. He could predict that snow would have certain characteristics wherever he would find it; he could predict that he would find it beautiful; he could predict that he could have fun with snow; and he could predict that his feet would get cold if he again went barefoot in the snow.

CONCEPTS OF OBJECTS

From his experience with snow my friend learned something about snow *as an object.* By "object," I mean any person or thing in your environment that you can respond to with your sensory equipment. At this point, I am not talking about events or qualities or abstractions.

My friend noted that snow fell from the sky to the earth in the form of flakes. He also noted that snow melted on his hands and left small drops of water where the flakes had been. He concluded that somewhere in the sky water had frozen into snowflakes, which then fell to earth.

My friend now had the general idea, in the literal sense, of what snow is. His language could have been more precise, for snow is actually water vapor frozen into crystals. But his language was good enough for anything but the most technical of discussions. My friend's idea, "snow is a form of water that froze into flakes and fell from the sky to the earth," denotes the literal meaning of snow. This denotive statement forms the core of his concept of snow. The statement identifies a combination of two characteristics putting snow into a class of objects. This combination of characteristics differentiates snow from other forms of water, including other forms of frozen water, and from other objects that fall to earth. For example, his combination of characteristics differentiate snow from rain, sleet, and hail—three other forms of water that fall to earth from the sky. His combination also differentiates snow from apples, leaves, and other objects that might fall to earth.

From this example, we may define a concept as *ideas about a class of objects and the characteristics of those objects that differentiate the class from all other classes of objects.* That's a fairly neat definition; indeed, it's a fairly standard one. But something is lacking, and the lack is what makes so much teaching of concepts in social studies flat and nonproductive.

I part company with those of my colleagues who say concepts are simply a classification with precise characteristics that differentiate one class from all other classes. To me a concept is all that an object denotes and connotes, all the meanings and feelings that are both specified and suggested. To me, *an individual's concept of an object combines his ideas about a class of objects, the characteristics specifying the class, and the cluster of meanings and feelings about the object that give richness and detail to the concept.*

My definition and my examples may have misled you in two respects. First, I may have given the impression that concepts always begin with an idea of class and characteristics and then expand to accommodate a cluster of meanings. Actually, I expect most concepts begin with a small cluster of meanings; then expand to include more meanings and some idea of class and characteristics.

Second, I may have given the impression that in order to "have" a concept, a person must have named a class, have specified characteristics, and have developed a rich and varied cluster of meanings and feelings. Actually, for most objects, we do fairly well to have an unarticulated notion of class, no specific characteristics, and a general cluster of meanings and feelings. For example, I am sure you have a concept for dog and a concept for cat. I am sure you have clusters of meanings for each. And I am sure you could separate any number of dogs and cats into two groups, one of all dogs and one of all cats. But, I'll bet money that you cannot state the biological characteristics that differentiate dogs from cats.

When a child can group objects into class and when those objects have some meaning for him, then he has begun to develop a concept. As he has more experience with objects, he may add meanings, he may refine his idea about the class, he may identify the key characteristics of the objects in a class, or he may become increasingly articulate about the class, the characteristics, and the meanings. He may, at any given time, accomplish any of those operations singly or in any combination.

The implication for you, as a teacher, is this: if you are to help a child develop a concept, then you must be aware of his notions about a class and its characteristics, his cluster of meanings, and his ability to discuss any or all of those ideas. From time to time, you introduce the object into a pupil's environment and make certain the pupil interacts with that object and environment. Then you find out what thoughts he has about the consequences of his interaction with the object.

Beyond objects, however, there are at least three other types of things for which humans develop concepts: concepts of activities, concepts of qualities, and concepts of abstractions.

CONCEPTS OF ACTIVITIES

When we talk about planning, choosing, fishing, or studying, we are dealing with concepts about activities. Fishing is an activity, a series of related behaviors organized into a sequence for the purpose of obtaining fish. In effect, my concept of fishing was developed by thinking about what I do when I am fishing, what I have observed others doing when they are fishing, and what I have read about what others do when they are fishing.

If you knew little or nothing about fishing, I could help you develop a concept of fishing by taking you fishing.

Whenever you help a pupil learn from experience how to do something, then you are also helping him develop a concept of that something. In learning how to do something, a person develops a *behavioral definition* of that something. For example, if you teach a pupil to orient a map, then you are also helping him develop a concept of orienting. The same holds true when you teach such activities as planning, voting, leading, or mapping—for each of those activities can be behaviorally defined.

The idea of behavioral definition implies an important consequence for teaching. Anything that can be behaviorally defined can be acted out, and anything that can be acted out is a form of experiencing. Acting out an activity may not be as direct or as concrete as the actual act, but it is more direct and concrete than just reading about the act. If I can't take you fishing, I would rather get you to simulate fishing than just read about fish and fishermen. Of course, a good teacher will try to combine all three doing something, simulating doing, and reading—in helping a child develop concepts about activities.

CONCEPTS OF QUALITIES

Let's stay with our example about fishing to illustrate the idea of developing a concept about a *quality of an action*. You say, "OK, I know what you mean by fishing, but what do you mean by *good* fishing?" Good, in this case, is a quality related to fishing.

To begin, I can say, "By good, I mean favorable rather than correct or proper." In other words, I am *not* saying that good depended upon my casting my bait in exactly the correct manner prescribed by experts. Nor am I saying that my fishing manners were impeccable. When I refer to *good fishing* I am introducing standards, or criteria, into my behavioral definition of fishing. I am saying, "Good fishing means I caught my limit and most of the fish gave me a fight before I landed them." At this point, you might ask me to state the number defining my limit and to state the criteria defining "fight." But for the sake of space, let me beg those questions. My point is that if I give you something to do—perform the behaviors defining fishing—then you build a concept of fishing. When I add a standard or standards for judging *good,* then you will know my concept of good fishing.

Of course, your reasoning about your experiences and about my suggested standards might lead you to a quite different concept. For example, you might reason that you couldn't eat the number of fish that make up the legal limit, that fish should be conserved as a natural resource, and thus good fishing, for you, would mean that you caught only as many fish as you felt you would eat. In either case, each of us would know what the other meant by good fishing.

We also form concepts for *qualities of objects.* Balls, hemispheres, disks, cylinders, and circles are five different classes of objects. Yet all five classes of objects share a common quality: *roundness.* Roundness, as a word, is a descriptive adjective; it describes a quality that objects may possess. Any circular or curved surface or outline possesses the quality of roundness.

To illustrate how a concept of roundness might be formed, let's use an example of a teacher working with elementary-school children. Our teacher has collected a basketball, a soccer ball, a softball, a baseball, a tennis ball, a golf ball, a marble, a cube, and a pyramid.

"What is this?" the teacher asks of any four of the balls.

The pupils may say, "That's a basketball." Or perhaps they just say, "That's a ball."

Now what? The teacher asks, "What shape is a ball?" (Wait a minute! Do the pupils know what *shape* means? If they don't, the teacher must develop meaning for the word *shape,* or she must ask some other question. Let's say she helped her pupils develop meaning for shape earlier.)

Some pupil says, "It's round."

"Where is it round?"

"All over."

"Take the ball. Show us where it's round."

The teacher does this with several balls, trying to get every pupil to handle a ball. Then she sets the four familiar balls aside. She takes out the other three balls, the cube, and the pyramid. She shows them one at a time to the class.

"What is this called? What shape is it? Show us where it's round." The pupils have no trouble with two balls. Then she shows them the cube.

"What is this called?"

"A block."

"Is it a ball?"

"No. It's a block."

"Is it round?"

"No."

"Show me something round."

The teacher next goes to the last ball and then to the pyramid. By now, *each* pupil has begun to develop *his* concept of roundness (or to add to his previously developed concept). She has accomplished this by using concrete objects, by asking understandable questions, and by testing the class with a mixture of positive examples (the last three balls) and negative examples (the cube and the pyramid).

At this point, our teacher must make another decision. Should she stop and give time for this initial concept of roundness to "soak in," or should she go on to introduce the disk, cylinder, and so forth to the class. In part, her decision should be based on her answers to three questions. One, do her pupils have any immediate need to understand that some objects are partially round and partially flat? Two, has she thought out how she will handle the round and flat combination? And, three, does she have at hand a number of round and flat objects as concrete stimuli?

Helping pupils develop concepts for qualities of objects or actions is a difficult business. In fact, it is a fair criticism of much elementary teaching that the child never is led to specify standards for determining the meaning of such words as good, right, correct, just, fair, beautiful, and kind.

CONCEPTS OF ABSTRACTIONS

One type of abstraction common to the social studies occurs when classes are arranged into hierarchies of classes. Hierarchies are common in advanced science; for example, men and women belong to the kingdom Animalia, the phylum Chordata, the class Mammalia, the order Primates, the family Hominidae, the genus *Homo,* and the species *sapiens.* The subject matters of the social sciences do not fall so neatly into arranged hierarchies, but some terms are the products of arranging classes. For example, land-form does not refer to *an* object; it refers to several classes of objects—mountains, plains, hills, plateaus, valleys, mesas, and so forth. Weather is a collective term, and to say what the weather is like requires some reference to temperature, precipitation, sunshine and clouds, and wind.

Now, go back to my friend and his experience with snow. He developed a concept of snow, and part of his concept was the idea of snow as a class set off from all other classes by a combination of two characteristics. Let's assume my friend also has experienced rain, sleet, and hail. From each of these experiences, he has developed a concept. He now has four similar concepts, one each for snow, rain, hail, and sleet. For some reason, perhaps no more than idle curiosity, he begins to think about similarities among the characteristics of these four concepts. He makes some notes:

—Rain is water that falls from the sky to the earth.

—Snow is water vapor frozen into crystals that fall from the sky to the earth.

—Hail is rain frozen into small balls that fall from the sky to the earth.

—Sleet is a mixture of rain or snow or hail, each of which falls from the sky to the earth.

My friend has identified two characteristics common to all four concepts: each exists as some form of water; each falls from the sky to the earth. Surely, he says to himself, there must be some general class into which rain, snow, hail, and sleet can be fitted.

There is, of course, and the name of the class is precipitation. He says, "Precipitation is any form of water that falls from the sky to the earth." My friend has now formed an abstract concept about his concepts of rain, snow, hail, and sleet. In time, he may have to reorganize his concept of precipitation to account for dew. Dew is water from the atmosphere that condenses on (rather than falls on) the surface of the earth. His revised idea would be that precipitation is the depositing of moisture from the atmosphere onto the earth's surface in the form of rain, snow, hail, sleet, or dew.

My friend now has identified a general class, precipitation; he has specified its key characteristics; and his cluster of meanings include all the clusters of meanings attached to the subclasses of rain, snow, hail, sleet, and dew.

Another example of an abstract concept would be *social class,* the idea that a population can be divided into groups of real or assumed differences among the groups. In many respects, building a concept for social class is a difficult proposition. The teacher has to work with words and loose definitions rather than with concrete objects or activities. She can point to examples of how others have used social class as an analytical tool, but at the root of her problem is the fact that there is no clear definition of the term. Even the scholars who use the term are not in complete agreement about the meaning of social class. What then is the teacher to do?

In teaching fifth grade, I found the idea of social class useful in dealing with the Puritans, the Revolutionary War, the writing of the Constitution, and the events leading to the Civil War. First, I built these ideas: class refers to groups of people, the people in a group are alike in certain ways, and the people in a group are different from other people in other groups in certain ways. Second, I helped the class identify nine characteristics of social class. These nine characteristics were terms for which the pupils had to have concepts. The nine were (1) *basis* for membership—commonality based on birth, money, profession, and so on; (2) *position* of the class in some ranking of classes; (3) *legitimacy* through recognition by custom or law; (4) *power* or lack of power to influence other classes or institutions; (5) *privileges*—assumed rights to behave in certain ways not extended to all people; (6) *expectations*—ways of behaving and levels of achievement assumed to be proper and reasonable by others in the class; (7) *mobility*— the likelihood for moving out of one class into another; (8) *subdivisions* —the idea that those in a class could divide themselves into upper, middle, and lower positions; and (9) *focus*—the notion that the defining characteristics of class could be sharp and distinct, or fuzzy and overlapping. A pupil's concept of social class thus depended on his ideas of class and his meanings for each of the nine characteristics. The pupils and I then found we could use social class as a tool for analyzing the behavior of different people with different ideas about such questions as what should go into the Constitution.

Primary-grade teachers can also work with abstract concepts. *Change* is an abstract concept, but even five-year olds or six-year olds can deal with change and its characteristics. Quite simply, change means to make different or to become different. If I were to use change with upper-grade pupils I might deal with causation, value, intensity, rate, and magnitude as characteristics of change, but with primary graders I would avoid those terms and get them to ask questions about change. What made this change? Is the change good or bad? Was it a big change or a small change? Was the change fast or slow? Was the change important to a few people or to many people?

Those questions can be asked about changes in the weather, in seasons, in family compositions, in new rules, in learning a new game, and so on. The point is that with these five questions, a pupil could go beyond saying, "It changed."

Somehow or other, the elementary teacher must make an effort to translate abstractions into experiences with concrete objects, actions, situations, or questions. The teacher who will not attempt this, or who cannot do it, is reduced to leading children to manipulate words without meaning.

GENERALIZATIONS AS FACTS

Children are continually making inferences from their experiences. These inferences often take the form of generalizations. If you continually "put down" a child who wants to challenge a statement in his textbook, he is apt to generalize about his experiences with you and textbooks. He thinks to himself, "If I argue about what's in the textbook, then I will get bawled out." Or he may think, "Arguing over what's in the textbook is bad." In either case, he has acted and his actions have had consequences; he has also thought about the relationships between the set of actions and set of consequences. His conclusion about the relationship has taken the form of a generalization.

A generalization is a *factual statement of a widely applicable relationship among concepts*. The generalization stated above—"If I argue, . . . then I will get bawled out"—has a factual basis in the pupil's prior experiences. It also states a relationship between two concepts—arguing and getting bawled out. It is widely applicable to the extent it has held true in the past with the child's teacher and because it is likely to hold true with that teacher and her pupils.

Generalizations can be memorized, but mere memorization is a characteristic of poor learning and bad teaching. A memorized generalization is seldom understood and thus lacks the power to be useful in producing new learning. However, generalizations produced through thought about experience tend to be understood to the extent that they may be used to explain new but similar situations.

Let's use our earlier example of the concept of roundness to create an example of a generalization. "Round things roll," is a factual statement. It states a widely applicable relationship. And the relationship connects two concepts, *round things* and *roll*.

Assume that a group of pupils have concepts of *roundness* (and thus, of round things) and of *roll*. They know roundness applies to balls, disks, and cylinders, and they can tell rolling from similar actions. The teacher begins with a variety of objects with round surfaces (positive examples) and some with no round surfaces (negative examples).

The teacher begins by reinforcing the concept of roundness. "What is this?" "What shape is this?"

Then she rolls a ball. "What am I doing?"

"You are rolling the ball."

"What is the ball doing?"

"It is rolling."

She repeats this with another round object or two. Then she asks, "What kinds of things roll?"

"Round things roll."

"Will all these round things roll?"

"I think so."

"OK. Try them." The pupils try to roll the round objects. They all roll.

"Do all round things roll?"

"Yes."

Then, as a test situation, the teacher mixes a few new round objects with the negative examples.

The pupils have generalized. They created a generalization that covers the round objects at hand and that can be extended to cover a wide range of round objects not available in the classroom (automobile tires, hula hoops, bowling balls, oranges, and so on).

In time, the teacher will use this generalization and another dealing with "round things spin" to help develop a concept of rotation and then apply that concept to a study of the movements of the earth and of globes.

The process described above was largely inductive, but the process could have been deductive. The teacher could have said, "Round things roll. Do you believe that? Can you show me it is true that round things roll?" In this case, the process is deductive, even if a syllogism isn't stated formally. The inquiry process operates in either case. The poor teacher uses neither induction nor deduction; she just says, "Round things roll. Remember that. It will help you later."

The use of the concrete objects and operations tends to insure insight into the nature of the relationship between the two concepts. Their use also tends to insure that a pupil can demonstrate that round things roll and can give a variety of examples of his generalizations.

Three types of generalizations appear often in elementary-grade materials. A *definitional* generalization reminds or informs: "A bank is an institution for keeping, lending, exchanging, and issuing money." A *primary* generalization states an uncomplicated relationship: "Every society has ways for transporting goods." A *functional* generalization states or implies an *if, . . . then* relationship: *"If* the supply of raw materials becomes scarce, *then* the price of goods made from these materials rises."

THE VALUE OF CONCEPTS AND GENERALIZATIONS

Two characteristics of being human are the abilities to internalize one's environment and then to manipulate those internal representations intellectually. Your concepts and generalizations save you time and effort; they give you power and insight.

Your concepts and generalizations free you from the anarchy of particular stimuli, and thus save you from constant concentration on details. When you developed your initial concept of horse, you had to respond to a particular stimulus—that horse in that field. Once you had an initial concept of horse, you had the ability to respond to horses in general. Every experience with horses taught you more and thus your concept was enriched. Your initial learning may have been slow and faltering, but your subsequent learning should have been more rapid and more precise.

When you group objects into a class, you can then think about the class as a whole and use the idea of the class to test new objects to see where they fit into your scheme of ideas about your world. *Your concepts and generalizations free you from the tyranny of constant relearning, and thus save you from always acting in a trial-and-error manner.* If your concept of horses was developed from experiences with work horses, you are freed from learning about race horses as if you knew nothing about horses. Race horses are different from work horses, and you will learn new things about horses from your experiences with race horses, but you won't approach a race horse as if it were a cow or a grizzly bear.

Your concepts and generalizations free you from viewing every object and every environment as completely discrete and unique, and thus they give depth and continuity to your experiences and learning. You gain depth when you connect one concept to other concepts in the form of generalizations. For example, a man with a scythe can cut a limited amount of hay in a day, but a man with a horse-drawn mower can cut considerably more hay. In this case your concepts of manpower and horsepower are related to agricultural production. These combined concepts, in turn, help you explain a relationship between invention and production. And that explanation, in turn, helps you understand the influence of machine power on an industrial society.

Concepts also provide you with the power to analyze an unexplained situation. For example, the transformation of the Plains Indians from farmers to hunters can be explained by the introduction of the horse into the culture of those Indians. Concepts and generalizations provide continuity in learning when what you learn today rests, in part, on earlier learnings and when what you learn today provides, in part, for learning from subsequent experiences.

Your concepts and generalizations free you from testing every proposition by overtly acting on it, and thus they permit you to judge probable consequences in an imagined experience. For example, if you have learned that going barefoot in snow results in cold feet, you need not go barefoot in sleet to be able to predict that the consequence will be cold feet. You can test that proposition intellectually and thus save yourself a certain amount of misery.

SUMMARY

Facts are something known to be true or to have occurred. Facts, as we deal with them in schools, take three forms: facts as information, facts as concepts, and facts as generalizations.

In dealing with facts as information, teachers must be aware that facts are not absolute. They do change with new knowledge or as new events take place. Some facts depend on specified definitions, some on authoritative decisions, and some on approximations.

Some teachers hesitate to accept the proposition that concepts are factual. To them, concepts are ideas hidden away in the intellect and thus much too difficult to get at in concrete ways. Actually, concepts are perfectly natural phenomena; every normal human being forms concepts as efficient and effective means of dealing with perceived reality. In essence, concepts are classes with all the meanings and feelings individuals attach to categories of objects, activities, qualities of objects and activities, or abstractions.

Generalizations are factual statements of a widely applicable relationship among concepts. Both history and the social sciences abound in generalizations, although historians are more cautious in stating them. Generalizations are found in three forms: *definitions* that inform, *primary* statements of primary relationships, and *functional* statements of if-then relationships.

Both concepts and generalizations may be learned either inductively or deductively, although the learning of concepts appears to be more naturally related to inductive inquiry. Both free the individual from particular stimuli, from constant relearning, and from viewing environments as unique. They thus save the individual from constant concentration on detail and from acting only in a trial-and-error manner. They provide meaning and continuity to experiences and learning, they provide the power to analyze new situations, and they provide a basis for judging the probable consequences of acting on an environment. They are the natural products of thinking about experiences. They are as factual as information, they are merely quite different forms of facts than those most teachers are used to working with in classrooms.

Facts can be memorized and then either be remembered or forgotten. If facts are memorized for no other reason than to pass a test or to satisfy a teacher, they may be easily forgotten. If, however, facts flow from reflecting on experiences, they tend to be remembered. In particular, facts that take the form of concepts and generalizations tend to be remembered and thus are available as intellectual tools for dealing with future experiences.

NOTE

1.   *The New Information Please Almanac, 1969,* New York: Dan Golenpaul Associates, 1968, p. 463.

SUGGESTED READINGS

Beyer, Barry K., and Anthony N. Penna (eds.), *Concepts in the Social Studies,* paperback ed. Washington: NCSS, 1971. (A basic collection of readings on concepts.)

Bruner, Jerome, *The Process of Education*. New York: Vintage College Books, 1960. (The book that stimulated the reforms of the 1960's; brief, readable, stimulating.)

Dewey, John, *How We Think*, paperback ed. Lexington, Mass.: D. C. Heath Co., 1971. (In a way, this is the book that much of what is good in social studies teaching is based upon.)

Dewey, John, *Democracy and Education*, paperback ed. New York: Free Press, 1971. (If you didn't review this book ofter Chapter 2, do it now. The language isn't difficult, but the ideas are complex.)

Gagne, Robert M., *The Conditions of Learning*. New York: Holt, Rinehart & Winston, 1965. (The best brief psychology book on a direct application of theory to examples you will recognize.)

Hullfish, Gordon, and Phillip Smith, *Reflective Thinking: The Method of Education*. New York: Dodd, Mead & Co., 1961. (This is a highly reasonable and readable restatement of Dewey's ideas. Particularly good for junior-high application.)

McDonald, Frederick J., *Educational Phychology*. Belmont, Calif.: Wadsworth Publishing Co., 1959. (Chapters 5 and 6 on cognitive processes are sound and interesting; the author knows both psychology and real out-of-the-laboratory children.)

Travers, Robert M. W., *Educational Psychology*. New York: Macmillan Co., 1973. (A highly readable new book that ties research to practice. The chapters on transfer and memory should be particularly useful to elementary teachers.)

Womack, James G., *Discovering the Structure of the Social Studies*. New York: Benzinger Brothers, 1966. (Strong emphasis on generalizations and their role in building a social-studies program.)

EXERCISES

1. Look up the definition of *fact* in your dictionary. If you use it as a criterion, how does the definition used in this chapter hold up? If you prefer another definition, how does it change the views expressed here about information, concepts, and generalizations?

2. Take any object that stands out in your mind, and try to recall experiences you have had with that object. What are its characteristics? Which of its characteristics are exclusive, which are shared with other similar objects? What feelings do you associate with the object? Do you agree with the definition of a concept used in this chapter? If not, what is your definition, and what are the consequences for you in using yours in thinking about social studies?

3. Join with two or three of your classmates and pick an event familiar to all of you. Now take two or three words that modify the activity (good, fair, honest, and the like), and see if each of you can be specific enough about the criteria you would apply to each term, so there is little doubt about what every one of you means when you use that term.

4. Suppose you are working with fifth graders on the meaning of *city, state,* and *nation* as they apply in the United States. What are the characteristics of these three concepts? How are they related? How would you go about handling this task with pupils?

5. Read the relevant sections of Gagne or McDonald to see what positions they take on concepts and generalizations. Are their positions fundamentally different from those in this chapter? How? What, if any, consequences do you see for teaching social studies based on these differences? If you see no fundamental differences, what does the chapter mean for you in thinking about the subject matter you will be working with in social studies?

Attitudes and Values

Most lists of objectives for teaching include entries on attitudes or values. By and large, these entries provide window dressing, honor past practices in writing statements of objectives, and encourage a teacher to believe she works to achieve them simply because they exist in writing. They form a part of the *written* curriculum or course of study, but they seldom find reality in the classroom.

Further, an either-or dichotomy seems to muddy the classroom situation more than necessary. Teachers feel confused about the nature and function of values and attitudes and about the similarities and differences between the two. Should they work with one and ignore the other? Should they work with both? What differences in classroom practices flow from choosing to emphasize one over the other, or do both call for similar approaches to activities and materials?

Late in the '60's, partly in response to what was perceived as excess emphasis on cognition, writers spawned an increasing number of articles and books about values. Most of this writing, particularly the portion aimed directly at teachers, focused on values and seldom ever mentioned attitudes. This confused many teachers, because their foundation work in psychology and educational psychology usually focused on attitudes. This seeming contradiction flustered some teachers enough that they decided to skip this area and focus on content and skills.

This, of course, was unfortunate, because pupils—being human—combine perceiving, feeling, thinking, and acting as interdependent elements of behavior. Whether teachers care to believe it or not, attitudes and values are always present in the behavior of their pupils. This chapter aims at convincing you that values and attitudes are sensitive, but not impossible, areas for you to deal with in your classroom.

Teachers deal with the observed acts and expressed opinions of pupils, so teachers don't care too much about splitting definitional hairs between attitudes and values. In a sense, the teachers are right, for the process of prizing lies just beneath the surface of each term. Unless there are major characteristics distinguishing attitudes from values, why should teachers care about differences in definition?

One proposition followed in this chapter is that there are major similarities, but only minor differences, between attitudes and values. A second proposition holds that similarities affect teacher behavior tremendously, while differences have little operational influence.

UBIQUITOUS JOHNNY

Over the school year, you notice the following statements or acts:

Johnny says, "Artists are evil."

Johnny says, "Art is boring."

Johnny looks out the window during most of the art class.

Johnny's face grows flushed during art class when you say, "You aren't trying."

Johnny mentions that he never looks at art in people's homes.

Johnny's health is fine all day except during art class, when he develops headaches.

Johnny never is absent except on Wednesday, the day you teach art.

Johnny says you don't teach art as well as you teach other classes.

Johnny is observed destroying the art work of a friend.

Johnny wastes materials whenever he has to produce something in art.

From these statements and acts, what do you infer about Johnny's attitudes and values?

If Johnny believes artists and art are evil, then Johnny doesn't value art. For reasons unknown to us, he believes art to be valueless. He may have other values—honesty, courage, religion—but art lies outside the circle of things he believes to be good for him or for society.

Johnny has a cluster of attitudes toward artwork, art class, art materials, your teaching of art. All his attitudes toward art are negative. In Johnny's case, his lack of value and his negative attitudes are consistent.

Suppose, however, that Johnny values learning and success. The conflict between these positive values and his negative attitude toward art can't help but upset him and contribute to his headaches and absences.

CHARACTERISTICS OF ATTITUDES AND VALUES

They are inferences. Both "attitude" and "value" are abstract concepts. The two terms were created to refer to something that does not exist psychologically separate from an individual. Our grammar permits us to talk about values as if they were as real as trees, about attitudes as if they were as obvious as leaves. Actually no one has ever directly seen an attitude or touched a value; neither can be heard or smelled or tasted; neither is directly perceptible to our senses.

Attitudes and values are inferences drawn by observing acts or words and then interpreting the reason the person acted or spoke in the manner observed. If you see a person pick up a wallet dropped by a stranger and return it, you can infer that the person values honesty. That person believes it would be a better world for us all if we each were honest about lost money (and probably, honest about all things in all situations). If someone talks constantly about pie but never about cake, you might infer that person likes pie and dislikes cake (or at least likes pie better than cake). In either case, the attitude or value must be inferred, neither can be observed directly.

If attitudes and values are inferred, a teacher must be careful about inferences drawn from single examples. Repeated observation of acts and words is called for before a teacher can say with confidence, "Johnny likes neat papers" or "Mary is honest."

They predispose action. Emotions and motives are mixed into the nature and functions or attitudes and values. Emotion provides observable emphasis to words and acts, emotion raises the voice or flushes the cheeks. Motives involve a connection between arousal of the need system and the setting of a goal. An attitude is a form of anticipation about action, a state of readiness to act. The attitude or value provides a psychological foundation for specific motives. The child who wants to draw a map has motivation and a goal; underlying the motive is an attitude toward mapping or a value toward success, or both. In either case, the attitude must satisfy some motive, or must lead to an act intended to satisfy the motive.

Attitudes and values predispose a person to act in a preferential way, rather than merely to be puzzled when a person is faced with a particular situation. The implication of this for the teacher resides in her concern for motivation in learning. Attitudes aren't motives, but attitudes certainly can influence motives. Indeed, it seems fair to say that teachers who complain about lack of motivation among pupils do not understand the power of attitudes and values. It is a personal opinion, but I believe younger children are more easily motivated by teachers partly because the young child has fewer attitudes and holds them with less intensity than older pupils.

They are personal but shared. Attitudes and values exist as part of *an* individual's psychological system. I have my attitudes, you have yours. Mine are personal, so are yours, but chances are we also hold some attitudes and values in common.

If I am telling the truth when I say, "I like fishing," then you can infer my attitude toward fishing. I can impute the attitude of Professor Joe Park toward fishing by writing, "Old Joe, the philosopher, likes to fish." In each case, if true, the attitude belongs to the individual, yet we share an attitude toward fishing.

The probability of shared values is even stronger, for people have fewer values than attitudes. Small groups can be held together by sharing either attitudes or values, but large-group cohesiveness is usually based on commonly held values.

The teacher needs to be concerned about classroom groups sharing attitudes for two reasons. The larger the group holding an attitude with negative connotations, the more difficult it will be for the teacher to influence the possibility of change in the attitude. Second, if her attitude toward something conflicts with an attitude shared by a group of children, then the teacher must assess the effect of attempting to change the group.

They are responses to something. Any object, event, quality, or idea existing in your environment can provide the focus for an attitude or value. This subject-object relationship requires some sort of psychological response. You perceive, you have feelings about the perception, you think about the perception, and you act. For example, I just noticed my tobacco jar (perceiving), reacted favorably (feeling) to the memory (thinking) of smoking, and reached (acting) for my pipe. My attitude (I *like* something) was a response to something in my environment. The pupil in the earlier example about art was responding to things and events, his attitudes were responses that led to overt, observable responses. As teachers, we know pupils respond overtly to their classroom environments, but we often forget that attitudinal responses lay behind their obvious classroom behavior.

They have direction. You can have a positive attitude toward apple pie and a negative attitude toward liver. You can enjoy San Francisco, but not Philadelphia. You can prefer to live in a democratic republic rather than in a democratic monarchy. You can be for peace and against war. By analogy with chemistry, you can assign plus or minus valences to your attitudes. With values, the popular interpretation is to assign only plus valences; if you hold a value, you hold it positively. On the other hand, it is quite common for a person to assign a minus valence, or negative direction, to values of others with which he does not agree. For example, if you are for peace and I am for war, you are negative toward my valuing war.

There are some things you can be neutral about, but as an adult your neutrality is usually based on lack of information or concern. In the case of young children, however, lack of exposure to stimuli results in a lack of attitudes or values toward those stimuli. The teacher of early elementary grades tends to have more effect on attitudes toward a greater range of new things than will the teacher in later grades.

They have intensity. The most obvious examples are the scales requiring us to rank our preferences from "strongly disagree" to "strongly agree." A response to such a scale item toward, say, peace would indicate both direction and intensity. A person can be strongly against war but only mildly against a fist fight between two willing participants. Intensity usually tells us how much a person will invest in acting toward or against something. You might risk your teaching career by fighting a law requiring teachers to be fingerprinted, or you might think the law foolish but harmless and therefore not be willing to risk anything. Your overt response indicates the intensity with which you hold the attitude or value. Teachers can usually infer intensity of a pupil's attitude from his actions, especially if he is highly emotional. In fact, intensity is a good measure of attitude, because children often become good at hiding their real attitudes, while giving teachers verbal responses they believe teachers want.

They are relatively persistent. Once an attitude or value is acquired, a person tends to continue to maintain that attitude or value. A child who prefers blue to other colors tends to continue to prefer blue. If a youngster believes in education as an avenue for social mobility and if experience confirms that education leads to achievement of social-mobility goals, then education as a value becomes a highly persistent belief. Because attitudes and values are relatively enduring, the individual has a consistent means for interpreting stimuli and for responding to his or her environment.

The notion of persistence is particularly painful to teachers in cases where a pupil holds an attitude or value conflicting with those of the teacher. The teacher who wants a pupil to change an attitude must take into account the strength of persistence. Attitudes or values are not changed with the ease of correcting misinformation.

They are learned. A child is born with the capacity to acquire attitudes and values, and the child lives in sets of environments from which attitudes and values may be acquired. The stimuli parents, teachers, and friends chose to put into an environment, or choose to call attention to, influence the *basis, direction, intensity,* and *persistence* of a person's attitudes and values.

A child learns attitudes and values from experiences and reflection about those experiences. As attitudes and values are expressed in behavior, all the pressures of rewards and punishments are brought to bear on the formation and expression of attitudes. To a great extent, identification with others seen as important influences the acquisition of both attitudes and values. The implications of these facts are similar to those drawn out in detail in the two previous chapters on concepts.

DEFINITIONS AND FUNCTIONS

From the characteristics discussed earlier, the following definition can be drawn: an *attitude* is

—a relatively persistent

—cluster of learned beliefs

—predisposing an individual

—to behave in a preferential manner

—toward someone or something.[1]

A value differs from an attitude in one major way. Value is based on a judgment of what is desirable for an individual and his society; values express what is believed to be good, right, just, or beautiful for the lives of people. Attitudes may touch on goodness (and the like), but more directly they are simple expressions of liking or disliking something. A value also differs from an attitude in some minor ways: values are one-directional, highly intense, and strongly persistent. A *value* is

—a highly persistent

—cluster of learned beliefs

—based on a judgment of what is desirable

—predisposing an individual

—to behave in a preferential manner

—toward someone or something.

These complex definitions aid one in thinking about or researching attitudes and values, but they are awkward to remember. For the sake of economy of memory:

—An attitude is a predisposition to like or dislike something.

—A value is a predisposition to believe something is good or bad.

Both are psychological responses inferred from acts or words. Both predispose action. Both become criteria for judging and for making choices. Both help orient a person to environmental situations, for we all select and organize stimuli on the basis of our concepts—and attitudes and values are conceptual elements. Either helps the individual select and organize stimuli into a perceptual whole. The old saws, "He saw what he wanted to see" and "She heard what she wanted to hear," have their roots in the functions of attitudes and values.

For two reasons—because the literature directed toward teachers deals primarily with the term *value* and because the major characteristics of attitudes and values are shared—I will refer only to values throughout the remainder of this book. My use of the term values, however, will refer to both attitudes and values.

THE OBLIGATION TO DEAL WITH VALUES

A major change in educational practices over the past decade has been diminution of the idea of *in loco parentis*. Our courts have reminded teachers that children are also citizens. Children today, particularly in upper grades, know they have certain rights under the Constitution. They can dress as they like, wear their hair as they like, and publish what they wish, as long as they do not endanger the lives and health of others and do not disrupt normal school operations.

A second notion, disturbing to teachers, has an "intellectual" hold on many children—everybody should do his own thing, be in her own bag, or whatever the current slogan may become. This notion has considerable validity if we believe in the dignity and worth of the individual, but lacks conviction unless limiting criteria are added, for example, "Everyone should do his own thing as long as he doesn't hurt anyone else."

A third problem is summed up in the current term "moral decay." Large segments of our society, from one ideological extreme to the other, insist all will crumble about us unless others join them in pounding sand down their favorite rat holes. The silliness of these demands, however, cannot hide the fact that we are in deep ecological, racial, population, welfare, violence, and school trouble. Most of us are uneasy about changes today, partly because a parent's very real history of depression, fascism, and communism is not the history of a youngster.

Many teachers believe they have no right to help a youngster develop certain attitudes or examine certain values. "The child has a right to become what he or she wants," they argue. "What right have I to influence that child in any way?" Other teachers say, "My job is to see that he learns his facts. He was sent to school to learn to think."

The first teacher makes a fundamental error. She assumes that dealing with values means indoctrination; she ignores the idea that becoming what one wants is a matter of choice and that the greater the range of options, the stronger the possibility the child will come to know what he wants to be.

The second teacher doesn't understand that very often the learning of facts is accompanied by the learning of attitudes and values toward the subject matter, toward the teacher, and toward the way the facts were taught and learned. The successful pupil not only learns the facts but also respects the teacher and values the way he learned. The unsuccessful pupil not only fails to learn the facts, he also learns to dislike the teacher and the way he was taught.

In the first chapter, Mrs. Jessup certainly helped me develop attitudes toward research and thinking about the future; Miss Shepherd helped me develop attitudes toward slavery and the value of freedom; even Mr. X, who ignored me, influenced my attitudes toward teachers and teaching. What was important about the first two was their help in making me aware of my attitudes and in helping me clarify my values. (Granted, Miss Shepherd was authoritarian in making me a slave. The democratic teacher today would probably talk me into "participating in an experiment.")

The obligation of the teacher to think about values in the classroom seems evident. Values are going to be learned, to be strengthened or diminished even if the teacher pretends they do not exist. The question to consider is not "will I deal with values," but "how will I deal with values?"

VALUING

Values predispose both overt and covert acts. If you return a lost dollar to someone who dropped it, you have acted overtly on the value we call honesty. If you decide, by thinking, to buy a four-door rather than a two-door car, you have acted covertly on the value of convenience rather than appearance. Whichever car you bought, you were *valuing*—a process involving choosing, prizing, and acting.

Valuing always deals with values or attitudes; the major difference between the notions of values and valuing is that values predispose action, while valuing requires action. The three names closely connected to valuing are Raths, Harmin, and Simon.[2] Their book identifies seven characteristics of valuing (I have paraphrased them).

Choosing freely. The person makes the choice rather than having a parent or teacher or other authority figure make it for him. The person, of course, may be influenced by someone else, but he is not coerced. Indeed, in most instances of coercion, the person merely talks and acts one way around the authority figure and quite another way when the "boss" isn't around.

Choosing from alternatives. Choice implies that at least two options are open to a person. In most cases, there are several options—picking up the dollar and keeping it, picking it up and returning it, picking it up and putting it in the Sunday-school collection, leaving it lie and ignoring it, leaving it lie but calling out that it had been dropped.

Choosing after reflection. Valuing depends partly upon reasoning. Choices are made after the possible consequences of each alternative action have been considered (what will happen to me if I keep the dollar, to the loser when he needs it but misses it, and so on?).

Cherishing the choice. The person who values his choice needs to be reasonably satisfied with that choice. He is convinced that he did what any right-acting person should do, and that the world would be a better place if everyone made the same sort of choice.

Affirming the choice. The person needs to have enough pride in his choice to affirm it publicly, to say that honesty is a good thing and that the right way to act in dealing with others is to act honestly. This does not mean the person should go around shouting loudly on every occasion about his honesty; it does mean that he holds his position on honesty in discussions about honesty.

Acting on choices. The person needs to act to confirm his choice, overt behavior reflects value choices. If the person says "honesty is good" but pockets the dollar, then he is lying to himself. He really values dishonesty on his part (although he is likely to become livid with anger if someone deals dishonestly with him). Indeed, a person's values are inferred from his overt behavior.

Repeating value choices. Every person's behavior has a pattern, and if a person persists in acting consistently on the basis of a value choice, then those who observe his behavior can have some confidence about the nature of his values.

One of the peculiarities of valuing is that choosing and prizing can occur instantaneously when action is required. The sorting out of alternatives and reflection of their consequences is sometimes a matter of split-second thinking. One advantage to dealing with valuing in the classroom resides in the amount of time that can be devoted to alternatives and to reflection. A further advantage lies in the opportunity to talk out the prizing of choices with others who may disagree with your views.

For generations, teachers have been concerned with values and valuing, even when they thought they were being quite neutral about many topics. When I emphasize inquiry in this book, I am valuing—I am stacking the deck of instructional cards so I can deal out a hand I want you to reflect upon. I'm not picking topics at random for inclusion in this book. I'm even aware that I choose the alternatives I mention, and sometimes my choices approach straw-manning. The same situation will hold for you when you teach. If you opt for textbooks, recitations, and grading on the curve, then you have made value choices, even if you aren't aware of it or won't admit it.

VALUING AS A SCHOOL ACTIVITY

I have heard teachers argue against dealing with valuing on the grounds that it is immoral to influence the choices of others. They argue that every individual is unique, and that the values and attitudes the individual holds are the source of that uniqueness. I quite agree with that statement about uniqueness, but I don't see how the immorality notion flows from it. Do they mean that valuational uniqueness is genetic in the manner of physical uniqueness? Do they mean uniqueness implies no common characteristics among humans? Do they mistake influence for coercion? Do they believe schools should deal with facts but not with feelings?

After some questioning and discussion, it usually turns out that they had a "close friend" who was forced to verbalize a set of value statements in school but who operated on quite another set of values outside school. The conflict between the two led to a sense of guilt over acting inconsistently. This guilt was painful and adversely influenced the self-concept of the "close friend." At this point I recognize that this person does not distinguish between values and valuing. They believe *any* discussion of values must involve the teacher forcing the pupil to accept (at least verbally) the values held by the teacher.

Actually, if valuing is to become a classroom activity of use in learning, the teacher must provide a psychologically fair climate. The teacher must be open to others who will press for value choices that do not agree with her's. She must accept the possibility of clashes over values by pupils, and she must be alert that cliques of pupils do not intimidate individuals with whom they don't agree. Beyond this atmosphere of freedom of expression, the teacher must be concerned about how to get pupils to let their values surface in discussion and to get pupils to clarify their value statements to themselves and to others in the discussion.

The Raths, Harmin, and Simon book provides you with a range of techniques—valuing charts, rank ordering, open-ended questions, value whips, voting questions, and public interviews are just a few. Several of the other books listed at the end of the chapter are equally useful, and in all frankness, I suggest you buy, study, and reflect on one of them before you try valuing techniques with a class.

In the chapters that follow, you should be able to pick out many of the strategies on valuing. They are not marked with red dots or blue arrows, but they are there.

NOTES

1.   Only the structure of these definitions is original with me. The basic ideas are drawn from Kurt Baier, "What is Value?" in Kurt Baier and Nicholas

Rescher (eds.), *Values and the Future,* The Free Press, New York, 1969, pp. 33–67; Frederick J. McDonald, *Educational Psychology,* Wadsworth Publishing Co., San Francisco, 1959, pp. 211–299; and Milton Rokeach, *Beliefs, Attitudes, and Values,* Jossey-Bass, San Francisco, 1968.

2.   Louis E. Raths, Merrill Harmin, and Sidney B. Simon, *Values and Teaching: Working with Values in the Classroom,* paperback ed. Columbus, Ohio: Charles E. Merrill, 1966, pp. 28–30.

SUGGESTED READINGS

Baier, Kurt, and Nicholas Rescher (eds.), *Values and the Future.* New York: Free Press, 1969. (A superb book for the future-minded; you may not want to read all of this one, but you should sample it.)

Barr, Robert D. (ed.), *Values and Youth.* Teaching Social Studies in an Age of Crisis, no. 2. Washington: NCSS, 1971. (An excellent combination of traditional theory and contemporary thought; for example, it deals with the values inherent in rock music.)

Gallagher, Arlene (ed.), "Special Issue: Children." *Law in American Society,* vol. 2, no. 2, May, 1973. (A journal issue worth its weight in intellectual gold, it combines philosophy, psychology, strategies, and theory on values and valuing.)

McDonald, Frederick J., *Educational Psychology.* Belmont, Calif.: Wadsworth Publishing Co., 1965. (My favorite discussion of values in an educational psychology text; two chapters are devoted to values and the second contains a fine review of the literature on what influences changes in attitudes and values.)

Metcalf, Lawrence E. (ed.), *Values Education.* 41st Yearbook. Washington: NCSS, 1971. (Rationale, strategies, and procedures on values clarification.)

Raths, Louis E., Merrill Harmin, and Sidney B. Simons, *Values and Teaching: Working with Values in the Classroom,* paperback ed. Columbus, O.: Charles E. Merrill, 1966. (For many teachers, this is the handbook that revived values and value clarification. It is filled with strategies for clarifying values, and these are strategies a great many teachers have tested successfully in their classrooms.)

Rokeach, Milton, *Beliefs, Attitudes, and Values.* San Francisco: Jossey-Bass, 1968. (A superior report on the topic, clearly written and packed with useful background information. This book is "must" reading for forming your own ideas on values.)

Simon, Sidney B., Leland W. Howe, and Howard Kirschenbaum, *Values Clarification: A Handbook of Practical Strategies for Teachers and Students,* paperback ed. New York: Hart Publishing Co., 1972. (Another excellent resource, building on the foundations of the Raths, Harmin, and Simon handbook.)

Zimbardo, Philip, and Ebbe E. Ebbesen, *Influencing Attitudes and Changing Behavior*. Reading, Mass.: Addison-Wesley Publishing Co., 1969. (A basic introduction to theory, methodology, and application of both to practice.)

EXERCISES

1. Turn back to Chapter 1, and see if you can find evidence of choosing, prizing, and acting in the examples of the three teachers. If you were Mrs. Jessup or Miss Shepherd, how else might you have helped me clarify my values?

2. Get a group of your classmates to vote (thumbs up for agree, thumbs down for disagree, thumbs hidden for undecided) on these statements:
   a. Do you believe you will raise your children less strictly than you were raised?
   b. Do you believe there are times when cheating is right?
   c. Do you believe school ought to be optional after the eighth grade?
   d. Do you believe classes can be taught for two or three weeks without the use of textbooks?
   e. Do you believe you could teach a month in a classroom without desks or tables for pupils?
   Keep track of the vote on each item, then discuss the vote and let your classmates discuss why they voted as they did. In view of what you know of values and valuing, what happened during this exercise?

3. Read Frederickson, Zimbardo, or Rokeach. List the influences on value changes and sketch out some classroom strategies for changing what you perceive as undesirable classroom behaviors.

4. Read either Raths, Harmin, and Simon or Simon, Howe, and Kirschenbaum, and identify some classroom strategies you believe you would be comfortable with. Then try one or two of them out on a group of your classmates. Report to the class on your success or failure.

Inquiry and Problems

Inquiry is both noun and verb, but the key to either form is action. Someone will inquire. Someone is inquiring. Someone has inquired. Inquiry involves action.

A quick look at Roget's *International Thesaurus* shows some of the nouns associated with the idea of inquiry: search, test, survey, review, contemplation, investigation, probe, exploration, check, analysis, diagnosis, question, query, problem, and issue.

In the same source, you will find these verbs as synonyms: ask, question, interrogate, seek, hunt, pursue, search, explore, grope, comb, trace, track, investigate, examine, inspect, and analyze.

The range and shades of meanings associated with inquiry indicate that inquiry may, quite properly, mean a great many somewhat different things to different people. A moment's thought about these synonyms reveals one particular characteristic: inquiry is a process, a set of actions occurring in some order. The doctor who diagnoses my sore throat as tonsillitis rather than strep throat does not perform a single act, but a series of acts. The detective who interrogates does not ask a single question but a series of questions. The same holds true for the chemist who analyzes, the lawyer who questions, the philosopher who contemplates.

Given this notion of inquiry as a complex set of acts, the small classroom answer to a small question doesn't qualify as such.

Inquiry deals with larger or more complex questions. Answers, or conclusions, are arrived at through a series of acts. Some of these acts are quite complex—say, tracing changes in the use of land within the present central commercial area of Chicago over the past 100 years. Some of the acts are quite simple—say, checking the population of Chicago for 1970. Inquiry involves a set of investigative actions undertaken to discover an answer or answers within a mass of evidence.

The phrase "to discover an answer" needs some clarification. I don't mean that the answer is actually stated somewhere in the mass of information. If it were, then a pupil would merely have to identify the statement as the correct answer. That's not inquiry. In the inquiry process, the answer must be invented or created through deduction or induction, through inference, hypothesis, and conclusion. To be sure, the answer usually exists, and the teacher usually knows the answer. Pupils discover or create relatively few new truths, but they can discover and state truths new to them. For example, the Pythagorean theorem is known to many adults, but it is a quite legitimate learning experience for a teacher to guide a pupil through its proof in such a way that the pupil feels he discovered it—not for mankind, but for himself.

Another key to the meaning of inquiry lies in the last paragraph. The pupil is the inquirer. Whether he acts as an individual or as a member of a group and whether he acts with or without guidance from the teacher, it is the pupil who does the inquiring. Inquiry means that pupils, with a minimum of guidance from the teacher, ask the questions and discover or create the answers.

INQUIRY AND THINKING

It is an axiom of good teaching that an individual must do his own learning. He must do some thinking for himself if he is to extract meaning from his experiences. Others may help him learn, but that help is valuable only to the extent that he will think about it. The quality of his thinking obviously influences the quality of what he learns. If he memorizes, then he won't have learned much of value. But if he analyzes and synthesizes a problem, his conclusion will be more worthwhile.

Let's say you have a brand new lightweight motorbike so you can zip around town. You show the new scrambler to your boyfriend. He admires it and then asks, "Where's your helmet? You know you ought to have a helmet. If you take a spill and don't have a helmet on, you'll smash up that pretty face."

Your boyfriend asked a question, cited something that passed for evidence, and drew a conclusion. Did you learn from this conversation? Maybe, maybe not. If you respect this man's opinion, you may accept what he says. Or, if you aren't sure about his opinions or judgment, you may ignore what he said.

Now, let's change the situation. You buy the new bike, but you don't buy a helmet. You read somewhere that your state legislature is considering the question of requiring every biker to wear a helmet. You ask yourself, "What good will it do to wear a helmet?" You think about this a bit and come up with some arguments for and some against the idea. One day you go in to have your motorbike serviced. You see three smashed bikes in the garage. "Wow," you say, "look at those!"

"You ought to see the people who were on them," says the mechanic, "two of them weren't wearing helmets. One was killed. The other is in the hospital for plastic surgery on his ear."

You think about this new evidence. Then you buy a helmet and you wear it. *You* asked your own question. *You* considered the evidence. *You* arrived at a conclusion. This kind of learning is more effective in most cases than simply remembering that someone gave you some advice.

It works the same way with children. For example, it is a fact that nearly all the most heavily populated cities in the United States are located on navigable bodies of water. A good question is *why* are they located on navigable bodies of water.

The easy response for a teacher is to tell her pupils the answer. The more difficult alternative is to guide a pupil (or group or class) to find evidence that bears on the question and then draw some conclusion from the evidence. It takes time and resources to help pupils sharpen the question to involve the dates these cities were founded and then to consider why they developed into large cities. The teacher must be certain that materials containing the evidence needed are available to her pupils. She will have to live through the process of drawing a number of conclusions from the evidence. And she will have to give her pupils time to present their findings.

The answer (and it is a complex one) to the question may not be sophisticated enough to please an urban historian, but it will likely be highly satisfying to fifth graders, it will likely be remembered by them, and it will likely be applied to other questions involving the location and development of large cities in other parts of the world. Further, the pupils have learned a way of learning; they have learned a way of answering a question, as well as an answer to a question.

QUESTIONS ABOUT INQUIRY

A teacher, of course, is bound to have a number of questions about learning through inquiry. How can she be sure her pupils are interested in this topic? Why should children rediscover knowledge known to adults? And, is every question worth learning through this time-consuming process?

The answer to the question of interest lies in two facts. First, the teacher decides on general topics for study. This is not to say that teachers should make every decision about topics, for teachers can share many of these decisions with pupils. But in most school situations, the teacher is legally responsible for dealing with a generally specified body of subject matter. She makes her decisions about the best approaches to the study of that subject matter. Then, she shares decision making with pupils in a great many situations. Sometimes, she may have good reasons for having the whole class deal with one large and significant question. Other times, she may be delighted to have five groups working on five different questions, plus three or four individuals off working on their own questions.

The second fact is that teachers can stimulate the development of interests held by pupils. Pupil interests often spring from their experiences. If the teacher provides them with activities and materials calculated to develop interest, then interest may well be created. It is a sentimental fallacy to imagine that all pupils of the same age bring exactly the same interests to the classroom. Of course pupils bring their interests to the classroom, but the range of differences among pupil interests is staggering. The alert teacher takes advantage of these interests; sometimes by using them to determine a topic for study, but most often to encourage groups or individuals to pursue subtopics within a general topic. Beyond this business of bringing interests *to* the classroom, a good teacher helps pupils develop new interests *in* the classroom. The teacher can't always wait for every pupil to develop an interest in a topic before she introduces that topic. But the good teacher recognizes that unless she can stimulate interest in the topic, there won't be much worthwhile learning by her pupils.

The answer to the question of rediscovering what is known to adults can be hinged on one proposition. The way to learn to do something is by doing it. If you want pupils to be able to ask questions, to locate and evaluate evidence, and to draw conclusions, then there should be opportunities to perform these acts. They need not be performed constantly, but they must be acted out often enough that they become established patterns of behavior. You don't learn to locate information only by being told how to find it. You don't learn to arrive at conclusions only by memorizing the conclusions of others.

It seems obvious that not all that might be learned is worth learning through the inquiry process. There seems to be no point in discovering the names of the five Great Lakes. Why waste time discovering the names of our presidents or the capital cities of the 50 states? The fact that the lake I see from my office window is called Lake Michigan is a matter of associating a particular name with a particular lake. What psychologists call signal learning, stimulus-response learning, chaining, and verbal association are not worth learning through the inquiry process. Multiple-discrimination learning, concept learning, generalizing, and problem solving are naturals for the inquiry process.

What is changing in teaching under the influence of concern for inquiry is not that everything is learned through inquiry, but that *some* things—the most important things—are learned through inquiry.

INDUCTION AND DEDUCTION

The inquiry process described to this point has been primarily inductive in nature. This is because the inductive process generally works better than the deductive process with children of elementary-grade ages. There are some teachers who maintain that inquiry *must* be inductive in nature; that is to say, if a pupil does not reason from particular facts to a general rule, he has not engaged in inquiry. Nonsense! Every good thinker, amateur or professional, shifts back and forth between inductive and deductive reasoning as he or she deals with questions or problems of any complexity.

Suppose a fifth-grade class has gotten into the question of why the price of corn products rose in a given year. After two or three days of digging into factual information about corn production and the prices of corn products over a period of years, the class notes a relationship between the two; when corn becomes scarce, the price of corn products rise. The class arrived at this conclusion inductively. Someone (the teacher, as a last resort) asks if the same relationship holds for other raw materials. The class restates its problem thus: when raw materials become scarce, the prices of finished products rise. Then they deduce a set of restatements: tomatoes are a raw material and catsup is a finished product; thus, when tomatoes become scarce, the price of catsup should rise. This conclusion can be checked against the facts.

Another example involves the teacher who begins with a general rule and asks that it be proved or disproved with the use of evidence. The teacher says, "In the United States, high prices tend to restrict consumption and stimulate production. You can divide into groups and spend the next three days trying to find evidence that will let you accept, reject, or modify that statement." The process here will be largely deductive, although inductive reasoning will also play a major role in the inquiry.

There are two rules of thumb about the use of induction and deduction in teaching. If you are working with youngsters or with new ideas, use the largely inductive process. If you are working with older students or with semifamiliar ideas, use the largely deductive process.

INQUIRY MODELS

Models are dangerous, for any reduction in scale tends to obscure or eliminate details. I have said "a set of actions occurring in some order" is a characteristic of inquiry. What kinds of models do we have for these actions and their order?

Model No. 1

1. *A question is raised and stated clearly.* The question may originate from any source—pupil or teacher, textbook or film, life in the classroom or the neighborhood. The question must be precise and clear to ensure that it is understood by those who seek to answer it.

2. *A tentative answer is developed.* The function of a tentative answer (hypothesis) is the narrowing of the scope of research. The tentative answer may be based on prior knowledge, reasoning, intuition, or prejudice. A class may arrive at a number of tentative answers, and different groups may investigate quite different possible solutions.

3. *Evidence bearing on the tentative answer is gathered.* Evidence must be located and collected. Evidence must be tested for accuracy. Relationships among bits of evidence must be sought.

4. *A conclusion is drawn from the evidence.* The drawing of the conclusion involves accepting, rejecting, or modifying tentative answers on the basis of reasoning from evidence.

5. *The conclusion is applied to the original question and to subsequent similar questions.* The conclusion should provide an answer to the original question. It should also be tested against a number of other imagined questions of similar nature. And opportunities should be sought for applying the conclusion to future questions drawn from study and from life.

One problem with this model is the impression that these actions always occur in this order. They don't. Sometimes step 2 is skipped. Sometimes the order is 1, 3, 2, 3, 4, 5. Sometimes steps 4 and 5 occur simultaneously. At best, the model is an approximation of what actually occurs in the inquiry process.

Another model, largely inductive, looks like this.

Model No. 2

1. *A question is raised.*
2. *Evidence is sought and evaluated.*
3. *A proposition, or general rule, is inferred from particular evidence.*
4. *The question is tested against the proposition or rule.*
5. *In future situations, the proposition or rule is tested against new evidence.*

Still another model, largely deductive, looks like this.

Model No. 3

1. *A question is raised.*
2. *A known general rule is stated.*
3. *An answer is inferred from the general rule.*
4. *Evidence of the accuracy of the answer is sought.*
5. *Evidence is used to confirm the answer and the general rule.*

An historian's model might look like this.

Model No. 4

1. *Raising a question.*
2. *Researching the sources.*

3. *Interpreting the evidence.*
4. *Presenting the findings.*

One more example. In teaching fifth grade, I used to give my pupils an outline map of the United States with the current number of representatives to congress printed on each state. My question was, "Do the states with the largest areas have the most representatives?" They always discovered the answer was *no*. The next question was, "What is the rule for deciding how many representatives a state gets?" Now, they had to raise some tentative answers and figure out what evidence they needed to "prove their case." (Once in a while some good reader would go directly to the Constitution. My response was, "Can you prove that's the way it works?")

The business described above is a rather simple example of inquiry. Some teachers used to ask why I took so much time to help pupils arrive at an answer that could have been pointed out in a minute. The answer is simple: people tend to understand and remember what they teach themselves.

There is a second answer to the *why* question. Human beings are problem creators. Thus, some humans must become problem solvers. If I have read my history correctly, man's problems have spurred him to find solutions and his solutions have determined whether his society progressed or decayed.

If inquiry produces solutions, and if inquiry can be learned, then what's a little extra time to a teacher?

PROBLEMS AND INQUIRY

Some teachers are satisfied that problems are the questions printed at the end of a chapter. Sometimes these questions are problems, but too many of them read like these.

1. Who discovered America?
2. Who paid for the ships Columbus used?
3. What were the names of the ships?

Other teachers have the idea that problems must be currently without solution to be called problems. For example:

1. How do we eliminate poverty?
2. How can the United Nations get the nations of the world to disarm?
3. When will man stop polluting his environment?

The first examples are problems only in the sense that the word problem is used in arithmetic; that is, "do the first ten problems for homework." The second examples are problems in the sense that they are matters of doubt and difficulty to all of us. Examples of this second type of problem can be legitimate topics for study if the teacher and pupils recognize that they are arriving at tentative and untested conclusions.

The usual problem the elementary pupil faces, however, is somewhat less complex than the question of achieving disarmament. For example, a second-grade class in the Midwest was studying the Indians who lived in their area before whites settled there. In the course of their study, they learned the Indians depended on the buffalo for many things. A small group was putting on a short play. They shot the buffalo with arrows. They skinned it. They cooked it. One child wrapped himself in a buffalo robe.

The next day the play was presented again and included the acting out of the tanning of the hide. For their own purposes, these pupils had solved *their* problem. What was the process they used?

Model No. 5

1. *Feeling of confusion or doubt.* The pupil becomes aware that an obstacle to further activity has arisen and expresses puzzlement, concern, or doubt.
2. *Recognizing and defining problems.* The teacher and/or children try to state the problem as a question. "Can you state the problem?" "What do you think the question is?"

The teacher records the problem in children's terms on the board and usually asks one of the pupils to read this aloud.

The teacher then asks: "Why do we want to know this? How will solving this problem help us?"

If enough of the group seems enthusiastic about solving it, proceed; otherwise, drop it, at least for the time being. The teacher, however, must try to lead her class to consider the problems she feels of major importance to their progress. As an adult working with children, she must capitalize on pupil interest but must also seek to create interest where it may not seem to exist.

3. *Analyzing the problem and formulating hypotheses.* After the problem has been stated, the teacher asks: "What do you *think* the answer might be?" (Teacher accepts and writes all suggestions on the board, even when they seem preposterous.) The teacher and pupils discuss the suggestions offered. If the class knows them to be untrue or impossible, they are erased; if uncertain, they are left up and the group realizes the problem is not solved.

4. *Gathering evidence.* The teacher asks such questions as: "How do we find out if our suggestions are right?" "Where can we go for solutions?" Children list books, pictures, people who know, experimenting, films, trips, and so forth. If the children don't find a way, the teacher suggests it and helps pupils to decide whether one of these ways is best for solving the particular problem. Children agree on things to do—they may work in committees, with partners, or as a whole group; they may read, view films, question people; they may do an experiment if a problem needs it; they may go on a trip to find out answers, and so on. For primary-grade children, data gathering is completed in a day or two; older children may require a week or more if several research areas are explored.

5. *Verifying and interpreting evidence.* After research, the teacher asks such questions as: "What did you find?" "Did you check your findings?" "Did you learn something new?" Put evidence on board in usable order. Ask what it means.

6. *Formulating and accepting conclusions.* The teacher asks such questions as: "Shall we look at our list of possible solutions (suggestions, guesses, and so on) and see which are correct?" "Do we have a useful solution?" "How will our solution help us in our work now?" "Will the answer we found today always be true?" "Does our answer remind us of other answers to other problems we have solved in the past?"

7. *Applying conclusions.* Pupils go back to whatever activity they were engaged in when the problem arose—and continue this activity using the solution to the problem to lead into new experiences. At this point, the teacher seeks to stimulate reflective thought on the entire problem-solving procedure and to help pupils evaluate the consequences of the choices they made in the effort to solve their problem.

Problem solving in this model looks remarkably like the other four models dealing with inquiry. Are inquiry and problem solving the same thing? The answer is probably "yes." Problem solving has a long history in our literature, while inquiry, as a term, has been widely used in the past few years.

Each term came into use as some teachers revolted against teaching practices that stressed reading and recitation, against learning situations that never got beyond memorization and recall. The revolts led to calls for a shift to increased emphasis on thinking and on learning how to learn. Both revolts led to the use of certain key words: hypotheses, evidence, reasoning, and conclusions.

Both problem solving and inquiry make use of inductive and deductive reasoning. Both require the child to do his own inducing and deducing. Both call for observation, interpretation, judgment, application. Both need a classroom climate of intellectual freedom and the right to make mistakes while learning takes place. Both place restraints on teacher decisions and certainly on her verbal behavior. Both demand access to evidence through a wide variety of materials and activities. Both generate new interests, or they fail.

The decision *you* must make is this: inquiry, or problem solving, is a learned behavior. Do you feel it important enough to your pupils and your society to take the time needed to teach it?

SUMMARY

Inquiry is both a noun and a verb; in elementary education both action and its product are called for in dealing with important topics or problems. Pupils should learn to produce some of the knowledge they possess. There is information that can and should simply be absorbed through memorization. Conclusions, on the other hand, are of quite a different intellectual level. They should be arrived at, and the process of learning how to produce conclusions is at least as important as knowing the conclusions. If the pupil never inquires, then the pupil does not learn to inquire in school.

The products of inquiry are the products of reflecting on experiences, on the interaction of self with others and with subject matter. The nature of this reflection may be largely inductive or largely deductive, but in most cases arriving at a solution to a problem requires both inductive and deductive inquiry. For most teachers, the problems with inquiry are time and resources. Inquiry takes more time than simple memorization of information or someone else's conclusions. Inquiry into a problem when the resources needed to solve the problem are lacking is a generally fruitless operation.

Inquiry and pupil interest are tightly related elements in classroom practices. Pupils have interests and they should be utilized whenever possible. Pupils also learn to be interested. The creation of social studies subject matter is broad enough to foster a wide range of subinquiries and subactivities for pupils to satisfy their own interests.

Inquiry models must be viewed with a proverbial grain of salt. No matter who formulates them, they provide no more than general guides to the inquiry process. The teacher needs to understand them, to have them clearly in mind during class activities, but should never become upset if the order of steps becomes shifted or if steps become combined. The nature of the problem and the prior experience and learning of pupils quite naturally constricts or expands the inquiry process.

Lastly, the teacher must recognize that inquiry is a set of learned behaviors. Pupils do come to school capable of thinking; we know this by observing their out-of-school behavior. The teacher's functions are to refine the thinking processes of some, to stimulate those who doubt they can think about school topics, and to provide all with practice in inquiry into problems that provide them with the satisfaction that they are learning.

SUGGESTED READINGS

Dewey, John, *How We Think*. Chicago: Henry Regnary & Co., Gateway Editions, 1971. (A reprint of the forerunner. If you've read much Dewey, you can handle it in an hour or two.)

Fair, Jean, and Fannie R. Shaftel, *Effective Thinking in the Social Studies*. 37th Yearbook. Washington: NCSS, 1967. (A good review of inquiry, with more than usual emphasis on elementary-school ideas and practices.)

Gross, Richard E., and Raymond H. Muessig (eds.), *Problem-Centered Social Studies Instruction: Approaches to Reflective Thinking*, paperback ed. Curriculum Series No. 14. Washington: NCSS, 1971. (A good quick source providing a review of inquiry principles and their application at various levels of education.)

Haddan, Eugene E., *Evolving Instruction*. New York: Macmillan Company, 1970. (An interesting and profitable book, better as a review of all topics to date than just inquiry; it seeks to convince the reader of the function of theory in teaching.)

Kaplan, Abraham, *Conduct of Inquiry: Methodology for Behavioral Science*, paperback ed. Newcastle, N.H.: C. Chandler Co., 1964. (A fine source

for a foundation in the role of inquiry in the behavioral sciences; a book
for the serious student.)

EXERCISES

1. Select from your curriculum library a copy of a pupil text for the grade
    you want to teach. Pick a chapter on a topic you like. Analyze the con-
    tents of the chapter carefully. Then pose two or three inquiry questions
    that will stimulate pupils and that will cause them to use the book as a
    source of information for arriving at conclusions. Work through, in your
    mind or on paper, the processes (group, intellectual, and research) that
    pupils will be likely to engage in as they solve the problem.

2. Examine the neighborhood in which your school is located (a real school
    or one in your imagination) and select a question appropriate for your
    pupils. How do people know where their land ends and someone else's
    begins? How does Mrs. Twinky make a profit in her candy store? What
    keeps us safe in this neighborhood? How do the people who live here
    feel about the way their taxes are used? What are the dangers of living
    around here, and can we do anything about it? Plan a set of inquiry
    activities to get at reasonable conclusions for your question, but assume
    all data required to answer it must come from the neighborhood.

3. Analyze the chapter by Crabtree in *Effective Thinking in the Social
    Studies*. Do you feel the teacher had the right answers clearly in mind
    before this unit was ever begun? Why? Can you work out a similar unit
    that would take possible pupil interests more into account than this
    chapter seemed to provide for?

4. Take any of the models of inquiry you like and sketch out what might
    happen with it if you were to apply it to a topic of your choice in a
    classroom. How does the model help you plan? How does it seem to
    restrict you?

5. Take a pupil text and pick a chapter at random. Read a few pages and
    then answer these questions: What might a child think as he read this?
    What questions might I introduce to turn pupils to inquiry in reading
    this? What questions might pupils raise about this material that would
    lead to inquiry? What resources beyond this book would we need if we
    did get into a decent inquiry about the topic? What conclusions, other
    than those in the book, might pupils arrive at by using this book as a
    springboard to inquiry?

PART TWO

Decisions, Decisions

THE superintendent of a Michigan town looked me over. "You look tough enough," he said, "and your transcript shows you're bright enough. Want to teach a sixth grade?"

I told him that if he knew what he wanted taught, I could teach it.

"This class put two experienced teachers in the hospital last year," he said.

I told him the only time I'd been in a hospital since I had my tonsils removed was to have two bullets cut out.

"I can get you a temporary certificate," he said, "if you'll take three education courses this summer."

I told him OK, and he told me the salary was $2850 and all the chalk I could eat. I figured I could fake out any man with a sense of humor like that, so I said OK again.

I'd been making $8000 as an engineer, but the chance to save the world seemed worth $5150.

The local college put me in a history of education course, a philosophy of education course, and practice teaching. Today I don't remember anything about the two courses, but I remember clearly that the critic teacher never let me teach. After a while, I began spending my time across the street drinking coffee and thinking about teaching. I got A's in the two courses and a C in practice teaching. I got my C mostly for putting a battery in the critic teacher's car. He was afraid of electricity and didn't want to electrocute himself by putting the negative cable on the positive pole. I also switched two wires on his spark plugs and hoped he would have a lousy time getting to Fire Island for his vacation.

Moral   *Courses in pedagogy are often useless if you aren't allowed to test what you are being taught.*

Moral   *Knowing what an administrator wants taught means understanding that he doesn't want your class to cause him any trouble.*

Goals and Teachers

Teachers hate to be taught badly, but almost all teachers do some bad teaching. The worst of it is that bad teaching, like bad apples, has its effect in time. It takes time and trouble to get rid of bad apples, and it takes time and trouble to get rid of bad teaching. Bad apples have to be thrown away, for no tetrocycline or penicillin will restore them to health. The only miracle antibiotic for changing bad teaching into good is rethinking your goals and the activities used to reach those goals.

Those who teach badly tend to believe in a laying on of labels. If the miracle word of the moment is *felt needs,* then they say they are teaching to felt needs. If the magic phrase is *stimulus-response,* then they claim to be stimulating responses in admirable fashion. The present mark of the golden fleece is *values.* Throughout the land resounds a great clattering of tongues as teachers lay claim to this latest panacea. The problem, of course, is that a bad teacher wouldn't know a value if one bit her in her academic bustle.

All teachers, knowingly or not, operate on the basis of a set of principles. Good teachers hate to admit that bad teachers have principles, but they do; some of these principles are:

1. "I know my subject matter." This means she read the textbook before she used it with pupils.
2. "My job is to teach; their job is to learn." This means that what she doesn't know can't be discussed.

3. "My methods are tried and true." This means that children memorize and recite all day everyday.

4. "Good discipline is an absolute condition for learning." This means, "Quiet you little beast or I'll tape your mouth shut!"

5. "The best textbooks are the old ones." This means I don't have to learn anything new and disturbing.

With such teachers, all thinking is memorizing. All testing depends on recall or recognition. All deportment is judged against standards of silence, immobility, and deference. Such teachers cling together within a faculty, reinforcing each other in the illusion that they are the best of all possible teachers. They have made certain decisions about what to teach and how to teach it; the question is, How sound are their decisions?

The next section of this chapter is a good example of bad teaching. I once watched a teacher cram so many new terms and so much unknown information into a 40-minute "lesson" that I was fascinated by the majesty of her errors. In the hope that you will react to the lesson much as her pupils did, I have translated her social-studies terminology into nonsense words you won't immediately recognize that allegedly refer to a sparsely occupied planet, Serin, which has just been discovered.

TEACHING ABOUT SERIN

To reduce overcrowding on Earth, whole families are to be rocketed through space to Serin. The people there speak a brand of English—the major difference being that their nouns are different from ours. The children of several departing families are being taught a lesson about Serin by a bad-apple teacher.

To play this game fairly, you must obey two rules. You must read this "lesson" rapidly, and at no point may you reread anything before you have taken the "test."

The teacher speaks: "All right, children, this is a globe that represents the planet Serin. Serin rotates once every day and revolves around a large, hot star, called Zup, once a year. Rotate means 'turn around' and revolve means 'go around.' Too bad you haven't studied the heavenly movements of our solar system or you would understand better.

"Serin rotates on its stigz, which is an imaginary line from the Chachee Spod to the Migo Spod. What we call directions, they call wazetoogo.

Chachee is the wazetoogo toward the Chachee Spod. And migo is the wazetoogo toward the Migo Spod. The other two wazetoogo are sumni and aber. Aber is where you see the zup in the early morgin, and sumni is where you see the zup in the ebning. Here, I'll put it on the blackboard.

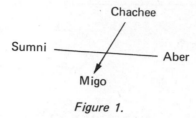

Figure 1.

"That's easy isn't it? But there is one problem. The magnetic rocks on Serin are all near the Migo Spod. So if you have a compass on Serin, the arrow will point at the Migo Spod. You'll just have to get used to Santa Claus living at the bottom of Serin instead of at the top of our Earth. Ha ha. That's a little joke.

"I'll draw a circle for Serin. They call a circle a zigle. A zigle has 1,000 milz in it. It is 1,000 milz around the zigle.

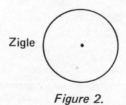

Figure 2.

"If you draw a line from the zup to the center of Serin and then raise a perpendicular line from that point, you can see that the stigz of Serin is inclined from that perpendicular. The angle of inclination of the stigz is 65.3 milz. Don't frown so, Bobby, I won't ask you to figure it out on the test. All you have to do is remember it, dear.

"Is all that clear? What are the cardinal wazetoogo on Serin, Barbara? Very good! How many milz in a zigle, Karen? Right! How many milz is the chachee-migo stigz inclined from the Zup-Serin plane, Bobby? You don't know? Take your hands out of your pocket, Bobby. Take them out!

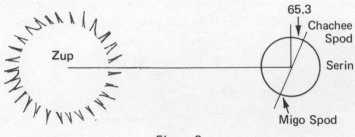

Figure 3.

Put them on your desk where I can see them. It's not good for young boys to have their hands in their pockets. The answer is 65.3 milz.

"Now that all that is clear, I want to talk about the dehavlinn. Oh, dear, I have only a few minutes left. Listen carefully now. The zigle that is exactly half way between the Chachee and Migo Spods is the dehavlinn. The dehavlinn is the 0 milz linn. The dehavlinn is a zigle. It is a true sumni-aber zigle.

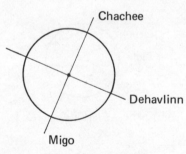

Figure 4.

"Chachee of the dehavlinn are many other zigles, usually 42 milz apart. These zigles are called litans. A litan is used to measure howfer by milz chachee of dehavlinn. There are also litans migo of the dehavlinn that are used to measure howfer a zigle is migo of the dehavlinn. Can you remember that? A litan is used to measure howfer chachee or migo of the dehavlinn. A litan is also called a pragagag because each litan is pragagag from all other litans. Bobby, get your hands back where I can see them! Pragagag means two linns that are always equal distance from each other from any two points on the two linns that could be connected by a perpendicular linn. Litans are pragagag zigles used to measure howfer chachee and migo of the dehavlinn.

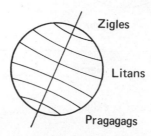

Figure 5.

"There is one more thing, but our time is up. The chachee-migo zigles on Serin are called loganoons. A loganoon is a chachee-migo linn used to measure howfer sumni or aber. A loganoon is a zigle but no loganoon is pragagag to any other loganoon. Now, clean off your desks and line up in two neat linns!"

Incredible as it may seem, this is the way some teachers "teach." Such teachers consider themselves the cream of the crop. In the 1920's, they would have said they were stimulating responses. In the 1930's, they were meeting felt needs. In the 1940's, they were at war with the Axis. In the 1950's, they were teaching subject matter. In the 1960's, they were teaching concepts. In the 1970's, they are valuing. Actually, in each decade they laid a new label on their same tired old litany of drill, drudgery, and damnation.

In analyzing what this teacher attempted, you realize that you must depend upon inference to know what her goals probably were. At no point does she really say, "This is what I hope you will understand." She does emphasize certain terms and bits of information, and you can assume those terms and bits of information were worth learning.

The opening paragraph is revealing. She speaks of a globe that represents a planet. She uses *rotates* and *revolves* in a single sentence and then defines those terms verbally in a manner that is open to confusion. There she laments the lack of prior experience on the part of pupils as a basis for

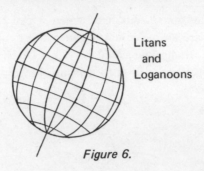

Figure 6.

Test   Name _____

1. Our new planet is called _____ .

2. It is _____ from Earth to _____ .

3. A linn of litan is a true _____ – _____ .

4. There are 1001 milz in every zigle. True. False.

5. The stigz of Serin is inclined _____ milz.

6. Are litans or loganoons pragagag? _____ .

7. _____ and _____ linns are used to measure
   howfer _____ and _____ of the dehavlinn.

8. I like my teacher. True. False.

Extra Points

9. How many milz chachee of the dehavlinn would
   the chachee zup zigle be? _____

10. Explain in 25 words or less why loganoons cannot
    be pragagag.

---

this new information. What has she done here to motivate anyone to want to learn anything? What has she done about readiness and transfer of knowledge, except to ignore the first and regret the lack of basis for the second? What about practice, even at the level of sheer repetition of the terms? Apart from one use of the clause "Serin rotates on its stigz," when again, even in the test, does she use either term in the clause? So even if we infer that she wants her pupils to recognize the two terms if they should hear or read them again, what chance is there that they would respond correctly to those two terms?

Assuming this teacher knows what goals she has in mind, what are the chances even a few of her pupils will achieve them? How well did you do? Could you follow what she was driving at in her lesson?

Come back to this lesson from time to time as you read this book and as you prepare plans for working with children. Look at its obvious errors, and then compare your own ideas and procedures with those of the teacher on Serin.

MOTIVATION AND GOALS

If a child is to learn in school, he must direct his actions toward a goal he is capable of reaching. All schools of psychological theory agree that a child must be motivated to learn. He can furnish his own motivation; that is, he can want to learn just because learning satisfies him. He can accept external motivation; that is, some pressure to learn from you or his parents or his friends. Or his learning can have been motivated both internally and externally. If a child feels motivated to reach a goal and if he feels successful because he did reach it, then in the future he is likely to be positively motivated toward reaching similar goals and toward repeating the method that brought him success.

Human beings possess or develop a complex range of physical and emotional needs. Hunger is the sign of a need to eat. The goal of a hungry man is food. His motive for eating is to fill his stomach so his need to eat will be reduced. Almost all of us have an emotional need for recognition. Our goal is a response made by someone else to our words or acts. The motive is to have someone else respond to us so the need for recognition will be satisfied.

The best social-studies lesson or unit is one that recognizes the needs and motives of children and provides experiences satisfying to those individuals. The best social-studies teacher is the one who helps, everyday, the greatest number of pupils to reach their goals.

The first step involves getting a child to state his goal. "Today I want to learn the location of ten states." "Tomorrow I want to draw a map showing how all the continents could have once been fitted together in one big continent." "Today I just want to read this book and see if it is interesting." Sometimes goals are difficult to achieve. Sometimes they are ridiculously easy to achieve. Most of the time, children's goals are quite realistic.

The second step is to be sure a pupil knows how to reach his goal. "I'm going to use the World Book Encyclopedia." "Billy is going to test me on the states." "I'm going to trace the continents on the globe onto this thin paper, and then I'll cut them out and try to fit them together like a jigsaw puzzle."

The third step, which can be skipped if the goal is very easy to reach, is to help a child know where he stands in achieving his goal. "Now that you have read about displacement, Jack, I think you are wise to test your finding with the fish tank." "Billy says you can locate six of your ten states already. That's a very good start." "Say, South America and Africa do fit together nicely!"

The fourth step is to help a pupil evaluate his accomplishments. "That's a good description of displacement, Jack. You helped me understand it better than I did before." "I think getting nine of the ten states today is fine." "It certainly does look like the continents could have fit together like that. I'm going to bring you a map I saw in *Scientific American* so you can see how some scientists think they once fitted together." A child makes his own judgment about goal achievement in most cases, but he usually wants some additional response from you.

No teacher has time to do all this with every pupil during every social-studies class. That's one good reason for working in small groups in social studies, since group interaction provides for some of these procedures. And every teacher can get to every child in some subject or activity everyday. Whether a child learns to like to learn depends in great part on how skillfully a teacher helps him connect his needs and motives to realistic goals.

THE FUNCTIONS OF GOALS

In the classroom, goals have at least three functions. The goal provides direction for the learner's behavior, and concurrently the nature of the goal influences the type of behavior needed to reach the goal. The classroom environment provides opportunities for learning and conversely sets limits on what may be learned. Thus, the goal indicates what materials must be present and what activities must be encouraged if the goal is to be reached. The goal also functions as the criterion for evaluating achievement; it is the standard for recognizing that a child has gotten where he said he wanted to go.

Pupil behavior can be either random or selective. Random behavior is seldom goal oriented, unless the goal is the avoidance of boredom. Some random behavior is acceptable, because all of us fool around part of the time, but constant random behavior usually produces conflict and problems for both teacher and pupils. Goal-oriented behavior may produce as much movement and noise as random activity, but it is purposeful and leads to some sought-after and agreed-upon end.

The nature of the goal influences the type of learning behavior needed to reach the goal. If a pupil wants to find out what the capital of Texas is, then certain research behaviors are called for. If a pupil needs to build a lighthouse for a model of a harbor, then construction behaviors are called for. If a pupil can't read his textbook, then certain listening or viewing behaviors are called for if he is to learn at all.

The classroom environment must provide a wide range of materials and activities useful in reaching certain goals. If a pupil wants to locate Texas, his environment must include maps. If he wants to build a lighthouse, his environment must include plans, tools, and construction materials. If a pupil can't read but wants to learn, his environment must provide other materials (say, films) and activities (discussion rather than recitation) from which he can learn. One of the advantages of social studies is that pupils can learn from other pupils. If one youngster can't read well, he can listen while someone else in his group reads something aloud; by listening he picks up enough facts and ideas to think about the topic being investigated. If the goal is clear to the teacher, then she should be able to deduce what must be present in the learning environment if the pupils are to have a chance to reach the goal.

Goals also function to determine the content of testing situations and of paper-and-pencil tests. If you write an achievement test, every item on it should be directly related to one of your goals. If you ask for performance ("Draw a compass rose on the map, Chuck"), then the act called for should be connected to a goal; if you don't really care about the idea of a compass rose, then you are wasting your time, Chuck's time, and the time of everyone watching you and Chuck. On the other hand, when your tests reflect goals that are clear to everyone, then pupils feel you are fair, and they tend to believe that they have been working toward something worthwhile.

SOCIAL-STUDIES GOALS

By tradition, social-studies goals have usually been stated in three categories:

Knowledge: The pupil should know the structure and functions of local, state, and national government.

Attitudes: The pupil should appreciate life in a democracy.

Skills: The pupil should get along with others when working in a group.

A major problem with these statements has little to do with the nature of the categories; the difficulty lies in the abstractness of the statements in the categories. These are motherhood and apple-pie statements, open to a wide variety of interpretations. How does a pupil show he knows how his local government functions? How does a pupil who appreciates life in a democracy act? What does it mean to "get along" with other pupils? Somehow or other, these statements must be brought down the ladder of abstraction to a point where they become specific and behavioral and thus have concrete meanings for teacher and pupils.

Let's take an example. A fifth-grade teacher says, "I want my pupils to know the names of the 50 states in the United States." The first problem is that the *task* is ambiguous; what does she mean by "to know"? The second is that we can't tell under what *conditions* the pupils are "to know." The one thing she is clear about is the *standard* she will apply—the pupils are "to know" all 50 states, not 42 or 34, but all 50 states.

A clearer statement would be, "Using an outline map of the United States, the pupil will point to and name each of the 50 states." The *condition* (using an outline map) and the *standard* (each of the 50 states) are clear and specific; the *task* (point to and name each state) is obviously a behavior any of us would recognize. The advantages of the statement are obvious; it is precise, specific, behavioral, and clear in its intent.

The problem with stating goals behaviorally—with the condition, task, and standard clearly specified—lies in the probability that any teacher can think up a thousand and one goals for any grade. As ridiculous as it sounds, a teacher could spend most of her preparation and free time just writing behavioral statements of goals. Somehow or other the teacher must find a middle ground between the mountains of abstractness and the swamp of specifics. The iron law of available time forces a teacher to decide which goals are of greatest importance to herself, to her pupils, and to their society, and then to translate those relatively few important goals into a slightly more extensive number of behavioral goals.

Before I suggest a set of goals I feel are important enough for you to consider in teaching social studies, let me specify three caveats. First, at this point, I am writing about goals that you as a teacher must decide upon, goals that will give direction to your behavior in helping your pupils learn. I assume we agree that these goals must be subsequently shared with pupils and that this sharing process will result in pupils accepting some of your goals, in your mutually modifying and perhaps rejecting some of the goals, and in their adding some goals to your list.

Second, some of my goals will apply as much to science or reading as they will to social studies. For example, if I refer to "research skills," I assume that using an encyclopedia to find out how a lever works is essentially the same process as using an encyclopedia to find out how ballots are cast in a presidential election.

Third, my examples will range over the grades, but most of them can be modified for other grades. Thus, if I write about fifth graders developing a concept of *labor,* I am assuming that in many instances, with particular groups of pupils or special materials or activities, the concept of labor can be developed in many earlier grades.

THINKING AND VALUING GOALS

Wherever I taught, from kindergarten through eighth grade, I had four goals dealing with thinking and valuing:

—These pupils need to develop concepts.
—These pupils need to create generalizations.
—These pupils need to solve problems.
—These pupils need to choose, prize, and act on their values.

To achieve any of these goals, a pupil must possess and utilize factual information. In addition, each of these activities is a complex rather than a simple process. For example, developing a concept requires observing, describing, contrasting, comparing, classifying, and generalizing.

Each of these goals also involves the use of deductive and inductive reasoning and thus the use of premises and conclusions. I do *not* mean that I always used these terms in working with children. When I worked with kindergarteners, I said, "Look at this carefully," rather than "Observe this." When I worked with first graders, I said, "Put all the things that are the same into a group," rather than "Classify these things," and I said, "Can you make a general rule out of all the evidence you found?" There were times and grades when I did use the more precise terms with pupils, but the decision to be precise depended on the verbal ability of pupils and on the possibility that the term would be useful in later learning. Indeed, with fifth graders I often found I could say, "What is your concept of _____? or "What generalization do you draw from all this?"

Why did I elect concepts, generalizations, problem solving, and valuing as important goals for social studies? First, each is a process important to historians, geographers, and other social scientists. Understanding the subject matter of the social sciences requires that a pupil develop concepts and generalizations, and a pupil can deal with the issues and problems of the social sciences only through some sort of problem solving. Second, each of these processes requires the use of other simpler processes. If I want pupils to develop concepts, I must help them learn to observe, to describe, to classify, and so on. If I want them to create generalizations, I must help them to infer, to analyze, to synthesize, to interpret. My goals were a middle ground between sheer abstraction and infinite specification. Third, I believe these are worthy goals because the people who make a significant difference in our lives exhibit the ability to develop concepts, create generalizations, solve problems, and act on self-selected and prized values. These men and women may be without formal education or they may hold academic degrees, but they share one attribute—it is their ideas and solutions that count in the long run.

Conceptualizing, generalizing, solving problems and valuing—and the processes associated with them—may not satisfy you as major thinking goals for social studies. That is not the point. The point is that you need your own list of goals regarding thinking and valuing. Without such a list, *your* behavior as a teacher will not be oriented to helping pupils think, and the classroom learning environment *you* create will likely limit pupils to memorizing and recalling.

SUBJECT-MATTER GOALS

Every teacher knows she deals with subject matter and must have some subject-matter goals. This subject matter falls into two rough classes: discrete bits of information and concepts and generalizations.

Bits of information take these forms: "There are 50 states in the United States." "The Atlantic Ocean is east of the United States." "Lansing is the capital of Michigan." "Pittsburgh is located at the confluence of the Allegheny and Monongahela rivers." "Texas is a major oil state." "East and west are opposite directions." The basic question regarding subject-matter goals is: How important is this information? There is no agreed-upon answer. A person might not be considered ignorant because he didn't know Lansing is the capital of Michigan, but what would he be called if he didn't know Washington, D.C., is the capital of the United States?

Three useful questions in thinking about information as goals are:

1. What information does this individual want to know?
2. What information does this individual need to know to keep others from thinking of him as ignorant?
3. What information does this individual need to develop concepts, draw generalizations, and solve problems?

My position is that the answer to the third question is the important one. I say that because I believe concepts and generalizations are *the* important elements in subject matter and because concepts and generalizations are based on factual information. Further, if I answer question 3, I have also likely answered question 2. However, a pupil's plea for information (assuming the topic isn't vulgar or criminal) should always be respected.

How can you handle discrete bits of information as goals? If you feel compelled to make lists, they might look like this one:

From memory, the pupil should be able to name:

1. each of the 50 states in the United States
2. each of the four regions of states
3. the largest state by area
4. the largest state by population
and so forth.

At first I thought it helpful to make short lists like this one, but as I gained experience I found they weren't so helpful after all. They do have one advantage—once you have them written out, they are good for impressing supervisors who adore lists. Incidentally, note that the *condition,* the *task,* and the *standard* are all present in the list.

Concepts and generalizations abound in social-studies programs and in most of the newer textbook series. The concepts usually are found in texts, but often the generalizations are only implied. The reason is that generalizations are a form of conclusions, and the authors want pupils to draw their own conclusions. For your convenience, the generalizations are to be found in teachers' guides.

In a first-grade book, for example, the child might be expected to develop concepts for *need, group, role, family, school, neighborhood, member,* and *leader.* The author would decide the order she wanted to introduce the terms in and the minimum number of times she would use each term; then she would provide enough information, description, and examples for a pupil to be able to develop a concept for the term.

Your first task with concepts is deciding the extent to which you will emphasize that concept. For example, I recently used a second-grade text in a class where the teacher was called out of her room for an hour. The part she was using dealt with roles; there was one page on sociology and four pages on roles. Should I give equal time to each concept? Should I give one-fifth time (one of five pages were on sociology) to sociology and four-fifths to roles? We skipped the page on sociolgy and spent all our time on roles. Why? Because a concept of sociology led to no generalizations or applications for second graders, nor could they solve any problems with it. We dove right into roles; we read and we discussed; we took the roles of others (patrol boy, principal, nurse, and so on) and acted them out; we discovered that each pupil played a different role in each group to which he or she belonged. (Note that the last is both a conclusion and a generalization.) We had a hell of a lot of fun—particularly when one girl role-played my behavior with them—and we got initial concepts of roles established with every child in the class, including the three that couldn't read the text.

In some cases, generalizations are to be found in textbooks, but the best use them as models from which pupils see how to frame further generalizations. For example, a first-grade book might include a paragraph like this one:

"All people must eat food to stay alive.

All people have a need for food.

What other needs must people meet to stay alive?"

Each of the first two sentences is a generalization summing up a great deal of factual information about the needs of people in all parts of the world and in all known times. The third sentence asks a question obviously intended to lead pupils to think, to conclude, and to state their own generalizations about other needs shared by all people.

Needs, people, and *stay alive* are the key concepts in the sentences; without these concepts, there could be no generalizations. Both the concepts and the generalizations should be useful again and again in studying people both locally and in other places and times. The example clearly indicates that the author and publisher believe concepts and generalizations to be important elements of subject matter. Your job as a teacher is to decide which of the concepts in the text are useful for your pupils. You emphasize those, and you ignore or move quickly over the others.

A second choice you need to make turns on the question of which important concepts for your class are not in any of the printed materials available to them. A corollary question is, Which important concepts are used as terms in the text but without the mass of factual information or examples needed to build meanings or feelings about the term? As an example of the first question, I once used a story on farming that provided adequately for a concept of *planting* in agriculture, but did nothing for a concept of *planning* the sequence of events required to bring crop to harvest. My class needed the concept of planning more than they needed planting, so I had to arrange a series of activities tied to the story, in order that my pupils could develop the concept that was implied but not in print in the story. As an example of the corollary question, I used a textbook unit on families. When one child kept asking, "But why is my name Braun?" I found a McGraw-Hill film on families that answered his query perfectly and also reinforced many of the other ideas we had been studying about families. This notion of finding the "hidden" goals also applies to the matter of valuing. Values, as far as elementary textbooks are concerned, tend to be implicit rather than explicit. The opportunities for valuing are there, but they aren't underlined or marked with red stars. One or two of the latest series have units on values and valuing; those units do contain explicit value questions, but examine the rest of the book and draw your own conclusion about opportunities for valuing. The point seems obvious: Only when augmented by your questions will ordinary text materials produce valuing behaviors on the part of your pupils.

A third choice you must make deals with the number of social-science disciplines you want represented in your social-studies program. I started out stressing history and geography, but in a year or two I came to believe that a comprehensive selection gave me and my pupils better balance and greater utility. Many recent texts and programs clearly draw information, concepts, and generalizations from several of the social sciences. The emphasis may vary from grade to grade, but the pattern comes through as multidisciplinary. For example, in grade three the key concepts for a general topic on cities might be:

—*history:* change, settlement, development, time

—*geography:* location, landforms, resources

—*anthropology:* society, culture, interaction

—*economics:* production, exchange, consumption

—*political science:* government, voting, leadership

—*sociology:* groups, roles, communication

—*jurisprudence:* laws, justice, courts.

Someone must decide what subject matter goes into a program. The author must decide for his textbook. The curriculum specialist must decide for her course of study. But in the end, you have the power, for you decide to use or ignore guides, textbooks, and every other type of material produced for use in the classroom. If you like a guide, you will use it. If you like a text, part of your job has been done for you. But if you don't agree with the guide or text, then you have a professional responsibility to produce a list of subject-matter goals suitable to your pupils. Actually, in most cases, you will pick and choose from written courses of study and textbooks. You will emphasize the concepts and generalizations you feel are worthwhile, and then you will add other concepts that you believe are important to your pupils.

There are times when you must abandon textbooks and prescribed programs. Let us assume you have a class of poor readers; they lack wide previous experiences, they suffer from physical and emotional conflicts, and they lack pride in themselves. Faced with that sort of situation, you had better ignore the conventional program. Your goals might better become building concepts of cooperation, rights, responsibilities, pride, justice, and so on. Actually, these substitute concepts are respectable subject-matter goals, for each is part of one or more of the social sciences. The difference in this situation is that you ignore the stated goals of a program in favor of other goals desperately needed by your pupils. You may have to turn from written mtaerials to the life of the classroom and community events for content, but your goals still measure up as subject-matter goals.

SKILLS AS GOALS

From kindergarten on, elementary pupils engage in research, work in groups, and use maps and globes. Your responsibility for teaching specific behaviors in any of these three performance categories depends on the program of your school, the course of study for your grade, and your judgment of what your pupils know and need to know. The three sets of behaviors listed below will give you some idea of what you must consider.

Working in groups by:

1. showing respect for the rights and opinions of others
2. cooperating with others in achieving group goals
3. helping plan and carry out the planned activities of the group
4. acting as a leader or follower as the situation may demand
5. profiting from critical judgments about the strengths and weaknesses of one's performance and its products

There is little point in my being more specific about these behaviors, for specificity depends on facts unknown to me about your grade and pupils. For example, I might say using parliamentary procedure would be worthwhile, but only you can decide if that sort of behavior is appropriate to your class.

At this point, you will note that my statements are *not* as specific as they might be. This is a good place to point out that my middle-ground statements are open to a range of interpretations. Let's take the statement on cooperation (number 2) as an example. Does this mean a pupil must cooperate with any plan of any group for achieving a goal? Does it matter if you assigned Johnny to a group or he chose to work with a particular group? Does it matter how the group arrived at the goal—did the toughest kid insist on his goal; was there a vote; was the vote close? Is there any possibility for a minority report? Are there any circumstances where a lack of cooperation might be based on a principle of a higher order then cooperation? Even if you should accept my five categories for working in groups, you need to think each one through to your own satisfaction.

Using geographic tools by:

1. visualizing the nature and movements of the earth,
2. orienting oneself with directions,
3. locating objects and places,
4. calculating or estimating distances,
5. recognizing geographic symbols,
6. interpreting information contained in maps and globes.

Again, I have avoided specificity. For example, some kindergarteners can find cardinal directions, but it might not be until third grade that other pupils can do this accurately. You must decide if your class can handle location by the mathematics of latitude and longitude or whether it is enough that a pupil can say Mexico is a nation south of the United States.

Researching by:

1. locating information from:
   —written materials available in the classroom
   —written materials available in the library
   —audiovisual materials of any kind
   —maps and globes
   —field trips
   —interviews
2. evaluating information by:
   —distinguishing among statements of fact, fiction, and opinion
   —comparing sources for agreement or contradiction or the accuracy of factual information
   —recognizing bias, point of view, advertising, and propaganda
   —reserving judgment until the available sources are exhausted
3. organizing information by:
   —drawing reliable and valid conclusions
   —outlining topics and subtopics
   —supporting the main idea with fact and argument
   —using such criteria as pertinence, consistency, and sequence of information in preparing your product
4. presenting an attractive product (oral, written, visual) that meets the criteria of accuracy, exactness, clarity, and interest.

Again, it would be fruitless for me to say exactly what should be taught in your class, because I don't know you or your pupils, I don't know what their capabilities or interests are, and I don't know what previous experiences they have had. But, I do say that something from each of these four categories can be learned in any elementary grade. Kindergarteners can locate information—they can hunt through magazines and cut out pictures of farm animals. They can evaluate information—they can sort pictures of deer from pictures of cows by comparing both to a model in a picture book. They can organize information—they can draw conclusions (farm animals are used for food). And they can present an attractive product—they can put up a bulletin-board display of their pictures. I am always amazed at kindergarten teachers who say to me, "Five-year olds can't compare or classify or use criteria. Those words are too difficult for them."

Of course the words are too difficult, but what if the teacher says, "How are these things the same?" Isn't that comparing? What if she says, "Put all the things that are the same into one group." Isn't that classifying? What if she says, "Look at the picture of the cow in this book. Now look at the picture you cut out. Is your picture a picture of a cow?" Isn't that using a criterion? The word is not what is important; the meaning is important, and meanings are often developed before a word is pronounced and remembered.

SUMMARY

All classroom teachers operate within some set of principles regarding teaching and learning. These principles may be open or hidden, they may be consistent or contradictory, but they function to establish some of the parameters for what occurs in a classroom. Thus, it follows that you need to examine critically what you believe about the nature of the teaching-learning process.

Although goals are related somehow to any condition necessary for learning (motivation, readiness, transfer, practice, organization, and so on), they are most obviously related to motives. Motives influence acceptance of goals, the acceptable paths for reaching goals, and the acceptable standards for evaluating accomplishments regarding goals.

From a teacher's viewpoint, the functions of goals are: providing a direction and an end for learning behavior, setting opportunities and limits through the use of appropriate materials and activities calculated to aid pupils to reach goals, and establishing the criteria for knowing if and when a pupil has reached the goal.

There seem to be three orders of stating goals. There are the apple-pie statements that show our hearts are good and pure. These suffer from ambiguity and vagueness of meaning. There are behavioral goals where the task, the conditions under which the task is to be accomplished, and the standard by which achievement is to be measured are clearly, precisely, and behaviorally stated. The problems with these are that so many are needed and that they take time and care to produce. The third order comprises the middle-ground goals that are fairly precise and reasonably behavioral. These bring apple-pie statements down the ladder of abstraction, and there are not so many that they require an applaudable feat of memory to list them. Their shortcomings are lack of behavioral precision in the task and a complete lack of conditions and standards.

My bias is for the middle-ground type of goal as an organizing framework to ensure you do have some reasonable, comprehensive general directions; then, within this framework you can state a limited number of behavioral goals. Whether you do or do not accept my model, it should be clear that you need some system for establishing and stating goals to reflect your view of learning and to provide you and your class with some guide to action.

SUGGESTED READINGS

Bacon, Philip (ed.), *Focus on Geography: Key Concepts and Teaching Strategies*. Washington, D.C.: NCSS 40th Yearbook, 1970. (A fine resource on geographic goals and means of implementing them.)

Berelson, Bernard (ed.), *The Social Studies and the Social Sciences*. New York: Harcourt, Brace & World, 1962. (See the early chapter by Berelson and the late chapter by Lewis Paul Todd for views on the major purposes of teaching social studies.)

Bloom, Benjamin S., et al., *Taxonomy of Educational Objectives: The Classification of Educational Goals. Handbook I: Cognitive Domain*. New York: McKay, 1956. (One of a pair—see also Krathwohl, et al., listed below— providing the base from which most other behavioral-objective texts build.)

Chapin, June R. and Richard E. Gross, *Teaching Social Studies Skills*. Boston: Little, Brown, 1973. (The newest of the skills books; a highly practical handbook even though it is slanted toward the teacher of secondary social studies.)

Fair, Jean and Fannie R. Shaftel, *Effective Thinking in the Social Studies*. Washington, D.C.: NCSS 37th Yearbook, 1967. (Some good chapters on thinking; teachers seem particularly to like the chapter on Taba's ideas for developing concepts and generalizations.)

Flanagan, John C., Robert F. Mager, and William M. Shanner, *Behavioral Objectives: Social Studies*. Palo Alto, Calif.: Westinghouse Learning Press, 1971. (Specifically for the social-studies teacher; excellent for picking and choosing what you want; a great time saver if your district demands behavioral statements.)

Gronlund, Norman E., *Stating Behavioral Objectives for Classroom Instruction*. New York: Macmillan, 1970. (The best of the newer do-it-yourself manuals; clear, precise, useful.)

Harris, Chester W. (ed.), *Encyclopedia of Educational Research*. New York: Macmillan, 1960. (See the chapter entitled "Social Studies," by Richard E. Gross and William Badger, for an interesting discussion of subject-area objectives within the social studies.)

Krathwohl, David R., et al., *Taxonomy of Educational Objectives: The Classification of Education Goals. Handbook II: Affective Domain*. New York: McKay, 1964. (The companion volume to Bloom, et al.; perhaps the best examples around on stating values in behavioral terms.)

Mager, Robert F., *Preparing Instructional Objectives*. Palo Alto, Calif.: Fearon, 1962. (A handy programmed text that has saved many teachers on the subject of behavioral goals over the past decade.)

Piaget, Jean and Bärbel Inhelder, *The Child's Conception of Space*. London: Routledge & Kegan Paul, 1963. (A brilliant and influential book for the serious student; it provides a basis for developmental geography.)

Raths, Louis, Merrill Harmin, and Sidney B. Simon, *Values and Teaching: Working with Values in the Classroom*. Columbus, Ohio: Charles E. Merrill, 1966. (Still the best book for dealing with valuing. If you are serious about this process, you should own this book.)

Wick, John, *Educational Measurement: Where Are We Going and How Will We Know When We Get There?* Columbus, Ohio: Charles E. Merrill, 1973. (A witty, informative book written in an appealing style; the author talks with the reader instead of at her.)

EXERCISES

1. Go to your curriculum library, pull out a few curriculum guides, and see if you can find some examples of the apple-pie, middle-ground, and behavioral types of goal statements. What do you see as the advantages and disadvantages of each?

2. Go to your curriculum library or a local school and get a copy of a teachers' manual for a social-studies text for the grade you hope to teach. Examine the statements of goals, then check through the book to see if the content provides an opportunity for reaching these goals. Check one chapter or unit carefully. What goals might be implied in the chapter? What valuing might be done with the chapter?

3. Take a coffee break with two or three friends. Sketch out the middle-ground goals for an agreed upon grade. To what extent can you agree upon the meaning of the verbs in your statements of goals?

4. Take another coffee break, and see if you and your friends can translate your middle-ground goals into behavioral goals that include the *task,* the *conditions,* and the *standard.* Long coffee break, wasn't it?

5. Examine the Raths book. Try to write a *few* behavioral goals on valuing. Discuss them with some classmates. If you are fairly successful, pat yourselves on your backs, because this is a very difficult activity. If you can write these successfully, you can write behavioral goals on any topic. Note, please, the kind of thinking *you* had to do to accomplish this goal.

Goals and Tests

In teaching, a reciprocal relationship exists between goals and tests. If you see a list of behavioral goals, you know what the questions on a test should deal with. If you examine a test, you can tell what a teacher's real goals are. A goal defines the test item; the item reflects the goal.

The word *test* refers to testing in a variety of forms. If you ask a child what a story was about, you are testing him. If you ask him to orient a map, you are testing him. If you use a standardized, commercial test, you are testing him. The word *test* also implies that the child has previously learned something about the matter being tested. The child must have had the opportunity to learn the meaning of "orient a map" before your request can be considered a test situation. Without prior opportunity to learn, there can be no test.

Most of us dread taking tests; we shouldn't, but we do. We fear tests for four reasons. First, teachers fail to think through their goals, so their tests reflect their uncertainty—many test items are statements picked quickly from a textbook and restated as questions. Second, teachers fail to inform pupils of priorities among goals, so the test items appear equally weighted—a test on ancient Greece gives the impression that knowledge of *plinth, urb,* and *vase* are as important as knowledge of *democracy*. Third, teachers fail to use the test as a device for learning, so their tests fail to perform one of testing's most valuable functions—the missed test item provides cues on the effectiveness of prior learning and prior teaching. Fourth, teachers fail to use anything but the written test for grading, so test scores become the sole criterion for passing or failing, or for being ranked A, B, C, D, or F.

College students hate tests because they know most tests are bad tests. Elementary pupils hate tests because there is no joy in them or learning from them. Yet, teachers must test, or they fail to do their job well.

TESTS, BEHAVIORS, AND GOALS

Our literature contains many books on testing in social studies, and most methods books contain a chapter on tests—almost always at the end of the book. My quarrel with those books and chapters focuses mostly on what has been left out. My ideas on tests and testing reflect heresy, but heresy based on experience with pupils. Some specialists in testing won't like what I write in this chapter, because I believe tests should be used for the benefit of the pupil—not for the convenience of the teacher, the ego of the parent, or the status of the test specialist. If you want a conventional view of tests, don't read me, read somebody else.

Teaching is the process of helping pupils produce desirable changes in their covert and overt behavior. By *covert* behavior I mean what a person knows (information, concepts, generalizations), what he values, and how he thinks (conceptualizing, generalizing, and solving problems). By *overt* behavior I mean what a person does and how he does it. Overt behavior includes verbal behavior, but I am more concerned with what a pupil actually does than with what he says he should or would do.

Teaching blends three acts: stating goals, providing experiences through the use of activities and materials, and testing covert and overt behavior. Stating goals furnishes direction for behavior changes, points course materials and activities toward goals, and permits testing of learning *and* teaching. Materials and activities flow from the nature of goals, provide the opportunity for experiences as a basis for learning, and change when testing shows they have not been effective. Testing uses goals as the criteria for test questions, includes oral, paper-and-pencil, and observational situations, and provides a basis for reteaching and relearning.

Let me put this another way. The classroom teacher must ask three questions about an individual pupil, a small group of pupils, or her entire class.

1. Can I state the behavioral changes I seek in pupils?
2. Can I provide materials and activities useful in changing pupil behavior?
3. Can I differentiate between a pupil who can behave in a certain way from one who can't?

Chapter 3 dealt with three categories of goals—thinking-and-valuing goals, subject-matter goals, and skill goals. The question now is: If these goals are our guides to changes in behavior, how do we state them? My answer is that teachers need write only two types of statements to express their goals. Goals can be stated in terms of covert behaviors or in terms of overt behaviors. By covert, I mean that the cognitive process is primarily hidden from an observer; covert behavior is internal and unknown, and can be identified or inferred only when the pupil says or writes something.

There are times when a person should orient a map. If orienting maps is a geographic skill you seek to develop, then you want a pupil to know (a covert activity or state) that orienting a map means lining up the direction sign on the map with actual cardinal directions on the earth. Your covert goal would read: The pupil can state that orienting a map means lining up the direction sign on the map with actual cardinal directions.

When a goal is stated with this degree of specificity, the relationship between goals and test items is easily seen. The paper-and-pencil test item reads: "What does orienting a map mean?" You can also see how that item could be reworked as a true-false, multiple-choice, or matching item.

Now, there are teachers who are perfectly happy if their pupils can provide the right answer to an item on a paper-and-pencil test. And many of those teachers never give a moment's thought to the proposition that knowing something is somewhat different from being able to do something with what they know.

Let us assume you want a pupil to be able to orient a map. If you do, your goal could be stated in terms of overt behavior: the pupil orients a map when he uses it.

Or if you prefer more detail: when he uses a map, the pupil lines up the direction sign on the map with actual cardinal directions.

In the case of an overtly stated behavior goal, the appropriate test is performance. To test a pupil you hand him a map and ask him to orient it, or you ask a question whose answer depends on his orienting the map. If he orients the map, he passes the test.

An even better test is for you to watch a group of pupils working with a map in a situation where it should be oriented (say, a group of second graders on the playground working with a map of the immediate neighborhood). If they orient the map, you know they have learned. *That is the best of all possible tests!*

GOALS, PLANS, AND TESTS

Let us assume you are teaching fourth grade. Your class has just finished a study of the Northeast Region of States with emphasis on manufacturing. In studying that region, you made use of the model shown on the opposite page.

Your next unit deals with the North Central Region of States; it will emphasize agricultural production and reinforce what was just studied about manufacturing. The North Central Region includes 12 states arranged into two divisions by the U.S. Bureau of the Census.

East North Central Division	*West North Central Division*
Ohio	Minnesota
Indiana	Iowa
Illinois	Missouri
Michigan	North Dakota
Wisconsin	South Dakota
	Nebraska
	Kansas

Now, the question is: What subject-matter goals do you have in mind for your new unit on agricultural production in this unit?

You certainly will want to continue expanding concepts for DEMAND, RESOURCES, LABOR, CAPITAL, and so on, by applying them to agricultural production. To keep our example simple, you will introduce only one new term—RAIN—in studying this region.

For purposes of illustration, let us say you want pupils to learn that areas in this region specialize in the production of corn and hogs, wheat and cattle, dairy products, and some fruits. You decide to begin with corn and hogs. What might your behaviorally stated goals look like? The plan on the next page provides you with an example.

Once you have decided on your goals, you are in a position to begin

UNIT 1: Northeastern Region of States

Emphasis: Manufacturing

(1) Things people <u>want</u> to meet their <u>needs</u> and satisfy their <u>desires</u> . . . .

(2) create DEMAND for <u>goods</u> and <u>services</u> . . . .

(3) which are <u>produced</u> by combining RESOURCES, LABOR, CAPITAL, and TECHNOLOGY through MANUFACTURING based on a <u>division of labor</u>.

(4) <u>Goods</u> and <u>services</u> are made available to <u>consumers</u> in the MARKET . . . .

(5) which is made possible by use of <u>money</u> for <u>buying</u> and <u>selling</u> and use of <u>transportation</u> in getting <u>goods</u> to the MARKET.

(6) People <u>earn</u> <u>income</u> from their LABOR and use <u>money</u> to <u>buy</u> <u>goods</u> and <u>services</u> for a <u>price</u> . . . .

(7) some <u>income</u> is kept as <u>savings</u> and can be spent later or INVESTED.

Subject matter goals are <u>underlined</u> or capitalized. Underlined goals are economic terms for which pupils have concepts. Capitalized goals are economic terms for which pupils are to form initial concepts in this unit. Thus, a pupil should bring an initial concept of <u>needs</u> to this unit and that concept should be expanded in this unit. In this unit, a pupil should develop an initial concept for DEMAND.

planning the activities and materials needed to achieve them. I won't go into the question of getting pupils to accept or modify these goals at this point, because much of the remainder of the book is devoted to that question and to the question of how pupils can learn to achieve these or other goals. The point is: If I were substituting in your room, I could teach for you if I had this list of goals in front of me. My teaching might be orthodox or highly progressive, but I could get at the goals you had in mind when you stated them.

Topic: Agricultural Production: North Central Region

Subtopic: Corn and Hogs

Covert Behaviors	Overt Behavior
The pupil can name and locate the 12 states in this region. (information)	The pupil uses physical, soil, and rainfall maps to predict where corn will likely be grown in this region. (geographic skill)
The pupil can identify "water in some form" and "falling from the sky to the earth" as the key characteristics of rain. (concept and conceptualizing)	The pupil uses physical and corn production maps to predict where hogs will be raised in the region. (geographic skill)
The pupil can state that corn is used to fatten hogs. (information)	The pupil uses his concept of rainfall to analyze why corn and hogs are major agricultural products of this region. (problem solving)
The pupil can state that it takes 20 to 40 inches of rainfall during the growing season to grow corn. (information)	
The pupil can name the top-10 hog-producing states and state that they are all in this region. (information)	The pupil helps his study group plan their use of time in locating resource materials on hog- and corn-producing areas within the region. (human and research skills)
The pupil can provide examples to show that when raw materials (resources) are scarce, the price of the finished product rises. (generalization)	The pupil deduces that the price of bacon will rise if the supply of hogs becomes scarce. (generalizing and generalization)
(And review the goals dealing with RESOURCES, LABOR, CAPITAL, and TECHNOLOGY in agricultural production.)	The pupil uses complete sentences organized into paragraphs in writing a two-page report on corn and hog production in this region. (research skill)

Topic: Agricultural Production: North Central Region

Subtopic: Corn and Hogs (continued)

	Overt Behavior
	The pupil uses his concepts of RESOURCES, CAPITAL, LABOR, and TECHNOLOGY in analyzing agricultural production. "You just bought a farm in _____. What do you have to do to grow corn and raise hogs?" (problem solving)

I could also write a paper-and-pencil test based on your goals, or I could devise classroom questions or performance situations that would test achievement of these goals. For example:

Test

1. How much rain does it take during the growing season to produce corn?
    a.   0 to 20 inches of rainfall
    b. 20 to 40 inches of rainfall
    c. 40 to 60 inches of rainfall

2. Of the top ten hog-producing states, all ten are located in the North Central Region.   True.   False.

3. If the supply of corn becomes scarce, the price of _____ will rise.

Or I could ask: "Mary, show us the part of this region that gets 20 to 40 inches of rainfall each year." "Bob, have your group show the rest of the class the location of the top-ten hog-producing states in the United States." "What would be the result if these states only produced half as many hogs next year as they did this year? Why?"

Do all teachers use plans as detailed as this one? Do all teachers write out every goal in specific terms? The answer in both cases is *no*. After I taught two or three years, my plans for studying corn and hogs looked like this:

Corn & Hogs — No. Ctrl. RS

12 states — 8 of top 10 in corn — 10 of 10 in hogs

RAIN — "water" & "fall from sky to earth"
        20–40 inches for growing corn
Gnrlztn — scarce raw materials/price product rises

Needs: phys/pol map, & maps on rainfall, frost, corn,
        hogs
Need data sheets on corn prod. & hog prod.

Activities — map interp; study groups; 2-page report

TEST — have groups identify resources, labor, capital,
       and technology in corn & hog production

These "plans" were written on 5-x-8 cards. I could translate the goals into behavioral statements, and I did if I had any idea that I would be out of class and a substitute would have to take over. I could tell what activities and materials were needed (books pupils had found helpful were listed on the back of each card). From the card, I could write a test, or ask questions in class to test my goals. My 5-x-8 card system was just as effective as the longer type of plan, and it saved me a great deal of time.

MASTERY TESTS

A beautiful bell-shaped curve brightens a statistician's life, but a bell-shaped curve for pupil achievement should make good teachers weep. Yet many teachers brag about basing their grades on the curve. They don't know the enormity of their error.

A bell-shaped, or normal, curve is based on random activity or qualities, or on pure chance. Thus, the normal curve seems inappropriate for evaluating performances influenced by motives or effort. Heights of people at any given age distribute their measures into a normal curve. Shoe sizes for women distribute themselves normally. When suit sizes for men are plotted, the curve is bell shaped. Measures of intelligence are distributed normally. Why aren't measures of achievement distributed normally? Simple. The teacher and the pupil can use motives and effort and time to influence achievement scores.

I once taught in a school district where the director of research correlated achievement with intelligence. The lowest correlation for any class in the district was with my class. This worried my principal. He called me in and told me the low correlation made me look like the poorest teacher in the district. My answer was, like hell it did, it made me look like the best teacher.

The IQ's of my pupils were normally distributed, but their achievement scores were bunched into a narrow, high curve. When the two curves were superimposed on a single sheet of graph paper, the achievement curve clearly overlapped the right end of the intelligence curve. In other words, my "dumb" and "average" pupils were getting high achievement scores. The research director was called in. He plotted the two sets of scores on a correlation chart. The principal could now see the result—my class was overachieving. For the grade in question, my average class (average in intelligence) had the highest achievement mean and the tightest range of any class in the district.

Well, big deal. Was I a hot shot? Did I have magic ways? I didn't think so. I thought any teacher in the district could produce the same sort of results. In my opinion, I had gotten my results largely because I helped pupils use tests as a tool. I did not use tests as a weapon against the pupils.

Much of my testing was oral and a part of regular discussion. Pupils spent a lot of time questioning each other. I judged pupils primarily on their overt behavior in situations they never recognized as test situations.

Achievement tests guarantee failure to a high proportion of the pupils taking them. An achievement test is written to produce differences in pupil scores. When an achievement test fails to spread pupil scores out, then the test items are manipulated until the test provides some failing scores. Then teachers put red lines on their "curve" and say "everyone from here to here gets an A" and "down here we have our F's." Then they jiggle their red marks around so about half the students get C's. The other two areas are D's or B's. Don't let anyone kid you that most teachers who grade "on a curve" are more scientific than that. They aren't.

In an "average" classroom, about 10 percent of the pupils learn easily, about 10 percent learn with difficulty, and the remaining 80 percent range between ease and difficulty. The question is: What causes these differences in learning? Is it IQ? Is it the complexity of the task? Is it the amount of time available for learning? Is it readiness? Is it motivation? Is it something else?

With certain pupils in certain situations, any of these may influence learning. The orthodox answer is that intelligence largely determines what is learned or not learned, particularly with complex tasks. My position on the question is not orthodox: learning in the elementary grades depends mostly on time invested and an intent to learn. This is particularly true of the middle 80 percent of pupils.

My position has two major implications for teaching. Somehow or other *the teacher and the pupil must agree to try to reach certain goals*. Without agreement on goals, the teacher must use coercion as the goad to learning. Second, *the teacher must ensure enough time will be available for the pupil to learn*. This means the teacher must limit the number of goals she expects pupils to achieve and then give them plenty of time and help. If this sounds anti-intellectual, you might look at the chapter on forgetting in any psychology book. When pupils are asked to learn masses of unrelated information, they forget most of what they learn. They remember concepts, generalizations, and information on which concepts and generalizations are based. If the teacher limits her efforts to a reasonable number of goals and gives pupils plenty of time to learn, then achievement becomes mastery for almost all pupils.

Willingness to learn influences mastery. When rewards come frequently, when recognition of success follows effort, then the pupil will devote more time to learning. The intent to learn is the starting point; praise and success reinforce that intent. One marvelous characteristic of most children is a persevering faith in schools. In most cases, teachers must beat failure into children over a period of years. Most children come to school eager to learn, for they have five or six successful years of learning behind them. They expect, unconsciously perhaps, to go right on learning. The problem arises when faith is destroyed. Once a child labels himself a failure, it takes massive doses of success to restore his faith. Intent, motivation, purpose— call it what you will—it's one key to learning.

In spite of my objections to most classroom tests, I do believe in mastery tests. A mastery test differs greatly from an achievement test. A mastery test reflects only a few goals. And since pupils have agreed with the teacher on goals, they should have a good idea of what the mastery test will call for them to do. This agreement on expectations decreases the tension and anxiety most tests raise.

A mastery test is written on the assumption that at least 90 percent of the pupils will meet a minimum standard for passing the test. In other words, if there are ten items on the test and nine correct items sets the standard, then the teacher expects 90 percent of the pupils will answer at least nine items correctly. There are no A's, B's, C's, D's, or F's given. A pupil passes or he doesn't. There is no real need for letter grades in the elementary school. At the end of the year a pupil either "passes" or he doesn't. A's and F's are nothing more than a form of teacher short-hand for justifying promotion or retention. If she needs justification, it would be simpler to keep a small file of work produced. In fact, promotion or retention is based on teacher opinion based on impressions about class-room performance; the henscratches in a grade book represent nothing more than justification of opinion. It would be far better for pupils, learn-ing, and the teacher's mental health to teach for mastery of a limited num-ber of important goals.

Short mastery tests should be used frequently—twice a week, every other day, certainly at least once a week. I used to give a five-minute arith-metic mastery test every day and most items were review questions. Tested at the end of the year on a standardized achievement test required in our school, 90 percent of my sixth graders scored above the average for seventh graders. Frequency functions to ensure success and to maintain retention.

When a pupil doesn't meet the performance standard on a mastery test, the teacher diagnoses the probable difficulty and then discusses the items with the pupil. Next, she works with him on relearning or lets him work with some pupil of his choice. Then she gives him the test again and praises him honestly for improvement. Finally the teacher works his problem items into the next test or two as review questions.

What happens to pupils with this sort of test? Competition is reduced and poor performance is almost eliminated. Almost every pupil has con-crete evidence of his success—and success breeds success. Motivation to learn rises and discipline problems decrease. The impact of frequency of reward (passing the test) changes the self-images of pupils. Tests are no longer feared, for they become positive feedback about progress. The child who was always at the bottom of the heap now finds himself up with the gang; his views of himself, of the subject, of learning, of school begin to change.

,Goals and tests can make a difference—the difference between learning and not learning, the difference between remembering and forgetting, and the difference in your feelings about your own success or failure.

MASTERY-TEST ITEMS

The major problem in testing elementary-school pupils lies with reading. Primary-age pupils have limited reading skills, and a fair proportion of upper graders do not read at grade level. Teachers compound the problem because they err in making a very human, but false, assumption. They believe they know children so well that any test they write must surely be readable to their pupils.

I have taken teacher tests and applied readability formulas to them. The general result shows that teacher-written tests run one to two years higher in readability than the grade they teach. The major faults fall into four classes:

1. Teachers have been taught not to repeat a word too many times. In a test situation the precise word should always be used no matter how often it must be repeated.
2. Teachers substitute words with Latin roots for those with Anglo-Saxon roots. Almost without exception this raises readability.
3. Teachers use too many adjectives and adverbs. These tend to raise readability rapidly.
4. Teachers write long, complex sentences. The pupil finds he is struggling with types of sentences he has not yet come to grips with in his reader.

Under circumstances like these, the pupil finds himself being tested, not only for social-studies content, but for reading skills, for knowledge of synonyms, for syllabification, and for insight into syntax. Without meaning to, teachers can easily turn a problem into a puzzle.

Many primary teachers avoid the problem by using performance tests— asking questions of individuals at odd times or observing classroom behavior. They also use ditto sheets containing sets of pictures; the instructions for responding to the pictures are given verbally.

Draw a circle around the tree that doesn't belong in this group of trees.

Picture of a maple	Picture of a spruce	Picture of an oak	Picture of an elm

Number these pictures from one to four so they are in the order that farmers do their work.

Picture of weeding between tomatoes	Picture of plowing soil	Picture of planting tomato plants	Picture of picking tomatoes

When an upper-grade teacher writes a test for use with a class containing poor readers, she can also use the picture-type item in some cases. In addition, she can read the test item aloud as pupils follow the written words. I found that pupils who failed a paper-and-pencil test could usually pass it if I read the items aloud. There are, of course, teachers who believe these activities are condescending or demeaning; they also feel comfortable when they flunk kids on tests.

In the middle and upper grades, the nature or form of mastery-test items need not differ significantly from items on other types of tests. The items can be true or false, completion, matching, multiple choice, or any other type. For *thinking* goals, items might deal with these activities:

1. To state the generalization to be drawn from a body of facts.
2. To write an abstract generalization covering a set of concrete generalizations.
3. To identify the conclusion to be drawn from a chart or table.
4. To match the name of a concept with the characteristics that separate it from other concepts.
5. To write a hypothesis that might be tested to solve a specified problem.

For example, let us write a first draft of an item for category 2. It might read:

Write a generalization that will cover each of the following generalizations:

1. When corn becomes scarce, the price of corn flakes rises.

2. When tomatoes become scarce, the price of tomatoes rises.

3. When cotton becomes scarce, the price of blue jeans rises.

Now you have to ask yourself some questions. Do the pupils know the meanings of *generalization, cover, scarce,* and *price?* Have they had any prior learning experiences with abstract generalizations? Are the concrete examples apt to be familiar enough to seem real? If your answers are yes, then you may have a good item (you won't actually know until you have used it).

For *valuing* goals you might use items like these:

1. To match attitudes with their likely consequences.

2. To write the ending to story based on conflict.

3. To complete such sentences as, "Our work on Indians has changed my ideas about . . ."

4. To select comments from a story that reveal value judgments as opposed to facts.

5. To suggest why a person might believe as he does.

There are two other techniques I like to use with values. The first asks the pupil to choose between pairs of items. For example, let us say I want to know if a pupil prefers reading or viewing or doing. I can take sports as the topic and then, with pictures or words, pair each activity with each other activity and ask the pupil to select the one he prefers. For example:

Playing baseball vs. reading about baseball
Playing baseball vs. watching baseball
Watching baseball vs. reading about baseball.

If you use this paired-comparison technique with the same activities but with varied topics, you begin to get quite reliable information about what a pupil values. The second technique involves role playing (or, as it is presently called, role taking). You ask pupils to act out someone involved in a conflict situation. As a pupil imagines what dialogue his role calls for, he likely projects much of his own feelings in what he says. You need to exercise care with this technique, however, to ensure that the pupil is ready to face up to and reflect on the beliefs and feelings that surface in role playing. I strongly recommend that you read the book on role playing by George and Fannie Shaftel before you try this procedure.

For *subject-matter* goals, items might reflect these types of tasks:

1. To match vocabulary with definitions
2. To state facts drawn from tables or charts
3. To support responses on test items with data
4. To arrange the steps in a process into logical order
5. To place events or persons in a time line.

For *skills* goals, these types of items are common:

1. To use a table of contents or an index to locate information
2. To supply a missing step in a set of directions
3. To answer questions that require the interpretation of data in a table or diagram
4. To interpret an imaginary map
5. To identify the steps in cooperative planning of a library-research problem.

As you write items for mastery tests, I suggest you check one of the references at the end of this chapter for help in writing standard test questions and in avoiding common errors in item writing.

You can also create new types of mastery-test items. For example, the item below is a variation of true and false items. Yet, all the items focus on one central topic.

Put a check ($\sqrt{}$) by each sentence that you believe is true.

The 25 biggest cities in the United States all have:

___ a population

___ a form of government

___ a business district

___ a school system

___ public roads

___ a postal system

—— a major-league baseball team

—— a source of water for homes and industry

—— many kinds of churches

—— a police force.

In a sense the item is testing a concept, for cities are a classification within the general class of community, just as apples are a class within the more abstract class called fruit. The next time you use the item, you could repeat three or four of these items and add others dealing with area, production, distribution, communication, transportation, and so forth. The item also provides for discussion; it asks for an expression of belief rather than fact. This usually leads to argument which demands some sort of proof, and proof in turn demands some research and reflection. The item thus helps review a concept and calls for an extension of knowledge.

One further bit of heresy: If your district or school requires the use of a *standardized* achievement test near the end of the year, then you should obtain a copy of the test and analyze the items. My reasoning runs like this:

1. If your district uses the test, then it accepts the goal that lies behind each item on the test.
2. If it accepts a goal, then it assumes the pupil will have had some prior experience with that type of goal in a school setting.
3. If you have any concern for pupil achievement, then you will have given them the opportunity for experience.
4. Thus, *your* mastery tests should reflect both the goals of the achievement test and the form of items used in the test.

Note carefully that I have not said or implied that you should teach the item on the test. That is not fair to anyone; it's not even cricket. The item on the achievement test must remain unknown and novel, but if you fail to deal with the goal, then in my judgment, you are letting random factors influence achievement and are asking your pupils to guess at test items.

SUMMARY

Goals specify test items; test items reflect goals. And both, obviously, have a relationship to the activities and materials provided by the school. Pupil confusion about tests are influenced by lack of prior opportunities to learn, by lack of knowledge of priorities among goals, and lack of experience with tests as means for learning.

Goals are related to teacher's planning because they are a first-order item of planning and because they subsequently influence all other elements in a plan. Just as goals may be expressed in a variety of ways, so plans may take different forms. The experienced teacher may carry most of her plans in her head, just as she specifies most goals in some form of mental shorthand. Plans may be highly specific and written out in detail, or they may be suggestive and scratched out on a file card or an old envelope.

Mastery tests are preferable to achievement tests unless you wish to spread pupils out for ease in giving them grades. The psychology of the mastery test provides success, motivation, and satisfaction to all or most pupils, whereas achievement tests bring true happiness only to the top readers who have also become test-wise. Mastery tests invite the repetition of similar items and thus provide review. They let the teacher focus on a limited number of goals of considerable importance, and thus they stress high-value goals and are relatively free of the chaff items often used to fill out achievement tests.

The form of mastery-test items are highly variable; you can use all the standard type—true and false, multiple-choice, and so on—or invent new forms of your own. Any of these forms may be used with any type of goal; thinking and valuing and skill goals, however, are best tested in some sort of performance situation. Indeed, the best tests are usually day-to-day questions or observations that do not appear to be tests.

SUGGESTED READINGS

Berg, Harry D. (ed.), *Evaluation in Social Studies.* Washington, D.C.: 35th NCSS Yearbook, 1965. (A useful collection of articles; however, much of it is oriented to the secondary school.)

Bloom, Benjamin S., "Mastery Learning and Its Implications for Curriculum Development." In Eliot W. Eisner, *Confronting Curriculum Reform.* Boston: Little, Brown, 1971, pp. 36–45. (A very helpful article on mastery testing—I urge you to read this one.)

Ebel, Robert, "Writing the Test Item," in E. F. Lindquist (ed.), *Educational Measurement.* Washington, D.C.: American Council on Education, 1951, pp. 185–249. (An old but venerable discussion of writing test items; much of the new material is modeled after his work.)

Shaftel, Fannie R. and George, *Role-Playing for Social Value*. Englewood Cliffs, N.J.: Prentice-Hall, 1967.

Wick, John, *Educational Measurement: Where Are We Going and How Will We Know When We Get There?* Columbus, Ohio: Charles E. Merrill, 1973. (The best of the measurement books for the elementary teacher; I steal from it regularly and shamelessly.)

(See also the readings for Chapter 6. Almost all the books on behavioral objectives contain sample test items.)

EXERCISES

1. Pick out two or three skill goals and write one paper-and-pencil test item for each one. Then see if you can devise a performance test for each. Try them out on a classmate or two. Which really convinces you that the pupil knows and can do what you wanted?

2. Read the Shaftel book and set up a role-playing situation dealing with valuing. Try this out with a few friends. The purpose here is to ensure that you get some notion of how adults react in role-playing situations before you try them out with children.

3. Try writing (or preparing) a few paired comparison items for your classmates. Don't try to get too fancy at first—use VW's, Fiats, and Saabs, or blondes, brunettes, and redheads. The purpose here is to convince you of the stability of choices with this type of test.

4. Write a mastery test on something your methods class has dealt with. Try it out on at least ten members of the class. If nine of ten don't get an item correct, rewrite it until they do.

5. Get a copy of a standardized achievement test (try your guidance department laboratory), and analyze any items dealing with social studies. What can you do to give pupils experience with the goal implied by the item without teaching the item itself?

Psychology and the Social Studies

No single chapter in a methods book will tell you all you want or need to know about the psychology of learning, but my hope is that this one will help you survive your clinical experiences, practice teaching, and first year as a teacher. Unfortunately for all of us, psychology has not yet produced a comprehensive, comprehensible, and completely agreed-upon statement of the nature of learning. From time to time, a particular theory would gain favor and influence teachers, but in each case that theory would prove deficient and give way to another theory or to an eclectic collection of bits and pieces of many theories. As things have turned out, psychology has often been a cross hardly worth bearing.

This chapter focuses on two sets of ideas that have worked for me in countless classrooms. The first section deals with five psychological conditions that must be present if learning is to take place. The second deals with developmental psychology, particularly the ideas of Jean Piaget.

FIVE CONDITIONS FOR LEARNING

Readiness, motivation, organization, practice, and transfer—each is a necessary but not wholly sufficient condition for learning. That is to say, motivation is necessary for learning to occur, but motivation alone does not ensure that learning will occur or persist. Nor will readiness without motivation bring about conscious learning.

Readiness

The child must have reached a sufficient degree of readiness if he is to learn.
Readiness is a compound of maturation and prior learning.

Because of a lack of maturation, a two-year old cannot ride a bicycle
and a six-year old cannot drive a car. Furthermore, neither the two- nor
the six-year old has enough prior experience to master these tasks. Primary
teachers do not panic if every child does not read equally well at exactly
the same time. They make adjustments for the immature or inexperienced
child. What primary teachers hate to do, however, is to look at the other
side of the coin of readiness. They do not always take advantage of advanced maturation or rich experience to start a child on something when
he is ready to start. For example, the first grader who finishes the first
reader in March does *not* move on to the second reader. Instead, he is given
a different first-grade book and made to mark time for six months.

From grade four on, the teacher errs in the other direction. Everybody
starts at the same time in the same book, especially in science and social
studies. This makes no sense in most classes. Readiness for learning is as
valid in grade five as it is in kindergarten. The fifth grader who, at best,
can read a third-grade text is not ready to learn from a fifth-grade basic text.

By the very nature of the bell curve, some 20 percent of our children
are nowhere near ready to read at grade level. In many classrooms, the
figure is closer to 50 percent. There are many large cities where the average
reading ability of eleventh graders is below sixth grade. The point is that
unless the classroom materials you are using range widely in reading difficulty, you are at odds with the principle of readiness.

The best teachers today (best in my judgment) give a great deal of
time to the development of concepts and generalizations. Readiness plays a
crucial role in such development. Let us say your pupils have meanings for
planet, earth, and *globe.* If you are trying to help your pupils develop a
concept of *rotation* of the earth, you must be also sure they understand *axis*
and probably *turn* or *spin.* And you may have to teach *axle* to get at axis.
When a child understands *axis* and *turn,* then he is ready to try to understand rotation.

If a teacher is interested in more than memorization, she must constantly ask herself what does a pupil need to understand before he can
understand _____? (You supply the term.)

The principle of readiness holds equally well for learning a generalization. Let's say you want your fifth graders to arrive at this conclusion: When villages are located where major transportation routes join, they tend to develop into large cities. Readiness must be present in two instances before understanding can take place. First, the child must have concepts for *village, location, transportation, routes, develop,* and *large cities.* If any of those terms lacks meaning for a child, then he cannot completely understand the generalization. Second, the child must have enough factual examples for the generalization to convince him that it is true. The examples might be any combination of New York, Chicago, St. Louis, New Orleans, San Francisco, and so on. For elementary-school pupils the conclusion, in the form of a generalization, is best drawn *after* a number of specific examples have been identified and examined. Once the generalization is drawn, however, it can be tested again with further examples.

A child may memorize a generalization, he may be able to recall or recognize the generalization, but he doesn't understand it and he can't apply it until he has concepts for its component terms and examples of its validity.

Motivation

If a child is to learn and remember what he has learned, he must want to learn and he must enjoy success from what he has learned.

It has always seemed to me that motivation, like a coin, has two sides. The first side has to do with an *intent* to learn; the other side with the product of *success* in learning. The term *intent* implies purpose and desire. You want to accomplish something specific—not "maybe do it," not "do this or that." You have an end in mind and you intend to gain that end.

A good deal of garbage has been written about intrinsic and extrinsic motivation. If motives are intrinsic, they are self-generated and come from within the learner. If motives are extrinsic, they are generated by others and originate from outside the learner. Naturally, everyone agrees that intrinsic motives are the better of the two. Thus, teachers are harangued to "get pupils to use intrinsic motives"; this statement, however, is a near contradiction of terms. If your motivations of the pupil are extrinsic by nature, how are you to pluck his intrinsic strings? The answer lies in an indirect approach: You create a rich, varied, and attractive environment and then stand back to see what effect that environment has on the pupil. If you've hit on the right combination, then he will go into action, or at least he'll begin to say, "I want to do this" or "I'd like to learn that."

Actually, a good deal of motivation in the classroom is extrinsic; it flows from you and is accepted to some degree by your pupils. If you say, "You'll need to know the names of the first five presidents for the test on Friday," then you have provided most of the pupils with a touch of motivation. If they don't learn those five names, then they will get hassled by you and perhaps by their parents. Most of us live with a lot of intrinsic motivation. Mother says, "Pick up your socks or no TV"; Dad says, "Take out the garbage or I'll give you a whack"; Teacher says, "Say good morning to the principal or I'll keep you after school"; The Boss says, "Cut down on the ice cream in those sodas or get another job!" Interestingly enough, intrinsic motives are most powerful during early childhood (learning to walk and talk), during adolescence (getting along with the opposite sex and becoming semi-independent of your parents), and after that point in life when you become more satisfied with your goals than with goals others set for you.

The cue in all this (other than the rich learning environment) is for you to get pupils to state their goals clearly and openly. If a pupil says, "I can get four of the five presidents by Friday," that's better than your insisting on five and his resisting you by getting only one. If Billy says, "I want to draw a map of Chicago showing the industrial areas," then why should you insist he learn school-district boundaries? I know I repeat myself, but why make kids learn 200 things in social studies when you know they will likely forget 175 of them? Why not cut down your goals to 50 things, get mutual agreement on 40 of them, and then see they are learned thoroughly and applied often, so 35 of them are remembered long after the school year is over?

The second side of the coin of motivation involves the notion of success. If a child learns and is satisfied that he has learned, then he feels success. And success breeds success. Not only in the content of what is learned but in the means used to successfully reach a goal. In other words, the child who reasons through a problem to a successful conclusion likes both his conclusion and the pattern of reasoning used to produce the conclusion.

One of the soundest propositions in psychology is: Unrewarded behavior is extinguished. Your job as a teacher involves seeing to it that reasonable and appropriate behavior receives its reward and thus does not die out like a spark on a wet blanket. Rewards take many forms. Praise is always welcome when it is deserved—the good word spoken in admiring tones, the little comment written on a map or a paper. The pat on the back, the appreciative wink, the nod of the head, the warmth of the voice, the thumbs up signal—all these provide signs of approval.

One bit of advice: If a child has grown accustomed to failure, then it does not pay to praise him profusely for what he knows is an unpraiseworthy job. You need to get the constant failure to state what he is willing to try to accomplish; then if he hits his mark, praise him. If, on the one hand, he falls far short of his stated aspiration, try to get him to scale down his goal until it seems realistic enough for him to achieve. If, on the other hand, he far exceeds his stated aspiration, try to get him to raise his goal to a higher level. Once his goals seem realistic to you—in view of his past record of failure—then praise him fully for meeting his goal. And then guide him to raise his aspirations bit by bit until he hits whatever you and he believe his potential might be. Realistic goals and praise for accomplishment and effort have made a tremendous difference in the lives of many pupils. Anyone who draws a teacher's pay can keep a failure failing; it takes a sharp teacher to turn a failure into a success.

Organization

If a child is to learn and remember what he has learned, he must understand meanings and be able to organize what he has learned.

The child learns most rapidly, remembers longest, and applies most readily those learnings that for him have meaning and possess organization. Isolated or unrelated bits of information are difficult to learn and easy to forget. Concepts and generalizations, on the other hand, are retained and even improve over a long period of time.

Forgetting is a topic most teachers won't discuss. They know it exists, and they know that the rate of loss of what has been "learned" is terrific. I have never understood why so many teachers insist on teaching information that will be forgotten shortly. Nor do I understand why so many insist on teaching in ways that insure that forgetting will occur. These teachers focus on the wrong things. They focus on information. Information is generally useful only when it can be organized into some association or functional relationship with other bits of information. If bits of information can be organized by pupils into a structure or a generalization, then the structure or generalization will be remembered. And there is an excellent chance that information will also be remembered as examples of the generalization or as parts of the structure.

For example, in the United States, people live simultaneously in a set of communities; they live in a family, a neighborhood, a city (or town or county), a state, a region of states, and the nation. The commas in the last part of the sentence divide it into bits of information. The sentence itself organizes the several communities into a structure based upon the idea of moving sequentially from the smallest to the largest of communities. The idea of belonging to several communities represents structure, and the idea of sequence helps us remember the parts in the structure.

The basic question about organization is, "Whose organization should be used?" The answer is, "It depends." Any organizing that is done by the pupil tends to ensure retention. But a clever teacher can lead a child to "discover" for himself an organization that the teacher already knows. Pupils will organize many ideas for themselves, and their notions about organizing ideas should always be encouraged by teachers. If they "discover" a way of organizing information by themselves, capitalize on it. If they don't, then you have to lead them to discover what you already have in mind.

In other words, your program of study should be based on subject matter that possesses a high degree of organization. You should concentrate your energy on ideas that can be organized into concepts and generalizations that have application to the lives and interests and problems of your pupils.

Practice

If a child is to remember what he has learned, he must practice, through review and application, what he has learned.

There is no point in developing concepts or generalizations if they have no application to what a child does or if they are not applied in what he does. The easiest example I can think of is *direction*. A first-grade teacher gets the ideas of north, south, east, and west across to her pupils in a week. Then, if she is a typical teacher, she never takes up direction again during the year. The second-grade teacher finds the pupils she inherits seem to know nothing about north, south, east, and west, so she teaches directions. The class seems to learn and that makes her happy, so she turns to other topics. "There's so much to learn in second grade," she says, so she never again gets back to directions. In the third grade, the whole process is repeated. Of course the children learn about north, south, east, and west more easily, because they are more mature, they have had more out of school experience with directions, and they really are relearning. The point is that no teacher has helped these pupils practice, through review or application, what they had learned about cardinal directions.

I know I beg the question of when children ought to learn the cardinal directions, but I believe teachers ought to decide on that question. They know their pupils, their school, their district. I don't. But I do know that it is a waste of time to teach directions unless the teacher provides for practice. One way for teachers to make a major improvement in what pupils learn would be to teach fewer things, but teach them thoroughly.

Something learned from a traumatic experience is seldom forgotten. But almost anything learned under other circumstances is subject to forgetting. There are, however, some practices that slow down forgetting. The suggestions that follow deal mainly with remembering discrete and unrelated bits of information.

Practice should be distributed over time. An hour on one day is less effective than fifteen minutes a day for four days. Fifteen minutes a day twice a week for ten weeks beats a half hour a day for two weeks. In general, the evidence shows that spaced practice produces three times the retention of massed practice.

Overlearning at the initial point of learning enhances memory. This is particularly true of learning lists of terms, such as the nations in South America, the duties of a chairman, and the major products of Japan. If it takes six repetitions to get the list right for the first time, then, to overlearn, the child should immediately repeat the list six more times. This sounds silly and unnecessary, but it works.

Self-recitation in learning is also a form of practice. One of the problems of maintaining a silent classroom during study time is that a child cannot mumble to himself or whisper to his neighbor. After a child has looked over a list of things to "know," the best thing he can do is recite to himself or to a neighbor. My experience with children leads me to believe that from 60 to 80 percent of study time devoted to memorization should be spent in pupil-to-pupil recitation. If you doubt me, ask yourself why the bull session or hen session is so effective for the college student.

What you need to consider are two factors in practice. The first is overlearning, self-recitation, and spaced review in *initial* learning. The second is review and application from time to time *throughout* the school year.

If you are not willing to apply these two factors, then you may as well forget about your pupils' remembering more than 20 percent of the isolated bits of factual information you ask them to learn.

Transfer

If a child is to learn and maintain what he has learned, he must transfer what he has learned in one situation to the solving of problems in novel situations.

Put a child at a desk, give him a yardstick, and tell him, without leaving his seat, to push a book off another desk two feet away. The chances are that he will use the yardstick to push the book. He either knew or figured out that a tool can be used as an extension of the arm.

Leave the desks and the book the same, take away his yardstick, and give him four one-foot rulers and a role of tape. The chances are he will overlap the rulers and tape them together. He then uses the tool to reach and push the book. The idea of the tool and the idea of using the tool were transferred from the first situation to the novel situation; the idea of taping the rulers together was the new element in his solution.

In one sense, transfer is the reason for learning. We learn to read from readers so we can later read other kinds of books. Much of what we learn in school is not learned for its own sake, but for the purpose of using it to understand other things or to solve new problems. If what you want a child to learn has no transfer value, why bother to teach it?

Strangely enough, most teachers don't, or won't, talk to children about ways to learn. Children are most often ordered to learn and then left to their own devices. I don't mean that every child should be told how to learn everything he is to learn. I give children more credit for creativity than that. But when I view the study habits of university students, including doctoral candidates, it is clear that no one ever convinced them that some ways of learning are better than other ways. Learning how to learn is a proper subject of transfer.

The key to teaching how to learn is more than just discussing the matter. You also have to provide a "test" that *convinces* the child that something (overlearning in memorizing or recall of a generalization in solving a new problem) will work for him. The "test" will also convince you that there are some exceptions to almost every rule about learning.

I used to discuss memorizing with children. I would let them "choose up" three teams. All three teams were given the same set of data. One team was told to "think about" the information. One team was to spend all of its time memorizing individually. One team spent half of its time discussing memorizing and half the time memorizing. Team number three always won and usually memorized three or four times as well as either of the other two teams. I then moved to a new topic and watched to see what methods the pupils used; the members of the third team always transferred what they had learned about memorizing to the new task. So, too, did a few sharpies from the other teams who had watched the third team at work.

In my experience, there are five things a teacher can do to insure transfer. First, as soon as you have taught something, demonstrate how it transfers. For example, with the yardstick-ruler situation, learning occurred with the use of the yardstick and transfer was demonstrated with the use of the taped rulers.

Second, point out the possibilities of transfer in other situations. It helps if you name a few specific examples, but just pointing out that something may be useful later will help.

Third, arrange for the application of transfer within a reasonable length of time. How did the Egyptians get water for irrigation from the Nile? How do fruit pickers harvest a cherry tree? How can you get back the quarter you dropped in a window well covered with a grill? How do fishermen catch fish?

Fourth, ask how the novel situation was explained or the new problem was solved. Then point out, if the pupils haven't, that transfer occurred.

Fifth, ask when transfer will work for them again.

There are three conclusions in all this for teachers. First, there is little point in teaching something that won't transfer to another situation or problem. Second, the principle of transfer (which is basically utility or use in the future) can be learned by children. Third, you ought to organize your goals, materials, and activities so transfer of learning will occur in a natural manner.

DEVELOPMENTAL PSYCHOLOGY

Jean Piaget's approach to developmental psychology involves qualitative research. He never was much interested in how pupils scored on tests, but he was interested in the *processes* pupils used in producing their answers, and he was as interested in incorrect answers as he was in correct ones. This emphasis on mental processes led him to develop a theory of cognitive development that holds up well in practice. Piaget's writings are quite difficult for most students (and most professors). Piaget deals with stages of development that span from two to several years. For example, the first four stages are:

The Sensori-Motor Stage (0–2)

Here you see the development of the sensori-motor reflexes, the coordination of the eyes and hands, the relationship of means and ends, and awareness of the permanent object. For example, if a baby in a crib shakes the crib to make toys suspended above him shake and move, then he has begun to grasp the ends-means relationship. Or, if you take a bottle away from a baby and put it under a pillow and the baby moves the pillow to get the bottle, then you see evidence of an awareness of a permanent object. Both of these foreshadow the future development of more sophisticated cognitive processes.

The Symbolic-Thought Stage (2–4)

Here you see the development of the symbolic function in language and play. For example, if a child picks up a doll and tries to feed it, you see the ability to let an object stand as a symbol of something else. Or, if the child points at a light and says "light," then you see the ability to let a set of sounds stand symbolically for something else. In either case, the symbolic function provides the basis for learning a language.

The Intuitive-Thought Stage (4–7)

Here you see the development of syncretism and transductive reasoning. Syncretism means to combine together to make something understandable. Children are interested in whole ideas rather than in analyzing parts of ideas. When a child hears a sentence in which meanings for one or two words are unknown, he will make up a meaning for those words so the sentence will make sense to him. For example, if you say, "The Fourth of July is Independence Day," and ask what that means, the child may answer, "It means you see fireworks on the Fourth of July." The child lets the difficult word *independence* slide, recognizes the meaning of *Fourth of July* from earlier experiences with July Fourth celebrations, and then interprets *independence* in light of the meanings he does possess. The child has combined a known meaning with an unknown to produce an interpretation satisfying to him. This characteristic, incidentally, causes the unwary primary-grade teacher some problems; if a teacher says, "All groups of people have some form of transportation. Do you understand that?" many children will answer yes because they gave meaning to the unknown term. Teachers are far better off to ask, "What does transportation mean?" The answer then indicates whether the child's meanings for transportation are reasonable or self-manufactured.

Transductive reasoning is a form of syncretism in which the child uses one of two related facts to explain the other. Teacher: "Why does it rain?" Pupil: "Because it is wet." This is an attempt at reasoning, but it is reasoning without logic; the reasoning moves from particular fact to particular fact. In time this transductive reasoning is replaced by inductive reasoning (particulars to general) and then by deductive reasoning (general to particular). It is a characteristic of intuitive thought for a child to give reasons immediately; they don't hesitate, they blurt out whatever connection they see. By eight or nine the same child is more apt to respond to a question by saying "I don't know," then by thinking a bit and offering a tentative answer. The nine-year old tends to know when he needs more information; the six-year old tends to believe he knows if he can make any sort of a connection.

The Concrete-Operations Stage (6/7–11/12)

Most kindergarteners and some first graders are in the intuitive-thought stage, but most elementary pupils fall within the broad range of concrete operations. During this stage the child develops two major intellectual abilities: He learns to group in his mind the objects he perceives in his environment, and he learns to draw generalizations inductively from concrete particulars. There are five characteristics of these thought processes. First, they are *internal;* the groupings take place in the child's mind. Overt action may accompany the thought processes, but they are not essential to it.

Second, thought is based on perceptions of the *concrete* world. The child manipulates internally what he has perceived (or perceived and manipulated overtly) in the real, concrete world.

Third, thought is *decentralized.* The younger child concentrates on but one element of a situation; the older child can decentralize his concentration—he can concentrate on two elements of a situation at the same time.

Fourth, thought is *coordinated*. The child can concentrate on two elements and coordinate them with each other. For example, a child can concentrate on both weight and length, and can coordinate a variation in one with a corresponding variation in another.

Fifth, thought is *reversible;* the child can work back to the beginning of a problem. This is done in either of two ways. In inversion (or negation) the child cancels out the effect of an operation through an inverse operation. In reciprocity the child compensates for the effect of an operation through a reciprocal operation.

These five statements are not easily understood without examples. If you give a child ten red wood blocks and five blue wood blocks, you can then ask, "Are there more red blocks or wood blocks?" The child who says "There are more wood blocks" can group red wood and blue wood boxes into wood boxes. (If you think all children can get this one, try it on a half-dozen five-year olds.) The same kind of question can be asked about pupils. "Are there more girls or children in this room?" The question requires that the pupil group two groups (boys and girls) into a single group (children).

A second type of grouping is that of ordering objects. For example, give a child twelve blocks ranging from one-inch to twelve-inches long. Then say, "Put these in order from the smallest to the largest." If the child can order it into a series, you know he can, first, *distinguish* between smaller and larger and, second, *relate* all the blocks into a smaller to a larger series. This operation implies the child has adequate concepts for *smaller, smallest, larger, largest,* and *order.*

To review, this is what these concrete operations have involved:

1. *perceiving:* synthesizing visual sensations into an awareness of objects
2. *discriminating:* perceiving the differences among objects
3. *classifying:* grouping similar objects into a class of objects
4. *ordering:* grouping objects into an order from smallest to largest.

It should also be clear that concepts are being formed, that some form of logic (for example, least to most) is being used, and that these operations are internal (intellectual), even though the objects are concrete. This word *concrete* is highly important in most elementary-age learning. For example, this type of question will *not* often be answered correctly unless the three boys (or their concrete representations) are present. Teacher: "There are three boys—Jack, Bill, and Tom. Jack is taller than Bill; Jack is shorter than Tom. Who is the tallest boy?" Without the three boys present, the problem is not one of ordering objects, but of thinking on a verbal level without concrete references. On the other hand, put the three boys in front of nine- or ten-year olds, and they get the answer without much trouble. Thinking in the elementary school depends on perceptible, concrete data; by thinking, I mean reasoning, as opposed to memorizing and reciting.

Every book on Piaget I have seen includes an example of his classic *conservation* problem. Two balls of clay, equal in size and identical in shape, are used. The researcher makes sure the child believes the two are equal. One of the two balls is then flattened into a clay pancake. Next the child is asked, "Are these two things equal? Which has more clay?" Around age seven or eight the answer is, "They're equal," or "You just flattened one of them, they are still equal." These answers indicate an understanding that shape was changed but the amounts remained unchanged. The child sees and understands that as the clay gained wideness (his term) it lost in height. The child combines two attributes, considers both of them at once, and conserves the attribute of quantity even though shape changes. In the social studies, conservation is the logic behind understanding that density of population may remain the same even though the distribution of population changes within an area. Another example would be that dollars can be changed into pounds without a change in purchasing power.

Another characteristic of elementary-school thought is *reversibility*. In this case, the child says the clay pancake can be rolled back into a ball again, and that the two balls will be equal in size and shape. An example in social studies is the idea that dollars changed into francs can be changed back into dollars again. Or a dollar bill can be changed into four quarters, then into 100 pennies, and then back to a dollar bill. Reciprocity is the logic behind understanding trade and tariffs. An increase in tariffs leads to a decrease in trade; a decrease in tariffs leads to an increase in trade; there is a reciprocal relationship between national tariffs and international trade.

At this point, some teachers are inclined to say, "Well, if pupils can handle those kinds of logic, all I need is a textbook." Those teachers have forgotten the earlier principle of concreteness that influences elementary-age thinking. If you try to handle trade and tariff on a verbal level, you face the problem of getting an answer to the earlier question of who was tallest, Jack, Bill, or Tom. You need three-dimensional representations; you need games and simulations, you need dramatic play and role playing to get this kind of reasoning with elementary children. Then you need films and film-strips, pictures and murals, models and field trips. Then, eventually, you can work only with words (with some children in the upper grades).

The last point I want to stress about elementary-age thinking is this: Inductive thought is much more natural to your pupils than is deductive thought. Collecting or observing objects and inducing a generalization about them is appropriate to the concrete-operational stage of elementary pupils. From this you can move to collecting and analyzing data and inducing a generalization from them. I have known elementary-age pupils who reason deductively, but they don't appear in great numbers in most classrooms. And the deductive reasoning easiest for many pupils seems to be based on generalizations *they* have previously induced. For example, your pupils have concluded that all cities in the United States have some form of government. You say, "We are going to take a look at a city called London in the nation called England. Do you think London will have a local government? Why?" The pupil answers, "We said all cities have some kind of local government. London is a city even if it is in England. So I think it will have some kind of local government." The next step, of course, is for you to say, "How can you find out if you are right?" To this extent, deductive thinking does occur—but you will seldom find it operating unless there is a solid base of fact behind the induced generalization upon which deduction begins. At this point I suggest you go back to the fifth chapter and reexamine the notion of problem solving. Would you say that data collection is called for before or after hypotheses (tentative generalizations) are formed?

In conclusion, let me offer you an old rule of thumb: with young children or new ideas, inductive teaching and reasoning work best.

CLASSIFICATION AND LOGICAL THOUGHT

Piaget has contributed considerably to what we know about classification as the basis for concept formation. When we are asked about classifications, we tend to think first of such terms as animals, cities, automobiles, storms, lakes, and the like. As we saw in the third chapter, however, objects can be classified on the basis of other criteria—color, shape, size, function, material, location, time, and so on.

Pupils need to become aware that because objects (or persons, events, and so on) are multidimensional, they can be placed in various classes if a particular attribute (such as color, texture, or function) is selected as the criterion for membership in a class. Apples are a class distinct from other classes. But because apples are multidimensional, they can be placed in several other classes. In this sense class membership is relative.

Class Names

Objects {	Apples	Curved Surfaces	Red	Foods	Grow on Trees
	Jonathon	Balls	Blood	Potatoes	Apples
	Delicious	Apples	Cardinals	Bread	Oranges
	Crab	Coins	Cranberries	Apples	Walnuts
	Macintosh	Disks	Apples	Eggs	Plums

After children learn to form and re-form classes based on a single attribute, somewhere around the age of nine they learn to build classes based on two or more attributes. For example, objects may be classified on the basis of function and location (large cities on navigable water), or size and function (box wrenches, sewing needles, vehicles), or texture and color (towels, shirts, rugs).

It seems reasonable to ask why teachers should worry about children becoming aware of the multiple attributes of objects. Isn't it enough to know that an orange is something to eat? Who cares if it has shape, size, color, texture, taste, a skin, seeds, and grows on trees? Actually, it isn't important that pupils learn all these things about the orange. What is important is that they learn that even simple-looking things are quite complex— they can be described in many ways—and that classifications are relative groupings based on some human purpose. It sounds silly to say that most of us have a stereotype about oranges, but we do. To test this proposition, make up a five-word association test including the word *orange.* Give the test to a half-dozen classmates; they will most frequently associate *orange* with *fruit* or *juice,* or they will give an alternate, *lemon* or *apple.* As children examine an object, as they search for attributes, as they say and hear others say *round* and *food* and *fruit* and *grows on trees* and *smooth with little dimples,* they sharpen their perceptions, pick up bits of information useful in identifying objects, and begin to form a logic for classifying.

Let's take a more complicated, social-studies example. Suppose you are studying Indians; what are the attributes of a tepee? Stop for a moment and answer that question before you read the next line. Did you think of size, shape, and color? What is it made of? What is its function? Can it be transported? Can it be decorated? Let me push you a bit: Why is a tepee conical? Is shape related to the availability and portability of poles? Is shape related to building a fire inside the tepee? Why is the hole at the top of the tepee? Now, how is a tepee similar to other types of dwellings? How is it different? Why didn't the Plains Indian build concrete-and-steel apartment houses? Why don't we live in tepees?

If you deal with such questions by asking questions of pupils, then they must discover the attributes that are important, they must provide the labels for the attributes, and they must do their own thinking. You don't list the attributes, name them, and say remember these!

Take a fifth-grade example dealing with the Revolution. Find some pictures of King George and George Washington. What will pupils say about likenesses—both have the same name, both are men, they dress alike, both are leaders, both are white. Now you ask why five times. Why do they have the same first name? Because they share a common culture in which the name "George" is frequently used. You then go on with the other four points. Next you can have the pupils read about the two men and then ask how they were different. Out of all this can arise discussions about the roles of men in those days, of social class, of power, of qualities of leadership, of influence on our lives, and of cooperation with other important people. In all of this the child is making use of classification and is practicing logical reasoning.

SUMMARY

Readiness combines physiological maturation and prior learning. There are some physical and intellectual tasks that cannot be accomplished simply because the child has not matured enough. In the same way, there is learning that depends upon prior learning. Because of this you must always ask what earlier concepts must exist before a new concept may be developed.

Motivation involves both intent to learn and success from learning. The first, whether the source is intrinsic or extrinsic, gets learning underway;

the second reinforces future intent. If a pupil learns best what he wants to learn, then you must share goal setting with pupils, and you must arrange a classroom environment that satisfies existing interests and promotes new interests.

Organization in learning provides a powerful tool for exploring new knowledge and offers efficiency in remembering what has been learned. The principle of organization involves you as well as pupils, for your goals should be reasonably limited in number and closely tied together in logical ways. If organization of ideas facilitates learning, then you should strive to help a pupil use concepts and generalizations to integrate new information with his existing structures of knowledge.

Practice influences initial learning and strengthens retention of what has been learned. Overlearning, spaced review, and self-recitation are major aids to initial learning; periodic review and application of learning to new and novel situations provides practice and convinces the child of the utility of what he has learned.

Transfer explains why we learn; we learn so we may transfer what has been learned to later problems and situations. Without transfer, we would be constantly relearning—a highly inefficient situation. Transfer involves learning to think, to value, to know, and the ways of doing things. In working with elementary children it is important to lead them to anticipate transfer and for you to see that it may occur.

Piaget's developmental psychology has powerful implications for elementary teaching. The thought processes of the school child are characterized by internal reasoning based on perceptions of a concrete world. Thought is decentralized so a pupil can concentrate on more than one element in a situation, and thus the pupil can coordinate a variation in one element with a corresponding variation in another. Thought is also reversible in either inversion (canceling out an operation with a negative operation) or reciprocity (compensating for the effect of one operation through a complementary operation). Piaget's work on the thought processes of classification form the basis for concept formation and thus for the drawing of conclusions.

There are other valuable lessons in psychology that apply to learning. No psychologist will be happy with my choices of concepts or my examples. You may not be either. All I ask is that you think about these ideas and test them in practice. Their source is the classroom, and with a little adaptation to suit your personality, they might make the difference between drawing your pay and earning it.

SUGGESTED READINGS

Books by Jean Piaget

Judgment and Reasoning in the Child. New York: Harcourt, Brace & World, 1928.

The Language and Thought of the Child. New York: Harcourt, Brace & World, 1926.

The Psychology of Intelligence. New York: Harcourt, Brace & World, 1950.

(These three books are relatively easy reading and provide a basis for understanding Piaget's theories and procedures.)

The Child's Conception of Time. New York: Basic Books, 1969. (Difficult reading, but obvious connection to social-studies content.)

Books by Jean Piaget and Bärbel Inhelder

The Child's Conception of Space. London: Routledge and Kegan Paul, 1956.

The Early Growth of Logic in the Child. New York: Harper & Row, 1964.

The Growth of Logical Thinking from Childhood to Adolescence. New York: Basic Books, 1958.

The Psychology of the Child. New York: Basic Books, 1969.

(These are fairly difficult reading. I suggest you read *Psychology of the Child* as an overview and then then others for their social-studies applications.)

Books on Piaget by Others

Elkind, D. (ed.), *Six Psychological Studies*. New York: Random House, 1967.

Furth, H. G., *Piaget for Teachers*. Englewood Cliffs, N.J.: Prentice-Hall, 1970. (A slim volume especially for use by teachers; contains an interesting section on symbolic logic.)

Gorman, Richard M., *Discovering Piaget*. Columbus, Ohio: Charles E. Merrill, 1972. (A favorite of mine, particularly because it is self-instructional and aimed at teachers.)

Sigel, Irving E. and F. H. Hooper, *Logical Thinking in Children*. New York: Holt, Rinehart & Winston, 1968. (A collection of research interpretations based on Piaget's theory; some good applications for teachers.)

EXERCISES

1. Think back over the past month or so of your own studies. Identify some idea you had initial difficulty in understanding. What prior learning as a form of readiness would have helped you learn more quickly?

2. Take the first ten presidents of the United States and memorize their names utilizing the principles of overlearning, self-recitation, and spaced review. Memorize the next ten, but use your old methods. Which took you longer? Test yourself on the two groups in six weeks. If this doesn't work for you, try it with some children.

3. When was the last time you used something you knew to solve a novel problem? What transferred in your solution? Spend a little time examining a pupil text to see if you can find evidence of possible transfer built into its content. If you find none, what does this imply for you as a teacher?

4. Why is "Thirty days has September" an example of organization? Tie why you remember the ditty to what you know of motivation, practice, and transfer.

5. Get one of the easy books on Piaget (say Gorman or Furth), and try some of the simple experiments on some friendly captive children of a variety of ages. Pay particular attention to the content of their answers, not just to rightness or wrongness. Do you begin to see how thought processes develop?

American Issues

It seems reasonable to assert that a child growing up in the United States today should know something of the long-term issues facing his nation and the world in which that nation exists. It also seems reasonable to suggest that teachers make choices about domestic and international issues based on three criteria: first, on what is specified in their course of study; second, on the availability of materials that are to be read by their pupils; and third, on their own knowledge and judgments of what pupils ought to know.

The course of study varies tremendously within and between states, but some general tendencies do exist. The emphasis in the primary grades remains on the family, school, neighborhood, and local communities (and *local* may include any or all of these—town, city, suburb, county, metropolitan area). The initial, and major, emphasis rests on the nature and function of these communities in the United States, but in a great many instances the focus shifts to some setting in another nation so comparisons and contrasts may be drawn by pupils. This increased attention to the international scene has, in my judgment, strengthened primary-grade social studies and will likely remain a viable part of the course of study.

The upper-elementary, middle-school, and junior-high courses of study bounce back and forth between the domestic and international arenas from grade to grade. Thus, comparisons and contrasts must be drawn more from year to year than within each year. Nonetheless, the nature of the local course of study tends to limit the number of choices you can make about emphasizing either domestic or international issues or topics.

The second criterion—availability of readable materials—influences your choices most often in a negative way. You won't find what you want, so you will either have to prepare your own materials or depend primarily upon a lecture-discussion format. (A later chapter on literature and the library provides you with some clear examples of what is available from trade and library sources.) Chapters 15 through 20 also offer you a number of alternatives to merely reading about the United States or other nations.

The third criterion, your own knowledge and judgment, are highly influential, but are tempered mightily by two elements. The first involves your ability to create appropriate conditions for learning, while the second involves the willingness of your local community to accept what you want to stress. Usually, however, unless you are a propagandist for extremely variant ideas, the community interferes with your choices far less than most prospective teachers expect.

FOUR AMERICAN ISSUES

Ours is an urbanized, industrialized, technological, and multiethnic society. From this set of facts flow any number of implications, topics, issues, and speculations within the realm of social studies. My own judgment of our times and our probable future leads me to stress four significant topics: population, ecology, violence, and minorities. Each of these is tied to other issues; for example, population has rather direct relationships to poverty, health, and opportunity, and thus, to expand on health, to starvation, malnutrition, and delivery of medical care. Further, each of my four topics is mutually related; for example, the health issue differs for different ethnic groups. And as a further complication, the domestic issue always has web-like extensions to international issues; for example, although we are but a fraction of the world's population, industrially we consume a major proportion of the world's fossil fuels.

The difficult question for you does *not* lie in identifying four or six or ten topical issues; the problem is how you organize these so they fit into your social-studies program. I suggest you begin by outlining a page or so of topics and their relationships. I'm providing a rough-draft outline on the next page as an example.

After I have drafted the outline, I can see that I need a few more resources for myself, especially on poverty and opportunity, to make certain I'm not running purely on my own prejudices. After a few hours' work in the library, I will have located, read, and abstracted a few more resources for each subtopic. For example, I'd have found these for item 1:

Commoner, Barry, *The Closing Circle*. New York: Alfred Knopf, 1971.

Ehrlich, Paul R. and Anne H., *Population, Resources, Environment*. San Francisco: W. H. Freeman, 1970.

Hinricks, Noel (ed.), *Population, Environment and People*. New York: McGraw-Hill, 1971.

My reading of these will also probably lead me to change a few of my outline items. What do I do next?

Depending on the grade I teach and the topics assigned to that grade by the course of study, I have to decide what, if anything, of my outline I can work into my social-studies time.

If I'm a first-grade teacher with an assigned emphasis on home and family, what are my possibilities? Well, the general notion of population can be demonstrated concretely in a study of the family and the school. If I deal at all with economics, and it is an increasingly more popular unit in first-grade texts, I can explore what my pupils consume—food, clothing, books, recreation equipment, desks—and what resources were used to produce those items. Under poverty, if it isn't a slap in the face to my pupils, I can deal with slums and the types of housing different families have. Every family has some means of conserving and protecting health; income levels can be related to types of housing and to health care. The same is true of nutrition, a common first-grade health topic. Opportunities as a topic is more difficult to make concrete, but we are seeing ever more realistic treatments of jobs in textbooks: who gets what jobs, who gets promoted, how is pay determined. In a recent manuscript for grade one, I saw these lines spoken by a woman to her daughter: "We want jobs and we want good jobs!" And first graders can be led to examine their own reactions to television advertising.

In each of these cases, I can ask questions that will probe the influence of more family members on disposable income, the result of greater numbers of sick persons, the increase in older persons in a family. I'll grant that my influence on learning about population may be quite small, but I might be laying the groundwork for easier understandings of population questions in the future.

Population: (Poverty, Health, Opportunity)

1. Meaning, trends, age groups, mobility.
    What do these mean for business? for use of resources?

2. Poverty
    2.1 General: definition of poverty, relative nature
                 : distribution of wealth by social class, last 5 decades.
    2.2 Use of income: high proportion for food, shelter, and other
                         necessities.
                      : sales taxes hit low-income groups hard.
                      : some luxury items, like TV, culturally neces-
                         sary and acceptable.
    2.3 Welfare: who really gets it? Be careful of myths.
                   welfare to individuals and welfare to corporations.

3. Health
    3.1 Early deaths, old-age problems, adolescent problems.
    3.2 Delivery of medical care — need for innovative system.
    3.3 Starvation and malnutrition in midst of plenty; tie to consumer-
         ism.
    3.4 Psychological counseling (doubtful topic for elementary?).

4. Opportunities
    4.1 Relationship of disposable income to who gets what.
    4.2 Advertising, TV, and rising expectations.
    4.3 Who gets and holds what jobs. Ethnicity. Sex. Pull.
    4.4 Ethnic recompensation and quotas; ethnic capitalism.

My Resources
1. See Barry Commoner, The Closing Circle; Paul Ehrlich, Population
    Bomb; census Abstracts, and World Almanac.
2. Hamilton's Economics of Poverty; Kotz' Let Them Eat Promises;
    Seligman's Permanent Poverty.
3. See Scientific American in general; specifically, April 1970 and
    April 1973.
4. See Scientific American, April 1967.

At this point I could provide the same sort of examples for third or fifth or eighth graders, but it isn't necessary or even efficient. I don't especially want you to accept my substantive topics in this case, I just want to convince you that this sort of thing can be done and that there are reasonable procedures for getting the job done.

There are two topics, however, that I want to explore a bit further with you. The first is the problem of race, the second of sex. The reason for choosing these two revolves around the fact that one is present in all classrooms in public schools and the other is present in most classrooms.

With the recent changes in attitudes toward women, the business of women's rights and aspirations and women's history can be easily defended as elementary-school topics. The textbooks your pupils read and the films they see provide them with instance after instance of favoritism toward boys and masculine activities. There is a prize winning film on Malaysia (by McGraw-Hill) that shows the boy going to a school where he receives instruction in both his vernacular and the English language, while the girl learns only the former; he has a pillow on his bed, she has none. The team that shot the film intended no sexism, but differential treatment of the sexes is a way of life in much of the world. A teacher should not refuse to use the film because of the sexism; indeed, it seems to me a marvelous opportunity to get a discussion of the sexes down from a purely verbal level to concrete examples. What should gall you would be similar situations in films on the United States, where the sexism gets either direct or subtle approval.

The other topic, race relations, can easily be defended as a topic of study. The empirical evidence of difficulties between the races is overwhelming. That is fact and from that fact flows a value judgment. Until race (or ethnicity) is removed by both parties to a racial situation as a criterion for aspirations, achievement, opportunity, and treatment, Americans will not likely find lasting and satisfactory solutions to serious problems that do not originate in racial differences. Until the black rises or falls on his or her own abilities, without being hampered by the artificial barriers of racial discrimination, none of us is free.

RACE RELATIONS

The teacher and the child are the fundamental variables in any learning situation, and in most cases touching on the topic of race, both must change. The white teacher must be willing to learn (sometimes painfully) from the content of minority-group life, must develop a positive attitude toward minority cultures, and must hold high expectations for minority youths. The self-examination necessary for relearning proceeds slowly for many whites, and the teacher must constantly reexamine what she knows about, how she feels toward, and what she expects of minority-group pupils.

The minority child must have experiences calculated to enhance his self-concept and to strengthen positive attitudes toward his minority culture. To do the first, the teacher must stress motivation, not motivation based on pep talks and blackboard slogans but on the utilization of levels of aspiration, clear knowledge of mutually acceptable goals, and widespread doses of honest success. In my judgment, teachers should be quick to reject the standard course of study during the bulk of social-studies class time and substitute other subject matter and experiences with solid minority content. Chapter 16 contains examples of such experiences; the best self-disciplined social-studies class I have seen in a decade was a "ghetto" fourth grade in San Diego where the focus of study was the role of law in our lives. Our highest elected officials, some of whom believe in law and order only at a verbal level, could learn from the humane, rational atmosphere of those self-governing nine-year olds. My point is this: If you want pupils to change, you must let pupils experience—in concrete, behavioral situations—the process of finding solutions to the problems they face in a pluralist society.

For the teacher who wonders what it must be like to be in the minority, I recommend John Hersey's *White Lotus* or Paulo Freire's *The Pedagogy of the Oppressed*. For help with teaching strategies and content, I suggest James A. Banks and William W. Joyce's *Teaching Social Studies to Culturally Different Children* or Kenneth R. Johnson's *Teaching the Disadvantaged: A Rational Approach*.

Learning about race relations in our nation's history will not be one of the pleasanter areas of study your class will focus on during the year. Beating the British or carving a colony from the wilderness is sure to be more inspiring. It would be a mistake, however, to treat the historical past of black Americans as a temporary fad that will go away in time. Whether considered topically or thematically, race relations and black history have staked out a claim for important portions of the social-studies curriculum. Because the treatment of minorities is a crucial test of how well our democracy lives up to its ideals, the concern for such topics as slavery, the Civil War, Jim Crow, and the civil-rights movement is a legitimate one.

One of the most important considerations in planning this unit of study is your class itself. Is the group all white? All black? Or are the pupils drawn from several minority groups? Your own color and its relation to the class is an important factor, too. A white teacher in an all-black class is bound to encounter different problems than a black teacher with an integrated group. These factors will strongly determine the content, methods, and goals of your unit of study.

It is likely, for example, that a class composed chiefly of black pupils will want to study black history topically rather than as a subordinate of race relations or the Civil War or southern history. On the other hand, an upper-grade class of black and white pupils may choose to examine race relations during the periods of Reconstruction, the Great Migration, and the post-World War II era. Another possible alternative, that of studying black history as a problem in minority-majority relations, may be the tack taken by an all-white class. Whichever course is followed, you will want to gear your approach to the particular needs of the class, and these will depend heavily on its racial composition.

You should remind yourself that this, more than many other historical issues, is one whose consequences are very much operative today. Therefore, it is bound to be an emotional, as well as intellectual, investigation. Begin by acquainting yourself with your own emotions on the topic, and use that knowledge to deal sensitively with the emotions of your pupils. Consider ahead of time what possible controversies might arise, and think about some ways of handling highly charged situations. If no differences of opinion ever arise, chances are everyone is avoiding current issues altogether.

Whatever area you end up focusing on, each of the branches of the social studies has leading questions to contribute to your unit of study. Taken together, they serve as a model for studying race relations or any particular race's history. One short but extremely helpful book in this respect is Peter Rose's *The Subject Is Race*. It will suggest a number of leads for your teaching and fill you in on some of the recent research findings.

A good place to begin is with anthropology, by getting the students to define race. From there you can draw on many disciplines in achieving the unit goals. Economics stresses the profit in exploitation and discrimination. Psychology emphasizes the fear of differences that makes prejudice more than an emotion based on greed. In the case of blacks, for example, skin color is a highly visible difference that has become the basis for irrational beliefs and behaviors. Sociology can add to your understanding of how prejudice works. Stereotyping and scapegoating are two activities whose operative techniques are taught with ease to almost any age group. Historically, the experience of slavery, at least in this nation, makes blacks unique among Americans. No other group has been involuntary immigrants, and this experience has profoundly shaped the course of every black person's life, as well as influenced every white person's expectations about what black people are like. The politics of race relations is an excellent way to focus on the recent past. The questions of power, of who makes laws, and of how decisions are made are extremely important issues for black people. For years, most black people couldn't vote. Then when ghetto residential patterns in the North made political representation possible, a small base of political power began developing. One of the more interesting items of black history is that thrusts for power have not generally come through politicians but have been expressed through church leaders. Martin Luther King was never a congressman; Senator Brooke does not think of himself as a spokesman for the blacks of his state. Organized efforts for changes in the legal status of blacks did not spring from political representation; they were wrought by massive demonstrations and other measures of civil protest. While not unprecedented, the drive of black people for equal rights was a movement whose scope and duration were unmatched by any other minority in our history.

One of the more recent emphases in studying race relations is by comparison. The comparative approach would be a particularly instructive way to end your unit, whether it has been a study of race relations or of black history. Have the class look at the experience of other minorities in American history: the Indian, the Chicano, the Oriental, the Polynesian, the Eskimo. Each offers a perspective different from the black experience—the Indian was nearly exterminated; the Chicano, Polynesian, and Eskimo lived in areas that fell under American dominance; the Oriental was a voluntary immigrant. On the other hand, if you are dealing with a fairly sophisticated group of students, you may want to examine race relations in Great Britain, the Soviet Union, South Africa, or Brazil. Because Pierre Vanden Berghe's *Race Relations* takes this cross-national approach, his book would be particularly suggestive in planning out this portion of your unit.

Other studies you may want to consult as references are Michael Banton's *Race Relations,* John Hope Franklin's *From Slavery to Freedom,* and Gordon Allport's *The Nature of Prejudice.*

THE STUDY OF WOMEN

It isn't likely that anyone would propose a unit of study in men's history. The very notion seems absurd—aren't men and history the same? Why then should women be singled out as a special area for investigation? The answer is that for too long history has been synonymous with the activities of men. Men were even the writers of history. History has been the study of politics and politicians, the economy and businessmen, wars and soldiers.

Only recently have women themselves begun to challenge this view of history. Why, they want to know, aren't families legitimate areas of study? Changing sexual attitudes? Changes in childrearing? And, with the entrance of women into the historical profession, the operational definition of history has begun to change.

Attention to the study of women in the social studies is a much more recent phenomenon than black history. Nonetheless, we can expect that increased amounts of time and space will be allotted to the subject, both in the classroom and in the textbook. The outlines of this new topic still have not taken on a definitive character. Although clearly an embryonic topic, the study of women is not likely to be a passing fad with only temporary appeal.

It would be a mistake to proceed on the same assumptions as those underlying the teaching of black history. There are similarities to be sure: the nineteenth-century feminists were fond of comparing their position to that of the slaves. Both are minority groups in a behavioral sense. Both have experienced discrimination. But a fundamental difference between racism and sexism makes each case unique, in spite of obvious similarities in experience. Men and women, for whatever kinds of inequality have existed between them, need each other to survive. This imperative does not hold for the relationships governing blacks and whites; and that reason may explain why the exploitation of black people has been more overt, more brutal, and more destructive than sexism.

As sexism is a subtle phenomenon in many instances, the first place to begin your study of women is with yourself. Assuming most elementary teachers are women, their attitudes and feelings about sexuality have an important influence on pupils. Further, it would be a mistake to assume that just because you will be a working woman, you don't harbor certain biases against your own sex. After all, you will be entering one of the most traditional occupations for women that society offers. You may work and consider what you do a "job," or you may work only because you have to, or you may only be working temporarily until you are ready to have a family. Having an occupation is no proof that you haven't absorbed at least some of society's ideals about what is and is not proper for a woman to undertake.

There are many tests on this matter, whether you are female or male. Consider your behavior toward the students in your class. Do you encourage girls only in their aspirations for "feminine" occupations? When there is a class party, who serves the food and helps you clean up? Are girls encouraged to participate on an equal basis in physical-education activities with the boys? Is serving on safety patrol a prerogative enjoyed only by the boys? While these examples may on the surface appear unimportant, cumulatively they illustrate the subtle ways in which girls and boys are unnecessarily socialized along different paths. So begin your study by recognizing the ways in which your behavior reflects acceptance of unnecessary distinctions just because they have been customary.

Second, recognize that a tremendous shortage of traditional materials exists in this area of study. You'll have to put your imagination to use in planning what to do about it. The tendency may be to take the easy course, assigning biographies of "trailblazers" and focusing on attainment of the vote. But this "Susan B. Anthony approach" is limited, considering the many nontraditional sources of information you can draw on. Advertisements in magazines are a convenient source of information about sex roles. Television says a great deal about stereotypes. The observation among your pupils of job divisions within their own families enables them to make comparisons. The technique of role reversal in role playing has been a successful way of raising certain issues, quickly and humorously. Indeed, a simple polling of pupils on "what I want to be" is an easy way to introduce the unit with the class itself as your source of information.

Finally, as will become obvious in your planning, it is next to impossible to study women as an entity operating in an historical vacuum. Rather, they should be studied in a variety of relationships; as wife, as parent, as wage earner, as community volunteer, as feminist, as household manager, and so on. This approach opens enormous possibilities for helping students understand our society and its culture. Women can be studied in the context of male-female relationships. They can be studied as part of society's most fundamental group, the family. And because their experiences have so often been entirely different from those of men, their values show us a whole side of American society that historians have usually ignored.

An interdisciplinary approach will give you the best results. An excellent place to begin is biology, with the obvious question, "What is a woman?" Or, "What is a girl?" You may, if you haven't already, want to read Margaret Mead's *Male and Female* to get a woman's point of view. But don't expect the class to agree on the answer. The answer isn't as obvious as the question; even scholars don't agree on it.

The degree to which you examine women's experiences historically depends, of course, on the level of your class and its ability to handle certain concepts. A second grader may easily understand what a family is but not an industrial revolution or a suffrage movement. If you intend to get into a colonial period and you need to brush up on your own reading, John Demos' *A Little Commonwealth* analyzes, as few historical studies do, the nature of love, the structure of families, and the methods of childrearing in America's preindustrial society. On the other hand, if you need a refresher on more recent times, Eleanor Flexner's *Century of Struggle* covers a whole range of women's activities during the nineteenth and early twentieth centuries.

The study of women as an economic force can be approached in two ways. One is to look at their contribution occupationally to the economy; in this respect students have the opportunity to understand that women are not only underpaid, but are actively discouraged from entering certain "masculine" jobs that have high pay and status connected with them—occupations like doctor, engineer, physicist, architect, and lawyer. The second point is that by far the largest occupational grouping of women in this country is that of housewife, a career that is without monetary reward except at the will of each woman's husband. An interesting study in this respect is Michael Korda's *Male Chauvinism: How It Works;* a less recent but still sound study is Betty Friedan's *The Feminine Mystique.*

Sociologically, the emphasis on sexual differences and the socialization of children into accepting certain unquestioned norms should be easy to teach to pupils in any grade. The use of clothing is one convenient way to illustrate the process. Another would be to have the students write their impressions of their favorite female television star or talk about the impressions that Edith Bunker, Miss Kitty, and other TV roles convey. The point is that society's major political and economic institutions are run by men, and it is in their interest to hold women to a feminine ideal that reduces competition for males.

This exclusion from society's ways of expressing power is a monopoly. What pupils should realize, however, is that both sexes will vote at 18. This means that women can not only run for political office, but that women as a group can lobby for legislation on their own behalf. The Equal Rights Amendment is an excellent example of just such legislation. It might be highly instructive to foresee the future in reverse for a day and have the girls govern the class. Simulating a situation in which the practice of power is in the hands of one group exclusively should bring interesting reactions.

Finally, you may want to draw on anthropology and take a comparative look at the situation of women in other countries. In Israel why isn't it "unfeminine" for women to serve in the army? In Russia why are so many doctors women? In the Middle East why must Arab women walk behind their camel-riding husbands? In Luxembourg why don't women have the vote? Comparative studies give students a perspective that they would not achieve from telescoping in on their own situation. It enables them to make better judgments about their own experiences and to decide what changes they would like in their own society.

SUMMARY

The United States is always dealt with in elementary social studies. The primary grades deal with the more immediate communities of activity; the fourth, fifth, and eighth grades deal with some combination of regions and the nation. Except for the eighth grade, these studies are largely multi-disciplinary—although some "history" is usually found in each grade.

The question facing many teachers revolves around the business of teaching issues or problems. Are pupils ready to deal with issues? Dare we chance the development of a slightly critical view of our nation? Can we find readable, accurate materials dealing with issues? What issues should we select? These questions make it clear that more responsibilities for selecting goals, materials, and evaluative techniques fall on the teacher's shoulders if she does deal with issues.

The newer textbooks are giving more space to issues than earlier, blander texts. You can find woman's rights in job opportunities in first-grade books, slums in second, and suburban–central-city aggravations in third. Fourth-grade texts deal with regional problems of water rights and flood control; fifth-grade texts include more on the history of blacks. Still, there are persistent problems that do not receive adequate treatment in texts, and thus teachers add their own selection of problems to their courses of study. This self-selection process requires more than average preparation on the part of the teacher. At the least, it requires careful library research so the teacher has a secure grounding in the subject matter of the issue and has an idea of what the major research areas are.

The next problem for the teacher is translating the adult material into concrete experiences. Few elementary pupils are capable of abstract, wholly verbal thinking. Unless materials and activities can provide the basis for concrete-operations thinking, the teacher's efforts will be largely wasted. For some reason, teachers often fail to take advantage of existing, ongoing experiences children have outside the classroom. Children do have some experiences with adults and thus with issues facing adults. Poverty, for example, is both an abstract term and a way of life for many pupils; health care is a problem in many families; crime worries all of us. The day-to-day experience of children is a rich source of data if teachers will only ask the right questions.

Among the many issues we face, I strongly recommend the study of race and women in the elementary school. The basic reason is that these issues are fundamental to the solution of many other issues; 50,000 doctors drawn from minority groups and from women would contribute mightily to the solution of medical-care problems. Further, the basic elements of study—human differences in sex and race—are present in most classrooms. In either case, the teacher should be particularly careful to apply what she knows of the psychology of conditions for learning and of developmental psychology to the study of domestic issues. If issues are important enough to work into the social-studies program, then they are important enough to be taught as creatively as it is possible for you to teach.

SUGGESTED READINGS

Banks, James A. (guest ed.), "The Imperative of Ethnic Education." *Phi Delta Kappa,* January, 1972, vol. LIII, no. 5. (A special issue devoted to educational problems and a range of ethnic groups. This single issue is *must* reading; if you can only read one item in this list, read this.)

Banks, James A. and William W. Joyce (eds.), *Teaching Social Studies to Culturally Different Children.* Reading, Mass.: Addison-Wesley, 1971. (An excellent collection of readings by two perceptive editors; provides a theoretical base and specific suggestions.)

Levin, H. and J. Williams (eds.), *Basic Studies on Reading.* New York: Basic Books, 1970. (Contains a discussion of black dialect that you may find useful.)

McLendon, Jonathon C. (ed.), *Guide to Reading for Social Studies Teachers.* Washington, D.C.: NCSS, Bulletin 46, 1973. (Fourteen annotated bibliographies on societal problems and issues; a highly useful resource; also contains sections on the social sciences, on curriculum and methods, and on human development.)

EXERCISES

1. Check out the McLendon book and draw up a list of domestic issues, then add your own ideas on issues that are not included in McLendon. Order the list into priorities for a particular grade. Give some thought to the number of issues you can handle in a year.

2. Take the list you ended up with in the first activity, and see how many interrelationships you can find. Then ask yourself how many of these have further relationships to international issues. What sort of possibilities do you see here for transfer of learning?

3. Take one issue that appeals to you, and prepare an outline similar to the one provided in this chapter. Then go one step further and outline some of the concrete activities you could develop with your pupils to help them achieve some of the goals you had in mind. (See Chapter 6 again.)

4. Do you agree or disagree with my contention that race and women are suitable issues for use with any elementary grade? Regardless of your position, sketch out the argument you would use if this were to be a topic of discussion at a faculty meeting in your school.

International Issues

To my mind, Barbara Ward said it best: "The most rational way of considering the whole human race today is to see it as the ship's crew on a single spaceship on which all of us, with a remarkable combination of security and vulnerability, are making our pilgrimage through infinity." [1]

That sums it up well: bloody well if we continue to be able to record our history, bloody bad if we hit the buttons ending the written record. For me, sufficient justification for stressing international education in social studies exists in Ms. Ward's truth about the whole human race hurtling through space and time on a spaceship called earth.

BEYOND THE NATION

For years, our educational emphases with our fourth, sixth, and seventh grades have been on other places and other peoples. In some instances, the sixth grade dealt with ancient civilizations, but the general fare in most cases has been some form of economic geography. The usual approach was to take a region of the world, say, South America, and then proceed to memorize each country's capital and three leading products. Both teachers and pupils thus saw the nations of the world as marbles of varied size and color strewn across a sidewalk in some game called history. By and large, each nation was an entity with its own geography, its own people, and its own culture—which seldom touched the peoples and cultures of other nations, except by invasion and war.

In the sixties and seventies, this pattern began to change. Some people began to develop an international view of the nature of the world. Paul R. Hanna of Stanford was insisting that the nations of the Americas were emerging as a loose form of community, that the Pacific area and Atlantic area were also emerging communities, and that all nations were being drawn together by population growth, technology, and shared problems. Leonard Kenworthy, John Michaelis, Ralph Preston, Vincent Rogers, and others began to prepare materials on international education. Due in part to the pressure of these university professors, changes began to take place in materials available for elementary social studies.

These shifts in materials on other nations and other peoples during the late sixties and early seventies improved textbooks and programs in several ways. One of the most striking shifts was the effort to begin "international" study early, to include some emphasis on it in every grade, and to at least touch on it throughout the text or school year. For the primary grades, this meant a section of each unit dealt with other peoples and the final unit focused on some other society. For example, if a first-grade unit dealt with rules, then there would be two or three pages dealing with rules in, say, Italy, Germany, France, and Yugoslavia. The final unit in the book might be on life in Mexico or Japan, so children could compare family life in the United States with family life elsewhere in the world.

A second shift concerned our notion of what constitutes the rest of the world. In the early sixties, the rest of the world meant the rest of the Western world—Latin America, Canada, and the European nations. Today, there is more emphasis on Africa and Asia. Africa became important because colonies became nations and because of the interest of millions of black Americans in their heritage and cultural roots. Asia became important because of the resurrection of Japan as a major industrial power, because of the rise of India and China as great powers, and because of our involvement in three Asian wars. This shift to the Third World, as it is sometimes called, raises a problem of spectacular proportions. There are some 132 nations today, and who knows how many tomorrow? Which ones should be studied? What criteria should be used in choosing to emphasize one over another?

A third shift focused on the inclusion of affective, as well as cognitive, objectives. We have learned from experience with older "journey geographies" that studies of other nations and peoples can reinforce prejudices, create stereotypes, and stimulate misconceptions. "All Chinese are bad because they want to capture the world." "All Dutch farms have windmills." "All Africans live in the jungle." All three statements defy the facts. The Chinese may hope for and stimulate revolution outside China, but the facts show 800 million Chinese live in China, while only some 19 million live outside China. There are fewer windmills in the Netherlands than on abandoned midwest farms. And fewer Africans live in jungles than on grassland plains. Although the new materials were not entirely free of ethnocentrism, they were clearly superior, particularly at fourth grade, to older textbooks.

A fourth shift moved emphasis from learning from the textbook to learning from a wide range of sources. Film and filmstrip companies produced some excellent products, both in content and in technique. Loops, study prints, and transparencies found their way into the classroom. Trade books proliferated, and teachers began to draw heavily on libraries. Simulations and games of varying technical complexity were accepted by imaginative teachers. This shift to multimedia materials and activities was particularly useful in stilling the lazy soul who complained, "I can't teach about _____ because there are only three pages on it in *the* textbook."

The fifth shift was a philosophical one that began with a painfully simple question: "What is international education?" Was it the study of one nation after another? Was it the study of relationships among nations? Or was it the study of the world's peoples as a society? Lee F. Anderson opted for the third alternative in an article written for *Social Education*.[2] In his article, Anderson demonstrates the unprecedented interdependence of the human species at the global level. As a political scientist, he applies the concept of system to our species, and he demonstrates the "systemness" of modern life with four examples. There is a rapidly expanding number of worldwide human interactions among individuals, organizations, and governments. There is a constantly growing network of cross-national associations and organizations touching on all human activities. There is a growing similarity of social behaviors shared by all humans. There is an increasing awareness that the solutions to some social problems are possible only through international cooperation. On this basis, Anderson argues that the notion of international education must shift from the idea that the world is a collection of nations and peoples to the idea that the world is a system of nations and peoples tied together by common problems, institutions, and interactions.[3]

Just so you know my bias, I'll admit that I accept Anderson's thesis. I have long been influenced by Paul Hanna's notions, and it seems to me that Anderson has (knowingly or not) incorporated Hanna's thinking, bolstered it with social-science research, and produced a new theoretical position. The implications of studying humanity as a society are debatable, but one charge sure to be hurled at Anderson is not implied by anything he has said. He is not saying, "Let's scratch the United States." There is nothing in his writing to suggest he wants to incorporate the United States into some supernation or bend our nation's needs to the needs of some international political cartel. What he is implying goes something like this:

1. Let's start admitting that all humans are human and stop believing that some of us are more human than others.

2. Let's all admit that we have our ethnocentric biases and that these biases influence perceptions and ideas. Then let's attempt to transcend ethnocentrism to the extent that we will be able to view events from a global perspective.

3. Let's admit that we already possess multiple loyalties (to our family, our city, our state, our region, our nation) without being unpatriotic, and consider extending our loyalties to some transnational organizations and associations (for example, Catholics owe a loyalty to Rome, but that loyalty does not diminish their loyalty to the United States).

4. Let's begin to judge the institutions of others by the criterion that institutions are created to serve human needs, and thus are satisfactory to the extent they do serve needs.

5. Let's admit that change and diversity are inevitable features of human life and strive to enjoy life while surrounded by variety.

6. Let's admit that major value differences exist in the world about forms of political power and systems of production, and learn to live constructively with the inevitable conflict, distrust, and hostility existing within a loosely structured, emerging society.

Anderson, of course, also stresses the need for youngsters to think critically, comparatively, and conceptually about information they receive on international affairs. This is a wise suggestion, for all sources of international information have their biases; some are generally propagandistic; and some are usually unreliable.

It should also be readily apparent that attention to international education does not mean you ignore the United States. Far from it. In most cases, a study of international affairs includes an examination of our role, or at least the likely effects the affairs of others will have on us. In fact, the predominant social-studies sequence adapts quite readily to these new ideas. The textbooks and trade books presently available can be used with this modification, but they must be supplemented with simulations, data banks, case studies, short biographies and novels, and movies and filmstrips. The shift from studying nations as nations to studying nations as the elements in a larger network of relationships is within the grasp of any district choosing to make the change.

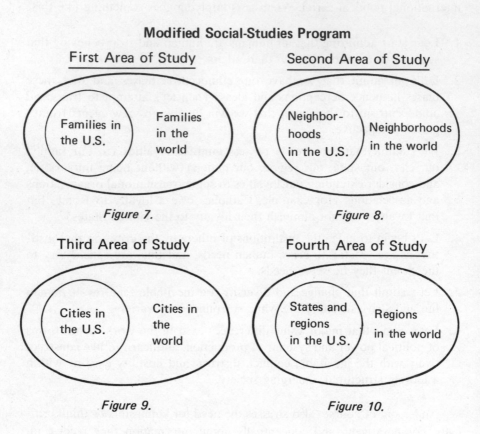

Modified Social-Studies Program

First Area of Study

Families in the U.S.   Families in the world

Figure 7.

Second Area of Study

Neighbor-hoods in the U.S.   Neighborhoods in the world

Figure 8.

Third Area of Study

Cities in the U.S.   Cities in the world

Figure 9.

Fourth Area of Study

States and regions in the U.S.   Regions in the world

Figure 10.

In each of these areas of study the emphases are:

1. All families are human, although the form of the family differs from place to place. (Substitute neighborhoods or cities or regions for families as you shift areas of study.)

2. All humans have needs; to meet their needs people engage in basic human activities; successful activities become institutionalized and valued.

3. Changes in ideas bring about changes in technologies; changes in technologies change our activities; changes in activities change our institutions and values.

4. Changes in technologies and human activities bring changes in the other elements of our ecosystem. Some of these changes are beneficial; some are not.

5. Likenesses among families are primary because all humans share them; differences are secondary because they form differing cultural solutions and differing environments.

Fifth Area of Study

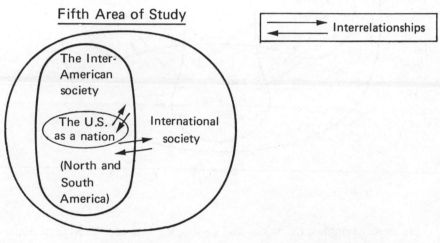

Figure 11.

Sixth Area of Study

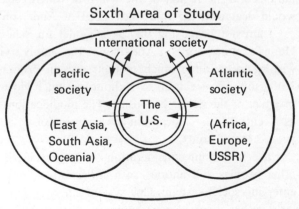

Figure 12.

Seventh Area of Study

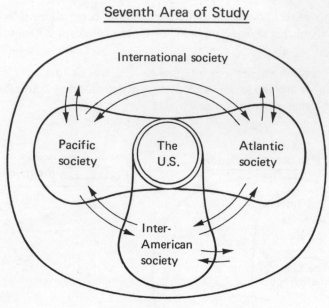

Figure 13.

In these examples, the initial and continuing foci are the United States as a nation and the international society. The secondary foci are the other nations and the region of the world in which each is located. Here pupils would deal with the more advanced of Anderson's objectives.

I am not proposing this as a model for schools to consider. It's not Hanna's model, nor is it Anderson's. I'm simply trying to show that districts wishing to conserve much of their present program *and* include some of Anderson's ideas can do so without too much violence to either the existing program or the newer proposals. The modifications retain the United States as a central focus and permit the inclusion of an international dimension in every area of study.

The important consideration, in any event, is the shift from viewing other peoples and nations as a *collection* of units to viewing them as an emerging social system. This system emerges, not because anyone particularly wishes it for its own supposed virtues, but because national communities by themselves no longer meet all needs, satisfy all interests, or solve all problems. In a way, people are inventing these new international interactions and arrangements just as they previously invented tribes and kingdoms and nations. The criterion for future growth of international institutions will be how well they help us solve problems that cannot be solved unilaterally.

Within the dimensions of international problems, I see two major types of issues in desperate need of solutions. The first involves the hazards of unforeseen results in exporting technology to "have not" nations; the second deals with the issues of conflict, war, and peace.

ECOSYSTEMS, LEAD PIPES AND SCHISTOSOMIASIS

Ancient Rome, the first large Western city, had an estimated population of 750,000 during the reign of Augustus (27 B.C.–A.D. 14). Its three main sources of water were the Tiber River, springs and wells, and the aqueduct system. The Tiber also functioned as a sewer for human, animal, and business wastes, and as a liquid cemetery for dead humans and animals. Quite obviously, the Tiber was not a wholly satisfactory source of water for drinking and cooking.

The Tiber was also subject to periodic floodings, and these high waters contaminated many wells, leaving them as undesirable as the waters of the Tiber. These floods were believed to be caused by angry gods, and thus, in the absence of medical and sanitary technology, solutions were sought in prayer and sacrifice rather than in civil engineering.

In time, the technologies of construction and metallurgy seemed to offer a solution. This involved the making of a system of aqueducts and pipes. The several aqueducts fed into the local system of lead pipes delivering water to some 1,200 fountains and 300 storage tanks. Technology provided a solution, but within the solution were the seeds of a new problem. Water flowing through lead pipes accumulates lead salts; lead salts in drinking water eventually produce lead poisoning; and lead poisoning, in time, produces sterility and death.

This factual anecdote makes a point. People create problems; they find some solutions to the problems; the solutions solve the original problems and create other problems which must subsequently be solved. Well, some people say, that was tough on those old Romans, but our modern technology is so sophisticated that it doesn't spawn problems . . . does it?

But yes it does. Because of its very sophistication, modern technology has spawned radioactive dust that finds its way to the bones of my unborn grandchildren, DDT which flows from my spruce trees into the lake's wall-eye pike and back to me, and new strains of venereal disease resistant to our good old solutions because the old solutions were used too often. Modern technology is polluting the oceans (if we can kill Lake Erie, let's try for the Atlantic), altering the temperatures of the earth (if we can smother New York in smog, let's try for the eastern seaboard), asphalting the surface of our cities (let's build over our cemeteries and golf courses; why should they produce oxygen?). Contemporary human behavior has erased natural frontiers as sources of safety—we popped our bombs; the Russians popped theirs; now the French and Chinese add to the mess; God help us when everyone else develops the technology and feels the need to test their jingoistic toys.

Oh, well, some of my friends say, everyone knows the danger in all that. If that's your only example, you begin to bore me.

All right, let me try more anecdotes. When I was a boy, back before World War II, I went to all the Gary Cooper movies. He always played someone like Old Leatherstockings or Wild Bill Hickok, so I assumed *The Story of Dr. Wassell* was a western. It wasn't, it was an eastern. The good doctor found out, as I remember it, that the dreaded Asiatic disease called schistosomiasis came from schistosomes, parasitic worms that live in certain species of snails.

You can imagine what schistosomiasis sounds like to an adolescent boy. My friends and I made up songs using the word, and we plagued our teachers with innocent mispronunciations as we asked purportedly academic questions about the movie.

In 1944, I found myself in the South Pacific, where my host, the army, cautioned me not to drink the water or swim in it. Fine, I remembered Gary Cooper and obeyed those orders willingly. The problem was that we spent a lot of time wading up to our armpits as we sought our enemy in the jungle. (There are few bridges across jungle rivers and streams.) You guessed it— I became one host in some schistosomes' life cycle. I asked the army doctors for a shot or a pill. Sorry, they said, we don't have a medical cure. Your only chance is plenty of rest, good food, clean living, and no physical exertion. Two dull years later they pronounced me fit. The only advantages to my bout had been separation from the army and salvation from a career as an athletic mercenary.

Now that you have some background on schistosomiasis and understand my concrete interest in the topic, let me tie this generally deadly disease to technology. After World War II, there were several humane plans for the "have" nations to share their goods and technology with the "have not" nations. Among these shared technologies were modern dams and irrigation systems intended to increase food supplies and decrease malnutrition and starvation.

For a concrete example, take Egypt and its new High Dam on the Nile. For hundreds of years Egypt has been plagued by the schistosome, particularly in the delta area below (or north of) Cairo. Life expectancy for males is 25 years, for females 27 years. The water in this area is slow moving, stagnant, and present the year round. Above (or south of) Cairo, however, floodwaters deposit silt and water in fields on a seasonal basis; the floodwaters are collected and stand in basins for gradual use during the growing season, but the Nile flows on with some force.

Construction of the New Dam will permit control of floods and bring irrigation water to the area in a regulated manner. What can we predict will happen in this area? First, perennial irrigation will create conditions favorable to snails throughout the year. Second, there will be a dramatic increase in the incidence of schistosomiasis, an increase from a few percent before the dam to something well over 50 percent now. (In some areas the entire population is affected.) In other words: There will be a man-made plague. The plague will, in turn, defeat the promise of science and the efforts of technology to bring a better life to the area.

By the time this book is published, the data needed to confirm or reject my hypothesis of plague should be available to you. The technologies of dams and perennial irrigation have been exported—for humane reasons but in ignorance of technological hazards—to Africa, Asia, and South America. Let me risk another hypothesis: Within five years, barring an atomic war or a medical cure for schistosomiasis, that disease will be the major cause of death among humans.

What is the international lesson in all this? There are a number: First, in spite of our sophistication with some technologies, we are ignorant about their multiple effects. Second, we are ignorant because we apply a single-criterion approach (efficient delivery of water for growing crops) to an incredibly complex environment. Third, we find what we should have known beforehand: if you screw up one element of a mutually interdependent natural system, you will probably mess up the entire system. Fourth, machines and power and ideas have not freed us from our dependence on the balance of nature. Fifth, although we do not know what the limits are, there surely is a point at which the balance of nature tips and our cup runneth out—and there likely will be no place for us for the next million years in the new nature that replaces the one we destroy.

Some would say this type of "lesson" rightfully belongs in science or health. Nonsense! The need was economic, the decision was political, the results were social. This sort of story, translated into simpler words or caught on film, is wholly appropriate for upper-elementary social studies.

EDUCATION FOR SURVIVAL

One of the ancient axioms beloved by writers about early man is Fight or flight! Supposedly early man, armed only with the most primitive of weapons, had only these two choices when he walked around the corner of a huge rock and came eyeball to eyeball with the infamous saber-toothed tiger. Although the axiom likely held true for the Neanderthal and Cro-Magnon, to apply it to modern humans is erroneous and dangerous.

If I turn a dark corner on a city street and find myself looking down the barrel of a gun, neither flight nor fight will likely do me much good, and either may hasten my passing. A far better choice, based on reason and statistics, would be to submit. If I hand over my wallet, I'm more likely to stay healthy than if I run or throw a punch. I can also placate, bargain, cajole, negotiate, or plead an immediate prior mugging. Any of these choices seems more appropriate than flight or fight.

Bringing peace to the world today appears as futile as plowing the great plains with a pickle fork. There are many reasons why peace remains a hope rather than a fact, but one basic reason is that many people hold to the fight-or-flight notion and never consider other alternatives to warfare. I will admit, naturally, that a stickup and a threatened invasion are not wholly analogous. There are degrees of submission. It's one thing to agree under pressure to remove your missiles from your ally's land that is within close range of the enemy. It's quite another thing to submit completely and let your enemy roll across your borders and dissolve your government. The first affects your nationalist pride; the second affects every part of your life. Fortunately, there are alternatives to violence as a means of resolving international conflicts. An education for survival in today's world includes some attention to the nature and causes of war, and an examination of nonviolent responses to conflict.

The nature of childhood learning requires concrete situations, rather than abstract theses. Certainly, children know when a major war rages, but they are far more aware of conflicts that engage them, their friends, or others in the perceivable local community. My suggestion, then, is that you start any study of war with a study of conflict—the very conflicts you and your pupils know so well in your own lives.

Conflict is a universal phenomenon. It is the basis for the literature of many cultures. There are stories of a person struggling against nature. There are tales of a person struggling to choose between two competing values. There are plots where one person (or group) competes with another person (or group). This third type, called social conflict, provides the subject matter of an education for survival.

Social conflict has certain characteristics. Two groups (or individuals) are interacting. These two groups communicate with each other. Each group has its goals, but the two sets of goals are incompatible. The goals represent something (tangible or intangible) in short supply. And the actions a group takes are intended to damage, control, or thwart the opposing group.

These characteristics are seen in all types of conflict situations. For example, the Burgers and the Hot Dogs are two preteen gangs. Somewhere on the boundary of their turfs lies a small playground with a softball diamond. The two gangs arrive at the playground. Each claims the right to use the diamond. The Hot Dogs suggest that two leaders fight it out; the Burgers send a runner to ask the help of some older brothers. Interaction, communication, incompatible goals, scarcity, intent to control—all are present in our little scenario. What happens next determines whether the conflict is resolved, stabilized, or escalated.

What are these scarce "things" that become goals in a conflict situation? They may be tangible goods or resources needed for life or thought to be needed for happiness. They may be intangible values—power, status, or ideology. The lack of any of these may be real or perceived as real, and either can lead to a sense of frustration so great that physical conflict will reduce the frustration even if it does not result in achieving the original goal.

The Burgers and the Hot Dogs both wanted, for their exclusive use, a scarce resource—the softball diamond. After a few minutes of interaction, the values of power (who can force the other to back down) and status (who gets the prestige of commanding use of the diamond whenever they wish it) began to be as important as the original tangible goal. Further, the perceived actions and reactions begin to be as important as the original point of conflict. The Hot Dogs offer to fight; the Burgers send for big brothers; the Hot Dogs pick up rocks; the Burgers look for bottles; and so on, and the conflict escalates. The ball game becomes forgotten. What now takes on importance is the content of threats and the possibility that push will become shove and shove will become hit. The goal has become to respond to the last response of the enemy.

This extension of our scenario illustrates several other characteristics of conflict. It is a process, an event rather than a thing. Communications break down. Actions are interpreted pessimistically. Original goals grow dim and are overshadowed by push-shove response goals.

Elementary pupils are all too familiar with these situations, but they seldom have analyzed them. They don't understand that all of us must live with conflict, that not all conflict must end with a fight, and that society has developed a number of ways of resolving conflicts.

An anthropologist, Paul Bohannon, has drawn these conclusions from his comparative research among societies: "Conflict is useful. In fact, society is impossible without conflict. But society is worse than impossible without the control of conflict." [4] Societies set up institutions—religions, laws, customs, mores, social arrangements—to institutionalize conflict. Institutionalized conflict is usually deliberate, organized, well led, legitimate, and restricted largely to nonviolent means. When conflict is controlled through institutions, there are appropriate ways for groups to reduce the differential distributions of goods or values so the "have not" group does not become so desperate they will take to arms. In our domestic issues, for example, the poor, working, and middle classes are always seeking a more equitable share of the nation's income. Minorities need to share in political and social decision making. If there are institutions influencing conflict resolution, then the "have nots" organize into a group, settle on goals, produce leaders, and approve and support the words and actions of those leaders. This organization gains legitimacy from its conduct and its appeals to the American creed, and thus has a basis for bargaining from power (the history of the labor movement is instructive in this sense). The influence of existing institutions tends to dampen escalation, tends to hold most behavior within the law, and provides opportunities for third parties to intervene before conflict produces bloodshed.

The role of law in our society is a highly proper subject of study for elementary-age youngsters. In our history, the law has always developed slowly. It has always grown out of conflict. It has always been abused and misused by some people (whether they were in or out of positions of power). But—and this is an important *but*—the law has promoted peaceful change. It has curbed domestic violence. It has limited commercial competition. It has settled civil suits without massive use of personal retribution. It has permitted domestic struggles for power to go on, but as an institution the law has limited the use of direct violence in these struggles. There are appropriate elementary materials on the role of law available.[5]

In helping pupils analyze conflicts, these questions may be useful to you:

1. Who is involved in the conflict? Are there any secret behind-the-scenes actors?

2. Are the goals at issue accurately identified? Are these the original goals or are they push-shove goals? Are the goals really important to both sides? Are the probable costs (time, effort, money, and so on) worth the possible gains to one side? Is it possible that the goals are broad enough so both sides can win? Are there shared but overlooked goals that might be given increased emphasis, in order to reduce conflict?

3. Does each group perceive clearly what the other group wants? Can a group be rational about its perceptions of the push-shove actions of the other group? Are there any institutional restraints on either group? Can one group act to de-escalate with any reasonable hope for a reciprocal act by the other group? Are there neutral or trusted third parties that can stabilize the situation through negotiation or arbitration?

This sort of analysis, plus a developing belief in the use of law, gives pupils an opportunity to understand some of the situations they encounter in and out of school. The first grader who learns concretely what rules are and how they function is ready to begin thinking about what he does in a situation where there are no rules. Primary-grade youngsters enjoy talking about the reasons that groups are formed and leaders are elected. They can understand the functions of laws, and they can apply standards to determine if laws are fair and just.

With these experiences as a foundation, the upper-elementary pupil can learn more about war than the sequence of battles. An examination of wars indicates a pattern of death and destruction constantly involving a greater proportion of the population in dangerous activities. Our Revolution, for example, was fought largely between armies, without widespread civilian deaths or property destruction. In this century, however, a war kills and injures as many civilians as it does soldiers; villages and cities are viewed as appropriate military targets; war from five miles up means woe to all and anything beneath.

It doesn't take youngsters long to realize the price wars extract: death, injuries, and the permanently crippled; damage to property and the natural environment; loss of irreplaceable natural resources; persecution of minorities suspected of possible disloyalty; strengthening of the military, which forges more alliances with certain industries; shift of governments' power from legislatures to executives, for efficiency in making decisions; and disruption of normal production and exchange of goods.

A bright, perceptive group of pupils will also spot some benefits for war: some people find a war exciting; individuals submerge their problems for the common good; national creeds are reinforced and the society becomes more cohesive; a ruthless enemy is destroyed; new inventions for war have applications to peacetime problems. The teacher who denies there are ever benefits from war finds herself in an awkward position. Our Revolution brought us independence; our Civil War strengthened the Union and ended slavery.

To my mind the problem is not one of admitting that some benefits do flow from war, but of sliding over into arguments about "just" wars. All but the most loving of pacifists agree that defense when attacked is legitimate. The difficulty is that attacks can be faked (Germany and Poland in 1939, for example). Further, there is empirical evidence to indicate that if leaders believe a war to be necessary, it can be made to seem just. After all, Europeans killed Europeans for the love of their souls; Christians killed Muslims for the love of God; Englishmen killed Englishmen for the love of a king. Some will claim a violation of a treaty is a just source for war; but history records nations will interpret anything as a violation of a treaty if it suits their purposes.

The communists have an interesting form of justification. They view capitalism as the cause of war. They say capitalism requires exploitation of labor and foreign resources and demands expanding markets at home and abroad. These requirements create dissatisfaction at home and imperialism abroad. Unrest at home leads to revolutions, and competition for markets and resources leads to war. Wars will end, they say, when workers seize power and build a communist society and government. A communist society ends exploitation, and abolishes capitalism, and hence eliminates the causes of war. Thus, they argue, communist revolutions and wars are always just.

The fact is that wars are expressions of sovereignty and instruments of national policy. The nation was a political invention forged from wars, as a response to the threat of future wars. Once established, the nation maintains itself by controlling internal (or domestic) violence for the good of all citizens. Political laws, social mores, economic customs, religious ethics—all get tied to efforts to reduce internal conflict. Thus the sovereign nation ends up with the sole authority to engage in violence—and the ultimate form of violence is war.

Some people extend this historical process of nationalism to argue that one last war must be fought to bring all of us together in one grand world nation. This action is unlikely to be successful, for the chance of surviving the last great war is slight. Further, at this point in time the notion of one grand world government strikes me as undesirable. Nationalism remains a strong, viable force in our thinking and values, both in developed and developing nations. If you add existing social and cultural diversity to the strength of nationalism, these attachments would always promote the possibility of civil war. Lastly, every time people create a new level of government, they lose a bit more personal freedom.

There is no reason, however, why youngsters should not debate the possibility of world government sometime in their lifetime. My own view is that time spent on the emerging world society and on the solutions to conflict would be more productive. For example, must we have a world government in order to bring international peace to a world of sovereign nations? Would honest recognition that all people are human and more alike than different in basic ways keep us from stereotyping whole nations? What ways, other than those familiar to us, do other societies use to resolve conflicts? From among all the means available to human societies, which ways of resolving conflict might be agreeable to all of us?

The topic of conflict resolution can be made concrete with youngsters, the need for laws and equitable application of laws can grow from their own experiences. Your goals regarding conflict as a topic can be as immediate as tomorrow's recess. The elements of concreteness and immediacy are not applicable to war and peace, but then, in the interests of ecology, haven't many of us planted seedlings that won't cast shade as trees until after we are dead? The early search for alternatives to violence is a topic worth your consideration.

SUMMARY

We live in an increasingly technological, industrialized, urbanized, over-populated world. Our technologies, like other earlier solutions to earlier problems, bring us mixed blessings and new problems. Technology is no longer the property of developing nations. Every nation seeks to employ new tools and techniques to its particular problems.

Actually, technology merely symbolizes the increasing and unprecedented interdependence of all humans throughout the world. Individuals, groups, and governments are rapidly expanding their volume of contacts across national lines. The network of cross-national associations and arrangements increases yearly. Social behaviors and customs (the blue jeans syndrome, for example) are increasingly shared among societies. And, perhaps most important of all, there is a new awareness among societies that solutions to increasing numbers of problems are possible through international cooperation.

For these reasons, there are major efforts today to include in social-studies programs the idea of international education as a system of nations and peoples tied together by common problems, interests, and needs into an international society. This notion, of course, can be rejected in favor of the old pattern of studying one nation after another as if each was an entity existing in a vacuum. Or, the present program may be adopted to bring international education into social studies as a partner to our present American focus. Or, a new program, emphasizing international education, may be devised and tested.

In either of the latter instances, teachers should consider two types of issues. The obvious one is conflict resolution, including avoidance of war. The less obvious one is the study of technological hazards that bring more unintended misery in the end than decision makers dreamed possible. In either case, international education must be made as concrete as possible if learnings are to be more than verbal and temporary.

NOTES

1.   Barbara Ward, *Spaceship Earth,* New York: Columbia University Press, 1966, p. 15.

2.   Lee F. Anderson, "An Examination of the Structure and Objectives of International Education," *Social Education,* November, 1968, pp. 639–647.

3.   Ibid., passim.

4.   Paul J. Bohannon, *Law and Warfare,* Garden City, N.Y.: Natural History Press, 1967, p. xii.

5.   See Robert H. Ratcliffe (ed.), *Law in a New Land,* Trailmarks of Liberty series, Boston: Houghton Mifflin, 1970.

SUGGESTED READINGS

Buchan, Alastair, *War in Modern Society*. New York: Harper & Row, Colophon books, 1968. (An interdisciplinary introduction to war and war prevention; good historical setting.)

Clark, Grenville and Louis Sohn, *World Peace Through World Law*. Cambridge, Mass.: Harvard University Press, 1971. (A great book in many respects, this readable account of bringing law to the world helps in understanding the limitations of the United Nations.)

Frank, Jerome D., *Sanity and Survival: Psychological Aspects of War and Peace*. New York: Random House, Vintage edition, 1967. (Excellent psychological work on violence and war; has specific slant toward education and raising children.)

Fuller, Buckminster, *Operating Manual for Spaceship Earth*. New York: Simon & Schuster, Pocket Books, 1969. (A great book for readers with high faith in technology and systems theory.)

Nesbitt, William A., Norman Abramowitz, and Charles Bloomstein, *Teaching Youth About Conflict and War*. Washington, D.C.: NCSS Age of Crisis Series, no. 5, 1973. (The best of the short books; ties conflict analysis and war together quite neatly. Good selection of references.)

Ward, Barbara, *The Lopsided World*. New York: Norton, 1968. (A book on a probable cause for war in the future—the growing gap between rich and poor nations.)

White, Ralph K., *Nobody Wanted War: Misperception in Vietnam and Other Wars*. New York: Doubleday, Anchor books, 1970. (A fine study of push-shove escalation resulting from misperceptions in World War I, World War II, and Vietnam.)

Scientific American. (This journal graces many coffee tables as a "cultural" showpiece, but among its deeper values are the many brilliant articles on international topics.)

War/Peace Film Guide, Lucy Dougall, 1730 Grove Street, Berkeley, Calif., 94709: World Without War Council, 1971, $1.50. (An annotated list of 200 films dealing with the problems of war and peace.)

EXERCISES

1. Examine the tables of contents for a year of *Scientific American*. List the articles dealing with international topics, and share them with your classmates.

2. Take any of the *Scientific American* articles and analyze them for content you might adopt for use with an elementary class. Use some notation system to indicate concepts to be developed, generalizations to be formed, and factual information. What thinking and valuing goals would go with your subject-matter outline? What research skills would you want pupils to display?

3. Role play a few confrontations in which extreme positions about international education are pitted against each other. Tape at least one argument, then analyze it for push-shove escalation.

4. Use the Nesbitt, Abramowitz, and Bloomstein book to locate a simulation your methods class could use. (See *Intercom* #71 on p. 94, $1.50.) Discuss how you would use this with your elementary pupils.

5. Ask your instructor to rent and show *The Hat* (McGraw-Hill Films). In class or small-group discussion, how would you use this film with elementary pupils?

PART THREE

The Squares

WORD got around town that one sixth grade would have a male teacher in the fall. The principals of three public schools, one parochial school, and the college demonstration school had their toughest sixth graders (two from each school) transferred to my class. I didn't know it, but I was a mighty popular addition to the school staff.

In September, I walked into my classroom. Forty-eight faces stared up at me. Thirty-eight kids who had proven they could hospitalize experienced teachers, ten tough kids from other schools. They stared and I stared back. They smirked and my throat went dry. They began to shuffle their feet, and my tongue stuck fast to the roof of my mouth. They snickered and I nearly went back to engineering.

I walked back and forth across the front of the room, praying that my saliva glands would begin to function again. Words began to tumble out. After a moment or two, I began to hear my own voice. Most of what I said must have been drivel, but I remember saying that I hoped I would learn to like them and that they would learn to respect me.

During my pacing, I noticed a 20-penny spike (a nail about 9 inches long) and began to toy with it. In my nervousness, I bent the spike double. "I understand some of you had problems last year." Forty-eight pairs of eyes grew larger. Ah ha, I thought, now I've got their attention. "I hear some of you even gave teachers some problems last year." I straightened out the spike. Ninety-six eyes opened to their widest. "I don't see why that sort of thing has to happen this year, do you?" Anxious about their answer, I bent the spike into a tight U. Forty-eight mouths popped open. "Are we going to try to get along?" Forty-eight heads nodded yes. "OK, let's go out to recess."

Fall is football time in Michigan, and I saw my stock go up when I tossed a 40-yard spiral to one of my tough kids.

I thought I was home free when I heard my principal's voice. "Mr. Lee, school has been in session only 15 minutes. What are you doing out here?"

The class gathered around to see how I handled this situation. "Well, sir," I said, "we're having arithmetic. We're going to see how many square yards there are on a football field. I'm, uh, letting them play for a minute or two as motivation." All the kids nodded their heads in agreement.

The principal stared at me for a long moment, patted a girl known to be a good citizen on the head, and went back into the building.

Moral   A liberal education and six hours of pedagogy aren't as much help as one bad gimmick in getting the attention of a class on the first day of school.

Moral   If you keep a straight face, and if you throw in a bit of jargon, you can convince a principal that recess is really arithmetic.

Programs and Courses

When you teach under supervision for the first time, you will probably be given some assignment in social studies. "Work up a lesson on the globe as a model of the earth." "Get ready to do a one-week unit on city government." "You can handle Chapter 12, 'Westward Expansion.'" "I'll do Brazil next week; then you be ready to handle Argentina." "Work with the class on a play for Thanksgiving." "Arrange a debate on the topic that urban life stifles individualism." You may be with a teacher who hates social studies and therefore shoves it all on you. Or you may get a teacher who loves social studies so much that you get to handle all the science classes.

But whatever you get to do under supervision, it probably won't quite prepare you for your first job. After my students sign their first contracts, they often come back to visit. One of their main concerns is the *course of study* in their districts. I can hear the concern in their voices when they say "course of study."

"There are so many things I want to do with social studies! Case studies! Dramatic play! Sociodrama! Biographies!" Their voices are eager and vibrant. Then the tone drops and becomes mournful: "But they have this course of study and the textbook isn't very interesting. What can I do?"

Some teachers give up, shove aside their desires to be innovative, and fall back on a course of study prepared by some curriculum specialist. In part, this chapter deals with ways you can handle this dilemma.

GUIDES, PROGRAMS, AND COURSES OF STUDY

All schools have a curriculum, and most schools have a curriculum guide. In essence, the curriculum specifies the subjects (reading, arithmetic, and the like) and special topics (tobacco, alcohol, and so on) taught in certain grades.

Curriculum guides state the why, what, and how for all subjects in all grades. When materials deal with one subject for all grades, then you have a social-studies program. When materials deal with one subject in one grade, it is either a course of study or a course program.

If a school district is rich and has a curriculum director, it probably will publish all sorts of curriculum guides, programs, and courses of study. Districts with less money will print fewer or shorter guides, programs, or courses. Poor districts will simply give you a set of books for each subject.

Reports on social-studies programs indicate that the most common pattern today looks something like this:

Kindergarten: Introduction to school life; very few social-studies topics specified. Teacher generally has great freedom of choice.

Grade one: Study of the family and the school. Some teachers ignore social studies and concentrate on reading. Some attention given to major holidays.

Grade two: Study of the neighborhood; usually includes a series of units on "community helpers." (This insipid term has largely disappeared from textbooks, but it lingers on in courses of study.) A unit on Indians is commonly found here.

Grade three: Study of the local community and, occasionally, some study of local communities in other lands.

Grade four: Two possibilities here: study of the state and regions of states in the United States, or study of children in exotic climates (hot lands, cold lands, wet lands, dry lands, and every other kind of land). There is some indication here of a shift to study of U.S. regions followed closely by a study of similar regions in other parts of the world.

Grade five: This is almost always a study of the United States. Most often this is a mixture of history and economic geography, but sometimes it is mainly history. The last few weeks are usually spent on Canada and Latin America.

Grade six: An economic and geographic study of all the nations outside the Western hemisphere. Or a study of the ancient "Western" civilizations, plus Greece and Rome, plus the Middle Ages and the Renaissance.

Grade seven: No stable pattern here. May be a year of climatic geography. Or may be a half year on economic geography (shared with sixth grade) and a half year of U.S. history (shared with eighth grade).

Grade eight: Almost always a chronological survey of U.S. history.

This listing of emphases by grades gives you some idea of what you are likely to face in most cases. Thus, if you hate history, stay away from grades five and eight in particular.

Scope and *sequence* are two terms frequently used in describing social-studies programs. Sequence refers to the major emphasis (or topic or theme) for study *from* year to year. Scope refers to a set of ideas used *every* year to give breadth to the major emphasis.

One of the more popular scope and sequence charts is shown below. Sequence is determined by assigning one or more of the expanding communities of man to each grade. Scope is given to each year through the use of ten basic human activities to be explored within each community of men.

In this pattern, communities in the earlier grades should always be compared and contrasted with similar and differing communities located in other parts of the United States and in the world. Thus, you move out from your own community even in the earlier grades. At the same time, whatever the pupils are learning about other communities should always be applied to the study of their immediate environment.

This organization for scope and sequence has several advantages. Almost all textbooks, particularly in the primary grades, are fairly closely related to these major activities and communities. The chart leaves the teacher great freedom for specifying particular goals and for selecting content from any of the social sciences. When a program is based on this pattern, the problems of providing continuity of experience from year to year are reduced. This particular pattern was developed by Professor Paul R. Hanna of Stanford University.

Today, many elementary districts are devising their own programs for social studies. The Evanston, Illinois, Elementary School District chart clearly reflects a decision by teachers to emphasize concept development. There is no one textbook to fit any grade, so the teacher must utilize a wide variety of materials. Her selection of activities must be suited to the development of concepts rather than to the memorization of information.

Courses of study are like the little girl with the curl in the middle of her forehead. They can be very, very good or they can be horrid. Courses of

	Home	School	Neighborhood	Local	State	Region of States	Nation	Inter-American	Atlantic	Pacific	World
Transporting people and goods											
Communicating ideas and feelings											
Producing, exchanging goods and services											
Creating new tools and techniques											
Organizing and governing											
Protecting and conserving											
Educating											
Providing recreation											
Expressing spiritual feelings											
Expressing aesthetic feelings											
Three			... history — time								
foundation			geography — space								
disciplines			philosophy — values								
Grade	1	1	2	3	4	4	5	5	6	6	6

Content
From economics,
anthropology,
social psychology,
political science,
sociology;
and the quasi-social
sciences,
jurisprudence,
medicine, etc.;
and . . .

Overview of Concepts and Topics*

Primary Level

Kindergarten	Grade 1	Grade 2
NEEDS, GROUPS, ROLES		
Families School Play group	Neighborhood Local community History of Evanston Pilgrims	City, suburbs, towns, farms Metropolitan area History of Chicago

Intermediate Level

Grade 3	Grade 4	Grade 5
RESOURCES, LABOR, CAPITAL, MANAGEMENT		

Early hunters
Early herders
Early farmers
Early miners
American colonists
	Early traders
	Explorers
	Early U.S.A.
	Industrial America
	Illinois
		Herding, farming,
		   fishing, and mining
		   today
		Manufacturing and
		   trade in the UNITED
		   STATES and world
		   today
		Free enterprise in the
		   UNITED STATES

Junior High Level

Grade 6	Grade 7	Grade 8
DEMOCRACY, STATE, and GOVERNMENT	COLONIALISM, REVOLUTION, and NATIONALISM	CONSTITUTIONS and GOVERNMENTS

Ancient Athens
The Roman Republic
17th century England
The American colonies
	The United States
	   to 1850
	Latin American
	   nations
	African nations
		Our local, state, and
		   national constitu-
		   tions
		The United States,
		   1850 to the present
		Totalitarianism

*The key concepts are capitalized.

study are frequently stolen, whole hog, from other districts. Sometimes parts of courses are stolen from many districts and put together with scissors and paste. University experts, curriculum directors, principals, supervisors, parents, and/or teachers may have had a hand in writing them. Their usefulness depends partly on how clear they are, how detailed they are, and how much you agree with their contents.

An example of a simple course of study for grade five might look like this:

U.S. History

Unit	Topic
1.	European background
2.	Exploration
3.	Spanish colonies
4.	Southern colonies
5.	New England colonies
6.	Middle colonies
7.	The Revolutionary War
8.	The Constitution
9.	Kentucky and Ohio settlements
10.	Cotton kingdoms and northern railroads
11.	The Civil War
12.	Reconstruction
13.	Westward expansion
14.	Etc.

Quite obviously you know you are expected to teach U.S. history. But the course of study does not state every major idea you will deal with, nor

Grade Three   Major Topic: Chicago

First Day

Facts	Activities	Resources
1. Chicago is a city.	Ask students what Chicago is.	
2. Chicago is located on the west shore of the south end of Lake Michigan.	Ask where Chicago is located. Ask a pupil to point to Chicago. Ask the name of the lake. What shore is Chicago on? Ask is Chicago near the north or south end of the lake.	Drafters Political Map of U.S., No. M3US (stored with office supplies)
3. The first man to build a house in Chicago was Du-Sable, a black.	Ask if anyone knows who the first man to build a house in Chicago was. Read story of DuSable to class.	Drawing of DuSable's house on north bank of Chicago River, #C1
		Stories About Chicago, Franzee Press, 1942, pp. 6-7. (Kept in school library or may be ordered from curriculum dept.)
4. Chicago was first called Fort Dearborn.	Show a drawing of Fort Dearborn and ask, Who knows what this is? Do you know the name of the fort? Where was it located?	Drawing of Fort Dearborn, #C2
		Photo of present spot where Fort Dearborn stood, #C3
5. Etc.	Etc.	Etc.

does it demand that you teach these units through any particular method. Within the limits of our history, you are free to stress almost anything you wish through any means you choose. The definition of clarity and the choice of details are left in your hands.

At the other extreme you might see the following sort of course of study. It represents just one of 350 pages of highly detailed statements. (This example is fictitious.)

This type of course of study is highly specific. If you can read, locate resources, and recognize a correct answer, you can use this. The first question is, Do you want to? The second question is, Do you have to follow it? My answer is no, but I need to qualify that no. As a beginner, I would be prepared to use it on any day the supervisor or principal might be expected to drop in. After you have been around awhile, you will find out what your bosses think of the course of study. If they think it's stupid, then you have been emancipated. If they think it's simply marvelous, you had probably best give the impression of using it.

It's also fair to say that the list of resources may be very helpful. If so, obtain the resource materials, and use them pretty much as you wish.

DECISION MAKING AND COURSES OF STUDY

As a teacher, you will be a constant maker of decisions. It doesn't matter whether you want to be or not, you *will* make decisions.

You can decide to use a single textbook, to teach its contents and nothing else. Or you can decide to let the most vocal pupils express their interests and then have the class pursue those interests. Or you can decide to fake the whole thing—gab sessions on Mondays and Wednesdays, movies (any movies) on Tuesdays and Thursdays, and then read them stories on Fridays. Or you can decide on a general outline for the year and then share day-to-day decisions with your pupils.

The decisions you make about your course of study will be limited by several conditions. I have already said that I advise the beginner to give the appearance of following the district's course of study. That advice is a limitation on decision making, but the advice assumes the alternatives are even more limiting. The advice also is based on this fact: I have never seen a course of study I couldn't teach in one-third the time available for social studies. Most social-studies courses of study just skim the surface anyway, so skim quickly and spend the rest of the time on what you and the class feel is important. (Of course, if you like the course of study, your decision is easy—follow it.)

Second, you have to decide if the materials available to you provide adequately for the individual learning capacities of your pupils. If every pupil reads above grade level, you are home free. If none of them reads up to grade level, you are in a bind. In any event, you will have to decide whether you have a range of materials that fits the range of reading scores for your class.

Third, you have to decide what activities will work with your pupils. The limiting factors here are your creative imagination, the developmental stages of your pupils, and the facilities you need for certain activities. For example, your class may have learned from other teachers to speak only when spoken to. In that case, if you want discussion, you will have to teach them to talk to each other (rather than just to you) in the classroom.

Fourth, you will have to find out what interests your pupils have and what value their parents see in schools. The interest of pupils, whether self-generated or stimulated by you, is the fuel on which good classes run. The values of parents tell you the extent to which they will support what you are doing in your course of study. If your pupils come from a neighborhood where every policeman is a natural enemy, then you should be dealing with problems that are not common to textbooks. If your pupils come from a silk-stocking neighborhood, then you have to be concerned with a myopic view of life. If your pupils have no pride in their race, then you have a special problem that isn't covered in most programs of study.

Your decisions about a course of study will be influenced by what you think you *ought* to do. If what is expected, what can be, and what ought to be overlap, then your decisions will be easy to make. If there is little overlapping, then decisions will be difficult to make.

In the past, I viewed my own problems with preordained courses of study as a matter of resolving an issue between two assumptions. When I signed a contract, I assumed I had agreed to follow that district's course of study. I also assumed I was hired to do the best possible, professional job of teaching. Thus, the course of study represented the minimum, while my judgment could take the class well beyond the district's printed statement.

I once taught in a school where the principal said a certain textbook was the course of study. He was very clear about the matter—my fifth graders were to read the book from cover to cover. There were 36 weeks in the school year and 24 chapters in the book. Leaving out pictures and charts and maps, there were about ten pages of text per chapter. The text

dealt with U.S. history and was written at about seventh-grade level. Of
38 pupils, I had 6 that read as well as the average seventh grader. I had a
dozen pupils who could read easy fifth-grade material. Five pupils could
read only second-grade material. The other 15 could read third- or fourth-
grade material.

I divided the class into seven study groups. Each of the six top readers
led a study group; I worked with the poorest readers. (As the year went
along, pupils elected to shift from group to group, and new leaders developed.) Each leader received a textbook in which I had marked key para-
graphs or passages. Each group leader also got a list of discussion questions.
The group leader read the marked passages to his group and then led a
brief discussion of the questions. Each pupil then skimmed the chapter and
reread the marked passages. The group then talked again about answers to
the questions. I did roughly the same things with my group of very poor
readers; by "roughly" I mean I read aloud and then they restated the
passage in their own words before we discussed the questions.

This group-study process took up two class periods per week for 24
weeks. This left us three free days per week for 24 weeks plus five classes
per week for 12 weeks. In other words, we spent 48 classes on the textbook
and had 132 classes for dramatic play, case studies, sociodrama, map interpretation, biographies, films, and general problem solving. In the main, we
stayed with the study of the United States; in fact, the history book stopped
with the end of World War I, but we worked up to the present and made
a number of wild predictions about the future. There were three fifth
grades in that school and as the newest teacher, I had been assigned to the
"dumbest" class. The principal gave all classes the same test near the end
of the year. There were no significant differences in the average scores for
the three classes.

TEACHING AND LEARNING

The course of study is the rough framework for planning classroom activities. Within this framework, teaching and learning take place. It helped me
to have a mental model of the teaching process. In my case, and perhaps
yours, the simplest model was most helpful. Learning is limited by psychological development, by inherent capacity to learn, and by the presence of
certain psychological conditions (such as motivation) that stimulate learning. Within those limits, I see three major acts in the teaching process.

The Teaching Process

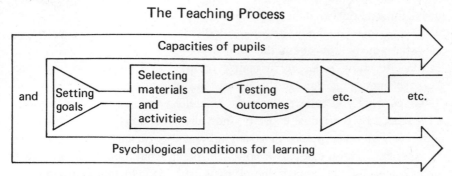

Figure 14.

The teaching process model indicates the major activities where you must make decisions. You decide what the major goals are, and you decide when decisions about setting specific goals are shared with pupils. You decide which materials and activities will promote reaching those goals, and you decide when pupils can share decisions about selecting materials and activities. You decide when a goal has been reached, and you decide the extent to which pupils may share in decisions about testing performance.

The Learning Process

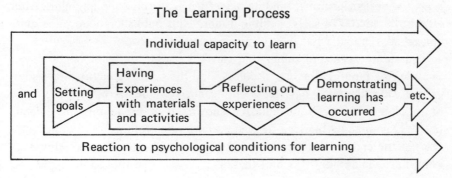

Figure 15.

The learning process differs from the teaching process in two important respects. Teaching usually involves a group, but learning is an individual matter. And learning (except for the simplest kind) requires that the individual think about what he has experienced.

Given what you know about the individual capacities of your pupils and what you believe about the influence of psychological conditions for learning, teaching is largely a matter of making decisions about setting goals, selecting materials and activities, and testing outcomes.

Given what you believe about the teaching process, individual learning is influenced by individual capacity, individual reactions to learning conditions, individual acceptance of goals, individual experiences and reflections on experiences. You can play a powerful role in what a pupil learns, but in the last analysis, the pupil is the ultimate authority. In that sense, as trite as it may sound, each child has his own social-studies program.

PUBLISHERS AND PROGRAMS

Publishers have dual purposes. They are in business to make a profit, and they have a genuine interest in helping pupils learn. There are dozens of elementary publishers of books, films, and other materials, and every one of them faces similar problems. A publisher puts anywhere from one- to two-and-one-half-million dollars into a six-grade social-studies series. This money goes for authors, editors, secretaries, artists, and a half-dozen other specialized personnel. The money pays for writing, editing, art work, graphics, design, printing, binding, advertising, storing, and shipping. After all this, the matter of sales is still in doubt. Thus publishers tend to be quite conservative about what they propose to sell.

There are dozens of things that can kill sales—the color of the cover, the title, the binding, the use of colors, and the types of pictures or photographs. Does the book have a "good" teachers' guide? Are there too many or too few minority-group children shown? Is it an inquiry or didactic book? How many American flags are seen in illustrations? Are there questions at the ends of chapters to keep pupils busy at their seats? How well known are the authors? Each of these is a serious question to the publisher, for he knows from experience that each has made or lost sales in the past.

These questions may be important to you also, but there are even more fundamental questions you must ask. Does the text (or series of texts) contain the ideas you (and your fellow teachers) view as basic to your social-studies courses or program? Does the text have enough range in content and readability to be useful and interesting to most of your pupils? If you wouldn't care to use the entire book, is enough of it useful to justify the cost? Are the authors known for their scholarship, both in subject matter and in the psychology of learning? If you can answer yes to these questions, then you apply the following queries as criteria for deciding whether you should recommend the book to your purchasing officer.

Accuracy

1. Does the content represent the real world or some rosy view of the best of our world?

2. Is the content based on scholarly research in the social sciences or is it based on the pseudoresearch of some politically oriented group?

3. When opinions or value judgments are expressed, is it made clear that they are biases, or are they cloaked to appear as facts?

4. Are the photographs and pictures accurate representations of reality or are they wholly aesthetic in value?

5. Is there enough factual (and therefore accurate) information to permit pupils to draw their own conclusions if they can't accept the author's conclusions?

Learnability

1. Can your pupils read the book; is it at least as easy to read as the readers they are using?

2. Does the writing have any literary qualities (style, rhythm, characterization, and so on), or is it purely pedantic?

3. Is the concept level controlled: that is, are new and unfamiliar social-science terms introduced sparingly and in logical sequence? Or are these terms dumped several at a time?

4. To aid in concept development, are there sufficient concrete examples and illustrations, or does each new term get only a few words of verbal explanation?

5. Is the content adopted, whenever possible, to situations reasonably familiar to children, or are they abstract and adult in nature?

Usefulness

1. Does the content have direct application to the pupils' out-of-school lives, or will it only apply sometime in the far-distant future?

2. Does the book help the pupil with what he will learn next in school (the principle of transfer), or is its content self-contained and isolated?

3. Does the book lead the pupil to use what he learns to examine his own life, his community, and his natural environment, or is the book an end in itself?

4. Does the book stimulate a pupil to examine and clarify his own values and those of others, or does it appear free of values?

5. Does the book answer and raise questions of interest to the pupil, or is it oriented to the narrow research interests of academicians?

There are other criteria you will want to add to this list, of course, but it gives you a place to start. You can also modify the questions and apply them to the selection of films, simulations, library books, and all sorts of supplementary materials. Whatever the type of material, it should be subordinate to the goals you and your pupils have for social studies.

Teachers have developed dozens of approaches to social studies. One of the best eighth-grade history classes I ever saw made almost exclusive use of film. A recent book by Kim Marshall rediscovers "learning stations" (in 1950 we called them "learning centers," and my mother says she called them "occupation corners" in the twenties). Not-so-incidentally, the Marshall book offers us a lovely success story of a teacher who creates a social-studies course that some people wouldn't call a course or social studies. I disagree with them, for Marshall did exactly what he should have done, given his values and temperament and his pupils. The book is worth the cost: *Law and Order in Grade 6–E,* Boston: Little, Brown and Co., 1972. Another useful example of the spontaneous course is found in Eliot Wiggington (ed.), *The Foxfire Book,* New York: Doubleday/Anchor, 1971. This book is about an English teacher in a rural, southern school. He drops his text and substitutes the writing of a magazine by students. The magazine uses material drawn from interviews with old folks in the area; to my eye, the content is superb social studies.

Thus, a social-studies course may be specified in great detail, or it may evolve day by day, guided only by the most general of goals. It may be materials centered or activities centered or a balanced combination of the two. It may be teacher oriented or child oriented. Most important of all, the program can be a hand-me-down from some specialist or publisher, or it can be created by you and your pupils—in either case the measure of its success will be desirable changes in the thinking, valuing, and behaving of your pupils as they decide, day by day, how they will live their lives.

SUMMARY

All schools have a curriculum, most have a social-studies program and some regulations about the scope of social studies for a given grade. Some of these courses of study are unbelievably detailed, leaving the teacher with little room for decision making. Some list only the textbook to be used; this is restrictive, but it still leaves the inventive teacher with roughly half her social-studies time free for nontext activities. Some courses list the bare bones of concepts to be developed or facts to be known. Some are so loosely identified that only the general topic for the year is specified. The conclusions are obvious: As you don't know in college just where you will teach, you cannot plan your social-studies course well ahead with any detail; as you don't known if you will work with a tightly or loosely structured course, the best you can do is develop some prior ideas about what you would most like to do—and understand that your ideas will likely be modified later.

If you are under contract, then by regulation or implication you have agreed to teach a particular set of courses for a particular grade. You should give every appearance of doing just this; however, if in your professional judgment your pupils need something more or something different, you can modify the required course to accommodate the additional goals, activities, and materials. This is particularly true when the materials furnished to your pupils are inaccurate, unreasonably difficult to learn from, and contain useless content.

If course goals are ambiguous, then you must make them behavioral. If course materials are highly abstract, then you must supplement them with concrete examples. If course activities are inappropriate, then you must substitute activities better suited to reaching your goals.

There are many models for teaching, some of them in the form of flow charts filled with boxes and arrows. Whatever else they may contain, they must specify three elements: (1) the setting of goals, (2) the using of materials and activities, and (3) the testing of outcomes to see if goals have been reached. In a sense the same is true for models of the learning process, except that one activity—reflecting on experiences—is so significant that it is singled out for emphasis. The two models presented in this chapter were drawn under the law of parsimony: The simplest, most easily remembered model is the one most apt to be applied. These models can accommodate any social-studies program (except one based on anarchy). They also make quite clear the major points at which you must make decisions about your social-studies course.

SUGGESTED READINGS

Surprise! I have none. Not that there aren't good books on the subject, but the best ways to learn about programs are listed under Exercises.

EXERCISES

1. Go to your curriculum laboratory and pull out four or five courses of study for the grade you hope to teach. Sketch out the major goals for each one. Do the same for the major topics or concepts. Compare and contrast your lists. Return again to the guides; which gives you the most freedom, which the least? If you do this for two or three grades, you may be able to decide which grade your college work has best prepared you to teach.

2. Your class should divide into groups for this activity. Each group should select one textbook company and examine its book for each grade carefully. What are the goals, the subject topics, the key concepts? Apply the criteria of accuracy, learnability, and usefulness to each book. Each of you should then report to the class on the strength and weaknesses of your book. You might also point out any parallels you found between the texts and the courses of study.

3. Break into groups again with enough members to cover each elementary grade. Each group should then plan its own sequence of courses for an imaginary elementary school. Put these on the board. Then regroup so all teachers for one grade are in a group; let each teacher for a grade explain to her fellow grade teachers why she chose to emphasize what she did. Then let the entire class ask each group any questions they wish.

4. Talk your instructor or curriculum librarian into setting up a display of some of the newer materials: data banks, M:ACOS (*Man: A Course of Study*), case books, game boards, and the like. If you had $100.00 to spend on your class, what would you buy?

Quick and Easy Lesson Plans

The organized elementary teacher lives a very busy day, but the teacher who does no planning lives a very hectic day. A teacher's time is valuable. She has too many pupils and too few minutes to give each pupil all the time she wants and he needs.

Planning and organization are needed to produce learning in a classroom. A school day contains just so many hours, and the curriculum guide contains too many subjects. Each subject contains a wealth of information, a great many concepts, and more generalizations than we care to deal with. The teacher must somehow bring a degree of order out of the chaos of time, numbers of pupils, and variety of subjects. She must keep from being ground to a halt by the business of taking roll, collecting funds, and the other administrative trivia that get piled on her already bent shoulders.

THE NEED TO PLAN

An analogy can be made between time and money. When you get a paycheck, your taxes, social security, group insurance, and one or two other amounts have already been withheld. When you cash that check, you know you have other fixed expenses—rent, car payment, utilities. You also have to plan rough amounts for other necessities—food, sundries, clothing, medicine, and so forth. What you have left can be shifted around to meet emergencies and have fun.

The teacher has so many minutes per day when children are in her classroom, but she can't spend all that time in any way she pleases. A certain amount of that time will be withheld from her.

"Your class, Miss Hopeful, will go to the gym teacher from ten to ten-thirty on Monday, Wednesday, and Friday. Those who play instruments will be gone on Tuesday and Thursday from two to three. The art teacher will take over your class on Wednesdays from one to two."

Now for fixed expenses. You may love social studies, but the "fixed subjects" are still the skill subjects of reading and arithmetic. Block out time for those and for recess. (You and your pupils need recess, preferably twice a day. They need to exercise their muscles, and you need to stop exercising your brain and tongue.)

You still have to work in other necessities—science, health, and social studies. Block those in and what do you have left? A few chunks of time, 15 minutes here and 30 minutes there. Those chunks can be used to meet emergencies, to stretch out other periods, or to give children a few minutes for themselves.

Have we missed anything? Spelling goes in with writing, so that's no problem. Oh, no, we left out vocal music—let's see where we can work *that* in. . . .

YOU AND YOUR PLANS

No one can lay out a plan for you in a textbook. I liked social studies so I taught it every day. It was one subject where every other subject could be *applied*. In social studies, I could tell if my pupils were learning to read and write and count. I could tell if science and art and music meant anything more than "book learning." But other teachers don't like social studies, so they give it a minimum of 30 minutes a day twice a week. You will have to do what everyone else does, work out a plan for yourself and then adjust it to suit your class.

Not only is your plan bound to be a bit ragged from hour to hour through the day, but it will also be uneven from day to day. The block of stories in the reader will take ten days. The science unit called "Machines" should take a week. "Transportation in Our City" will take from three to four weeks, depending on field trips. The chapter in arithmetic will take at least 12 days. These things just won't work out neatly, so you will have to make periodic adjustments.

Don't worry about adjustments. Worry if you aren't making changes. No one makes perfect plans, for no one has that keen an insight into the future. The same is true of plans for lessons. Most good teachers do three kinds of planning: planning beforehand, planning in process, and planning afterward. To some extent, you plan both *for* students and *with* students in each situation.

Many teachers plan for students beforehand. The beforehand lesson plan is your idea of what you want and what you think will happen. Planning in process is a characteristic of all good teachers, for children are human and no human is ever wholly predictable. Planning afterward is a matter of asking what worked, what didn't work, and what you should do with that lesson next year.

Experience tells me there are some exceptions to what I have written. You won't always have every lesson planned out before you teach it. Sometimes, but very seldom, I hope, you just have to fake a lesson. (A family argument or crisis can keep even the best teacher from making plans beforehand.) When that time comes, don't worry about it. You need a clear mind. Plan as you go, and draw the class into the planning process. If you have been doing a good job, the class won't be condemned to ignorance just because you blew one lesson.

One worthwhile tip—Have at least one model lesson for each major subject on hand for emergencies. It can be a new lesson or one that has been taught before. If a principal or supervisor walks in and sits down on a day when you were going to fake a lesson, whip out that model and show off. For example, the short lesson plan on the globe (see the next section) is one that *should* be repeated, with variations, four or five times during the year. Use it when the principal drops in and shows you his crocodile smile.

THE QUICKY

Some lesson plans are short, simple goal activities. The plan that follows is a *quicky*. It assumes that the globe has been introduced previously to these first graders. Note that I make a distinction between what I want pupils to understand about the earth and about the globe.

Anything in italic is something new to my class (everything else is review). For example, I want my pupils to develop meanings for *up* and *down*. To accomplish this, I will have pupils perform certain acts, and I will use certain language. I have to be sure they understand that language. Let's

Globe and Directions

Equipment Needed

Simple introductory globe; blue for water, brown for land
Apple or orange and knife

SM Goals — Earth

1. Planet earth looks like a very large ball.
2. Part of our earth is land, part is water.
3. Down means away from the center of the earth.
4. Up means toward the center of the earth.

SM Goals — Globe

1. A globe is a ball with a map of the earth on it.
2. On this globe, blue means water.
3. On this globe, brown means land.
4. Only half of a globe can be seen at any one time.

Activities

1. Stand in center of circle.
2. Find center of apple.
3. Climb up on chair.
4. Jump down off chair.

say I don't think they all know what *away from, toward,* and *center* mean.

"You six come over here. Do you know what a circle is? OK, get in a circle."

Ask someone not in the circle, "Did they get in a circle? OK, you six get in a circle. Now that six. And now this six. Billy, do you know what the *center* of a circle is? OK, who does? (The question is directed at the four or five pupils still in their seats.) Fine, get in the center of one of the circles. Now, Billy, can you get in the center of a circle? Good. OK, Mary, now you. . . ."

From here I can have everyone move *toward* the center of their circle and then *away from* the center. Perhaps I let them play "Simon says," moving *toward* and *away from* in their circles (the centers are "Simons").

Then I shift to the orange and ask its shape (they know *shape* from an earlier lesson). The orange is cut and we find the *center*. We try to establish that all round things have a center.

Next we work on *up* and *down*. "Climb *up* on the chair; jump *down*. Toss the eraser *up* in the air; catch it when it comes *down*. Look *up* at the floor. Why can't you?" And so on.

You can take it from here with the globe, but don't forget to go back to the cut orange and get at the meaning of *half*.

When I was a beginner, I got in the habit of making up 5 x 8 cards for simple lessons; I still find the habit useful. I used to put key questions and activities on the back of the card, but with two or three years' experience I stopped using a set sequence in procedures and played that part of my teaching by ear.

The lesson contains the simple elements of teaching. It indicates the *goals* I hope pupils will get to, it reminds me of the *materials and activities* I want to use, and the *testing* is built into the activities.

I tried to involve everyone both physically and mentally, and if I handled it well, the pupils became emotionally involved. They had fun, enjoyed learning, and stretched their muscles. They got in some review (a form of testing) and they acquired some new learnings they could employ in the future.

Did I need a lesson plan? I think I did, and I think most teachers do. I've seen too many teachers who want to teach *up* and *down* without bothering to teach *away from, toward,* and *center*. Their pupils memorized but developed no meanings; their pupils could repeat but could not apply what they could recall.

Did I spend hours on that lesson plan? Not on your life! I spent ten minutes. After I taught the lesson, I spent two more minutes polishing it. The second year, I spent a couple of minutes reviewing it before I taught it. The investment was small, the results were worthwhile.

There are many sets of quicky lessons that help out in social studies. Most of them deal with learning and remembering arbitrary associations or geographic skills. For example, most teachers expect children to know the names and often the locations of the 50 states. They want pupils to be able to locate the cardinal directions, orient a map, point up or down, or find an island, peninsula, and gulf on a map.

There are many ways of learning the names and locations of the states. My favorite requires some butcher paper, scraps of carpeting, an overhead projector, and a map of the United States. I would have some pupils pin butcher paper over the biggest bulletin board in the room. (The old 48 states were roughly 1,000 miles north and south and 3,000 miles east and west—so my papered area was three times as wide as it was high.)

At a time when four or five pupils who liked to draw had nothing else to do, we set up the projector, slipped in my map, and adjusted the table so the map rather neatly covered the butcher paper. The group then traced in the projected state lines (adding Alaska and Hawaii at some other odd moment).

At another time, another group cut out each of the states. The "cut-out state" was then used as a pattern. Turned upside down and laid on the *back* of a scrap of carpet, the pattern could then be traced onto the carpet. The outline was then cut out, turned over, and what did we have? A state, and one that would fit into a block of states.

(The map provided both accuracy and relatively consistent area. The carpet scraps were begged, extorted, or requisitioned from local merchants who couldn't stand to see children cry. The tracing of the map and the cutting of the patterns kept two groups of unoccupied hands from the devil's work.)

We then started with our own state and region of states. Down went California or Texas or Michigan. Other pupils had other states of the region in hand. They built in those states around "our" state, and each was named as it went into place. At first I did this with small groups—but eventually everyone got to do it. A simple political map of the United States hung on the wall for ready reference.

We then doubled the size of the group and added a new region. Before long the whole class was busy at once. They could put that carpet map together in no time.

Next, we began to reduce cues and increase the task. The big map came off the wall and an outline map (no names) went up. Two pupils had to do the whole job. Then the outline map disappeared. No matter, everyone could do the job by himself by now.

The pupils made up their own games with the map. They cut out the Great Lakes, they ran blue ribbon where major rivers flowed, they cut out circles and added cities. They learned to spell the abbreviations for the states. No pain, no fuss, no tears; 10 minutes here, 15 minutes there. And did you ever see the expression on the "poorest" kid's face when he realized he could do a school task as well as the brightest?

ADJUSTING THE QUICKY

One last point about lesson plans in general: Be prepared to plan in process. That is, be ready to add a new idea that just hit you. And be ready to plan with pupils, when they get an idea or ask a question.

Let's say you are teaching the quicky on the globe. Another globe hangs in the room. You see some pupils shifting their eyes between the two globes. The other globe is a physical representation, and you guess the pupils are wondering why the land is multicolored rather than all brown. You suddenly have a chance to put across another point about geographic tools: Different colors can stand for the same things on different globes. Should you bring that in? I don't know, because I don't know you or your pupils. But I do know it's important that you consider it.

Let's say that you and your class are working on your carpet map. Suddenly, a pupil looks up and asks, "Why is Michigan called Michigan? Why isn't it called Illigan or Minnigan or Canagan?"

You probably don't know, so admit you don't. Ask, "Where can we find out?" Someone will be smart enough to say the encyclopedia. Someone gets it. And someone looks it up. Now you all know. You have had a minilesson within an activity. You and the group had a goal, a plan, a resource, an activity; and you used all these to find an answer.

Sometimes, the ideas pupils have can't be handled in three minutes. If they are good ideas, and if there is general interest in them, then take time to get at them. The process is familiar: what do we want to know, how can we find out, what do we need, who will do what? You are teaching them to teach themselves—and that is a major aim of learning.

The short lesson involving activity and discussion is a valuable tool. It breaks up too much reading. It fills in odd chinks in a day's schedule. It works well with a small group that has nothing else to do. And, best of all, it produces learning and builds the attitude that not all things worth knowing must be learned from a book.

INTEREST AREAS AND DATA BANKS

Two "new" ideas floating around these days tickle me. The first is *interest areas;* the second is the *data bank*. Both are good ideas and worth your consideration.

The learning, or interest, area provides pupils with opportunities to do something they choose to do on their own time. It's also an antidote for discipline problems. Of all the various difficulties I have seen beginning teachers encounter, the problem of what to do with the Crows and Eagles while the Robins are reading seems most confusing. The problem extends, of course, to what happens to other pupils or other groups when you work with one group in any subject.

The average teacher, believe it or not, tries to make the Crows and Eagles stay in their seats and be quiet. That is unreasonable, for stillness and quietness are not natural states for children. Discipline breaks down under these circumstances. The teacher counters by giving the pupils seatwork. This seems more reasonable to pupils, but the work is dull and lacks motive power. And then the teacher must stay up at night correcting the seatwork assignments.

Casting frantically about for a solution, the teacher gives no assignment and puts no restrictions on movement or talking. Anarchy now reigns, and the teacher begins to think about working in a bank.

Actually, there are three principles for you to hold in mind about this problem. First, silence and immobility are unnatural for children. Second, if you want children to move freely but softly, and talk openly and quietly, then you have to help them learn these behaviors. Third, there must be enough opportunities for pupils to engage in something interesting enough to keep them willingly busy.

Many teachers are shocked when I say pupils need to learn to move about in a classroom without disturbing other groups of pupils. These teachers seem to believe this behavior is imparted genetically, or is hammered into kids by some Saturday-morning television cartoon. It would be great if it were, but the sad fact remains that you must teach this behavior. More about this in a moment.

As a teacher, I was always a scrounger. The more junk I could pick up and distribute around my room the better. In my room you could find such centers as these:

1. A practice bicycle-repair area, complete with tools and printed instruction sheets on changing a tire, tightening a brake, raising a seat, and so on.
2. A science area with fish or gerbils or plants, always with some experiment to try; or a tank of water for "discovering" displacement; or something mechanical or electrical to build.
3. An art area—near the water supply—with water-based paint in used frozen-juice cans and plenty of cheap paper; clay and beads and tile chips and leather thongs.
4. A knot-display board with a heap of clothesline ends for practice (don't ask why, but this was a great attraction).
5. A library table loaded with books with slips of paper placed in them at strategic points—often with questions on them: "How will Jonah get out of the whale?" or "Will the wicked baker keep the runaways to slave over his ovens?"
6. A construction area with scraps of wood, dull tools, and pictures of things to make.
7. A thinking area complete with cushions and a small rug, where silence was mandatory and reflection was optional.
8. An audio-visual area with a filmstrip projector and viewer and cans of film.

These areas could be used at any time, except when the whole class was in session or when a pupil was part of a working group. If at the end of a week, a pupil clearly had gotten behind in "regular" work, then he was restricted until he caught up his back assignments. Before long, pupils took over the operation of the interest areas. They changed the books, they mixed the paints, they brought in scraps of wood. Why not? Weren't the areas theirs? They also added areas—a music area, a map area, a games area, an arithmetic area. No more problems when the Robins were reading, no more stacks of papers to correct at night.

How did I teach them to handle this freedom to choose and to learn? I started them off by holding them to their seats for two or three days. Then I added the interest areas and let their mouths water for a day. Next, I asked if they liked the rule about staying in their seats. They didn't think much of it. What would they like? They'd like to use all that "stuff" around the room. Wouldn't that bother the Robins? No, oh no, they told me, if they could use that stuff they wouldn't bother anyone.Ok, I told them, why don't you show me how you would act. They tiptoed around and were as silent as they could be. Come on, I teased them, you can't be that quiet for more than a few minutes. Ok, they told me, we'll just whisper or talk in a low voice. How about moving around? Well, they told me, we'll walk quietly. How about running, I asked? No running, they replied. Ok, I said, now show me again how this idea of yours is going to work. They did, and it worked.

At one point they wanted to change a rule, and with some prodding they did. They also showed me what things would be like under the new rule—we then had an agreed-upon standard of behavior. Oh, they lapsed from time to time, but they were quieter and learned more than the adults who gathered twice daily in the teachers' room.

The connection between lesson plans and interest areas is this: Interest areas are *not* wholly haphazard undertakings; they are loose forms of lessons. Remember the bike instructions and the question slips in the books? Those were kickoffs for minilessons. When the principal dropped in and watched, he said, "My God, John, aren't they moving around a lot?" My answer was, "Yes sir, but did you ever see such good citizenship?"

I stumbled onto the idea of data banks with my first sixth grade. I was having a terrible time getting across the idea of percentages, particularly with a group of boys. Now, percentages were taught in the spring, and spring opens the baseball season. One day I asked a kid what his batting average was. "About .320," he replied. And a lightbulb went on over my head.

The next day I showed up with an almanac. There they were—won-and-lost records and percentages for baseball, basketball, and football. Away we went, and percentages were no longer a problem. One day someone asked me about death penalties. "Look it up in the almanac," I suggested.

From then on the almanac was a major resource. It had all sorts of information about nations, rivers, manufacturing, trade, and a host of other subjects. The next year, instead of assigning reports on countries, small groups of pupils were asked to collect all the information they could find about the nation of their choice. They tore up old almanacs, copied from encyclopedias, and cut maps and pictures from books and magazines. These went into resource folders. After a period of mulling over their contents, the pupils threw out some of the collection and organized the remainder so the information in all the folders was in roughly the same order. Now we were ready to ask questions. Did all nations have a government? Did they all have three branches of government? What were the alternatives? On and on they went, questions of comparison and contrast.

Eventually, some of the folders turned into looseleaf notebooks for major countries. The class kept a record of the comparison and contrast questions. "You'll need these for next year," they said. Year by year the resource folders grew. They were the products of group work, and although the poorest readers concentrated on maps and pictures, they also could name the nations with highest GNP's and could speculate on what would happen as populations grew and food production didn't. They predicted the Vietnam War (this was 1952) although they got the combatants wrong.

The resource folders were a crude form of data bank. The inquiry questions everyone made up were a form of quicky lesson calling primarily for the retrieval of stored information. At times, the information was used as a basis for comparison and contrast, and in these instances some first-rate reasoning took place.

The quicky lesson thus serves several purposes. It provides for minor skill development, for acquisition of isolated bits of information, or for utilizing fragments of otherwise useless time. It protects you during an unexpected visit from a supervisor. And tied to interest areas and data banks, it permits pupils to develop their own brief lessons while working on projects of interest to them.

SUMMARY

Teachers need to plan—not only their goals, how to reach them, and how to know when they have been reached—but also to plan how to manage a chopped-up school day. One way to fill in those odd chunks of time is to use quicky lessons—the brief lesson focused on an easily reached goal.

If the teacher is to conduct the quicky, then she should try to make the experience as concrete as possible (getting pupils into a circle rather than just talking about circles, for example).

The models for teaching and learning in a quicky lesson are the same as if you were planning a three-week unit (see Chapter 11). In addition to concreteness, teachers find the quicky has some of the qualities of a game. Learning becomes both efficient and fun.

Interest areas and data banks provide pupils with opportunities to create their own quickies. The resulting learnings are as substantial as any other school learnings, and the settings in which they occur stress thinking and research skills.

The quicky lesson thus serves both teacher and pupil well. It cuts down friction in some circumstances, and it permits effective use of short periods or free pupil time when the teacher is engaged with a special group. It permits movement and communication by pupils without imposing on the rights of others to learn.

SUGGESTED READING

Walsh, Huber M. (ed.), *An Anthology of Readings in Elementary Social Studies.* Washington, D.C.: NCSS, Readings No. 4, 1971. (Read Section II, "Inquiry-Oriented Teaching" and Section III, "Individualizing Instruction." There are 13 articles in these two sections. Also, see the Exercises listed below.)

EXERCISES

1. Divide the class so all 13 articles in Walsh are read and can be reported on; after the brief reports have been made, use discussion to review the notions of inquiry and individualized instruction.

2. Divide the class into four groups, each assigned to one of these journals: *Social Education, Social Studies, The Instructor,* and *Learning.* Review the articles in each journal for the past year and select those a group feels should go into a book of readings. Then discuss why each article should be included, and see if, from those reasons, you can induce a set of criteria for judging the worth of professional articles.

3. Draw up two or three quicky lessons on 5 x 8 cards; on the back spell out in behavioral terms part of the activity you would use to help reach the goal. Share these with some of your classmates, and let everyone comment (gently) on the strengths and weaknesses of the cards.

Using Textbooks

No textbook is perfect. Some are downright bad. They are, in fact, like people—some should be avoided, most should be treated civilly, and a few should be good friends. I never have used all of any textbook for elementary pupils. I did find a few texts that I used a great deal. I found many that I used great chunks of. And I found many where I could use only dibs and dabs.

Of all the criteria used in selecting a story from a textbook, usefulness gives teachers the most trouble. Yet, the reasoning behind the criteria of usefulness seems quite simple.

Pupils like what they learn if they can use what they learn. They want to solve problems they face. They want to answer questions their environment poses. They want to reduce the unknown to the known. If what you are teaching has no use, then it will decay and be forgotten rapidly.

You are merely kidding yourself when you teach useless information or ideas to children. And that is what many teachers do—they kid themselves into believing that useless information is useful if it is "covered" or if pupils remember it long enough to pass a test. Let me be blunt. If most of what you are teaching youngsters in social studies cannot somehow be applied to their immediate lives, then it probably isn't worth learning.

In the next section of this chapter there is a story (and a lesson plan for the story) called "The Plan to Grow Pumpkins." Pupils who read that story probably will learn something about pumpkins. That's fine, but to me what is important is that they should learn about plans and planning. I want them to know about plans. I want them to make plans. I want them to work with others in making plans. And I want them to use what they know about plans in dealing with their classmates and classroom situations, with their parents and home life, with everything that is important to *them*. I don't want plans to be the object of a story in a book. I want planning and plans to be a part of their behavior.

PLANNING THE TEXTBOOK LESSON

How do you plan to teach a lesson from a textbook? Obviously, read what you want pupils to read. Then read the teacher's guide. That may go against the grain. Teacher's guides are often pedantic, boring, prescriptive, and patronizing. All true, all too true, but people have gotten rich on silver mines turning out only 15 ounces of silver for each ton of ore. You only need one or two good ideas from the teacher's guide to make it worth the five minutes it took to skim the pages. The key words in using a teacher's guide are *select, adapt,* and *expand*. Take what is right for you and your pupils. Ignore everything else.

When examining a story, ask yourself three questions. What is the key idea used directly in the story? Is the meaning of that key idea developed? Is there any key idea or ideas that can be inferred?

If there are no key ideas, or if none are worth teaching to your class, skip the story. If there is a key idea, then use the story. But if meanings for that key idea aren't developed in the story, then you must plan to help pupils develop those meanings through other activities. The question now is, should those meanings be developed before or after the story is read?

There is no absolute answer, but I use two rules of thumb. The younger the child or the more unfamiliar the idea, the more I tend to develop initial meanings before reading the story. The older the pupil or the more familiar the idea, the safer I feel in checking on meanings after the story has been read.

On the matter of key ideas that can be inferred from a story, I almost always wait until the story has been read before I put a label on the idea. There is an old first-grade story about Tom and some tomatoes. I always liked that story, partly because Tom was an unwilling helper and partly because Tom's father showed a little emotion by yelling at him. The word *cooperation* was not used in print, but cooperation was the key idea. I used that story, in front of a dozen experienced teachers, with a group of first graders at the Stanford Demonstration School one day when the regular teacher had a bad cold. We whipped through the story, spent 5 minutes acting it out, and then spent about 15 minutes discussing cooperation. We tested our ideas in a number of ways. The class found that not one of them could move a desk with me sitting on it, but that six of them could push it easily. I put two children on opposite sides of the room, gave one a can cover and the other a pair of scissors, and asked each to draw and then cut out a neat circle. They had to cooperate. The class then set up two or three other situations that required cooperation. At the coffee break, I met with the visiting teachers. The oldest one offered a compliment or two and then said, "I must have missed something. I didn't see the word *cooperation* anywhere in the story. Why did you spend so much time on cooperation and so little time on tomatoes?" I told her, but she went away certain that I had broken some great, unspoken trust with textbook publishers.

THE MECHANICS OF READING

There are a number of tough questions about teaching from a text. Should everyone use the same text? Should you work with the class or with groups? Should the reading be silent or oral or a mixture? Should new words be "taught" before, during, or after reading? Should discussion be page by page, by groups of pages, on the whole story, or just on key ideas? Should you discuss questions by pupils?

I don't know that there are right answers to most of those questions, but I do believe there is but one right answer for two of them. The answers to the others depend greatly on your temperament, on the range of abilities and interests in your class, and on such other variables as how long pupils have been sitting, how hot and sticky the room is, and how badly you need a cup of coffee.

To the question of silent versus oral reading, I say flatly: Unless you want to punish a child, let him read silently before you ask him to read aloud. Always! Anyone, including you, can be made to seem idiotic by having him read a complex and unfamiliar passage. If you don't believe me, get yourself an audience—some of whom don't particularly like you and some of whom you really want to impress—and read them a page or two on the theory of relativity. Or pick up a Bible and begin with Numbers 33:28. If you pass the test, leave teaching and get a job in broadcasting— they need you.

To the question of considering children's questions about a topic, my position is that you are paid to help pupils with their questions. Children ask many questions, and many of those questions seem irrelevant. But irrelevant to whom? You? Or the child? Come on, earn your daily bread. If you cut off questions long enough, you cut off curiosity. If you cut off curiosity, you kill part of an inquiring mind. If you don't like inquiring minds, you probably believe that 1984 represents salvation.

When I taught a class with many poor readers, I used a mixture of class and group techniques. We got oriented to the story as a class; new words went on the board, were pronounced, and tentative meanings were explored. The class then broke into groups, although I made sure there was at least one good reader in each group. Everyone read silently as best he could, although anyone could ask for help within his group at any time. Then, in each group, a good reader read aloud while the others followed along.

The class then was ready to discuss the story. I seldom called on individuals. I would ask, "Group number two, what did you think of Pete and Kate's way of finding out what they didn't know?" "Do the other groups agree?" "What do you think the person who wrote the story thought was the most important idea, group number four?"

The members of a group could confer before an answer was given. Sometimes the answer was, "We can't agree, but we think it was . . . or maybe . . ."

If I wanted to check out an individual, I would ask, "Billy, why did you (or your group) decide on that answer?"

Somewhere in the questions we got at the meaning of the key idea or ideas in the story. Pupils would act out examples, set up simple demonstrations, or draw illustrations. Then we would tie those ideas back to earlier ideas, and we would try to predict what other new ideas might be learned later. But no matter what else we did, we applied the key idea to the lives and environments of the pupils.

For example, if a key idea was *capital,* we asked what a baseball game had to do with capital. A player's bat, ball, and glove are capital—they are the capital goods he uses to produce recreation. The ditto machine and the overhead projector were capital goods for producing learning materials. We used each to produce something we could consume in learnings—maps for each student or a projected photograph on a screen. Billy's dad needed tools as a carpenter, the tools were his capital goods. Everyone knew the ice cream man—what were his capital goods? Now then, how would you play a baseball game without a bat and a ball? Keep your patience when someone says, "with a stick and a can." He's right, but what are the stick and the can? Capital goods, right? But what if you had no stick or can? How would Billy's dad build a wall without his tools? Ok, so why is capital needed if we are going to produce something?

Of course, this kind of teaching is predicated on two assumptions. First, you know something about production and the factors of production, including capital. Second, you have taught the class, slowly, that there are many ways to learn. Youngsters who have spent four years in straight rows, with their noses stuck in books they couldn't read, do *not* automatically take to group responsibilities or open-ended discussion.

The point is this: If you ask yourself tough questions, if you use your imagination, and if you trust yourself to make some mistakes, you will find some exciting and worthwhile ways to use parts of textbooks with any kind of a class.

THE TACTICS OF PLANNING

What follows is a story written in somewhat orthodox style for, say, third graders. The capitalized words are descriptions of illustrations for the story; they are placed approximately where the illustration would be on a page. Along with the print you will see a certain amount of cursive writing. The "handwritten" parts represent teacher notes on what might be done with the story. Be warned, now. There are more notions about what to do with the story than you ought to try. They are there so you can see how much might be wrung from one short story.

These pages represent one type of lesson plan. You write your lesson plan on the pages of your textbook. Do this with pencil the first time you teach the story. Then, when you have taught the story, erase all the ideas that didn't work. Use red ink (or any bright color), and trace over everything that worked well.

By the end of the year you will have a set of lesson plans that grew out of your imagination and your experience. You can go on making changes from year to year as you grow wiser. Substitutes will love you. And you will have time to plan other matters.

To my mind, the key ideas are *plan, work,* and *decision. Plan* and *work* are in the story; *decision* must be inferred. Whatever else I might do with this story, those are the words for which I hope my pupils will develop concepts.

Pics
↑ Pumpkin
   Jack-o-lantern

TEACH NEW WORDS!
SILENT READING FIRST!!

What is a plan?
What is a plan good for?
Do plans always work?
Why not?

PLAN
PLANT
PLOWS
WORK
SELL

The Plan to Grow Pumpkins

SHOW HEADS OF 3 KIDS

Pete said, "Let's get to work.
Let's plant our pumpkin seeds now."

Kate said, "Let's ask Mother
if it is time to plant the seeds now.' } Mother as "resource"

3 KIDS AND MOTHER IN KITCHEN
GRANDMA SETS OUT MILK AND COOKIES

Kate said, "We want to ask something.
When do we plant the pumpkin seeds?"

Mother said, "I know when to plant seeds.
You plant pumpkin seeds late in the spring.
Grandpa plants his corn in the spring.
When the corn gets up to here,
then you can plant your pumpkin seeds." } Why plant Ⓟ w/corn?

MOTHER HAS HAND ABOUT 10" OFF FLOOR.

approximate?
exact?

BASIC IDEA

If you want something,
you
   1. make a decision
   2. make a plan
   3. do the work

ANCILLARY IDEAS

Seeds and growth
Seasons & different kinds
   of work
Cooperation

Q- What is mother
telling Pete and Kate?
Hook up and tell me
in your own words.

Q- If corn planted before
Ⓟ and both are ready
to be picked at same
time, which takes
more time to grow?

Q- For next page! What
can Pete & Kate do in
the winter so they can
grow Ⓟ? Let's turn
page and see!

Winter

This is what Mother said about the winter.

WINTER SCENE – KIDS ARE OUT IN FIELD
WITH MAP. STANDING IN CORN STUBBLE
AND LIGHT SNOW.

You make your plans in the winter.
You plan how many pumpkins you want.
You plan where you will plant your seeds.
You plan how to take care of your pumpkins.
You plan how you will sell your pumpkins.

When you make a plan,
you know what you want to do.
When you make a plan,
you know how you will do something.

DISCUSS PIC

— Is corn still growing?

— How do you know?

— Is this the way winter looks on farms around here?

— After winter is gone, what season comes next?

— What will (weather, trees, clothes, etc.,) be like in the spring?

Look up – Tell me, what is a plan?

If I want to wash the blackboard, how will I do it?

What do you think Pete & Kates plan will be?

Turn page and see.

Spring

TWO PICS

SPRING SCENE – BUDS OUT ON TREES –
GRANDPA PLOWING

CORN IS 10" HIGH – KIDS ARE PLANTING
SEEDS IN LOW (3") HILLS IN CORN ROWS

This is what Mother said about the Spring.

You will help grandpa in the Spring.
A farmer plows his land in the spring.
Grandpa will plow the land and plant corn.
You can help plow and plant corn.
Late in the Spring you will plant your seeds.

The Spring is the time a farmer
works his land and plants his seeds.

PIC

How can we tell that
the season has changed?

What season is it
now?

Why do we plant corn in
the spring?

— warm
— no frost
— sunshine
— rain
— long time to grow

What does a farmer
do in the winter?
— in the spring?

Summer

This is what Mother said about the summer.

SUMMER SCENE – KIDS ARE WEEDING
(NOT BETWEEN ROWS, BUT IN THE ROWS
AMONG THE CORN STALKS). SHOW CORN
UP TO THEIR SHOULDERS AND VINES OUT
FOR PUMPKINS.

WHY?

You will work hard in the summer.
You will weed the land in the summer.
You will have to get the weeds
out of the corn and the pumpkins.

PROTECTING
PLANTS

It takes hard work to grow something.
It takes hard work and a good plan
to make things grow on a farm.
The summer is the time a farmer takes
good care of his crops.

What season now?
How do you know?

— What does
happen to the
seeds?

— Why is it hard
work to weed
the land?

— Did Pete and
Kate know
they had to
work hard?

— How do you
think they
feel about
their plan now?

What season did
we talk

What season did
we talk about
first?

Then which one?

On this page?

Tell me all three
first???

Fall

This is what Mother said about the fall.

PIC

What has happened
to the pumpkins?

FALL SCENE — SHOW STAND WITH PILES OF
PUMPKINS. KIDS ARE UNLOADING WAGON.

You will pick your pumpkins in the fall. } TRANSPORTING
You will have to put them in a wagon.
You will have to carry them to the stand.
Then you will have to sell them for Halloween. } PRODUCING
You can sell your pumpkins to the people   A SERVICE
who come to our stand to buy food.

If you can do all that work,
then you will grow and sell the pumpkins.
If you can sell all the pumpkins,   DISCUSS WORK –SELL –EARN
then you will earn the money you want.

Have 4 CARDS on pumpkins (A)
and 4 CARDS on seasons (B)

(A) 1. plan   2. plant (P)   3. weed
4. sell pumpkins

(B) 1. winter   2. spring   3. summer   4. fall

(C) Kids put cards in sequence.

(D) Student tells story looking at cards.

(E) Student tells story without looking
at cards.

Pete and the Twins Work

USE POSTERS
AGAIN
A6   REVIEW

These are the things that Pete and the twins did.
They made their plans in the winter.
They got the pumpkin seeds they needed.
They made their map to show
where they could plant their pumpkin seeds.

Pete and the twins helped Grandpa in the spring.
They helped him plow the rows for the corn.
They helped him plant the corn in rows.
They saved places in the rows for the pumpkins.
They planted the pumpkin seeds in the late spring.

Pete and the twins worked hard in the summer.
They weeded the corn rows, and the corn grew.
They weeded by the pumpkins many times.
In the late summer, the corn was ripe.
The family picked the ripe corn,
and sold it to people at the stand.

The pumpkins were ripe in the fall.
Pete and the twins picked the pumpkins.
They put the pumpkins into Grandpa's wagon.
Grandpa helped Pete and the twins,
for they had helped him grow his corn.

BOOK LIST

Pete said, "Soon it will be Halloween.
Now is the time to sell our pumpkins."

SEASONS ① _____
② _____
③ _____

ACTIVITIES ?
POSTER
SHORT ACTING OUT
MAKE BOOKLET—base this on:
① decision
② a plan
③ WORK—so kids will use
all 3 ideas —

FARMING ① _____
② _____
③ _____

EARN & SELL ① _____
② _____

The pupils may also learn something about sequential activities in farming; they may pick up information about corn and pumpkins; they may reinforce their ideas about seasons—and if they do, more power to them. But *plan, work,* and *decision* are still the keys to my using this story.

You may have different priorities. Perhaps your pupils don't know anything about seasons. Fine, then teach seasons if that suits you and your pupils. But make sure that your subsequent activities stress the application of knowledge about seasons to the present lives of your pupils.

I have the same obligation. Decision making, planning, and working to carry out plans must become a part of the life of my class. Let's see now, the class has been wanting to put on a puppet show . . . and they want to build a television set big enough so they can get inside it and put on a news hour . . . and there's that field trip to the . . .

CONCEPTS IN STORIES

What follows is an example of my idea of how a textbook can be of help to a student in concept development and in valuing. These sections are taken from a first-grade book intended for use at about the time the pupils are reading at primer level.[1] The topic is *rules.*

THE ILLUSTRATION SHOWS TWO GROUPS OF BOYS, ONE GROUP OF TEN-YEAR OLDS, AND TWO SEVEN- OR EIGHT-YEAR OLDS. THE SETTING IS AN INNER CITY INDUSTRIAL AREA. THE GROUPS ARE INTEGRATED. THE OLDER BOYS ARE PLAYING "FOLLOW THE LEADER." THEY ARE KICKING A CAN. THE YOUNGER BOYS ARE TALKING TO ONE OF THE OLDER BOYS.

"Come on," Chuck said.
"Please let us play.
We want to play with you."

"Go away," said Mac.
"You are too little."

"We are not," Chuck said.
"We can run fast and kick a can.
We can play that game."

"So you can run," said Mac.
"So you can kick a can.
But do you know the rules?"

"Rules?" said Chuck.
"What are rules?
Who needs rules to kick a can?"

"So you want to play," said Mac.
"But you don't know what rules are!
A rule tells you what you can do.
It tells you what you can't do.
Rules tell you how to play a game."

Chuck said, "We want to play.
What rules do we have to know?"

THE ILLUSTRATION SHOWS THE OLDER BOYS PLAYING
"FOLLOW THE LEADER." THE LEADER HAS JUMPED OVER
A BOY AND IS WALKING ACROSS A BEAM. THE OTHER
OLDER BOYS FOLLOW. ONE OF THE OLDER BOYS IS TALK-
ING TO THE YOUNGER BOYS.

"I guess you can play," Mac said.
"I will tell you the rules.
We call the game 'Follow the Leader.'
We choose a leader and we follow him.
He kicks a can.
We all kick the can.
We do what the leader does.
That's the rule.
Do you get it?"

"Yes," Chuck said, "we get it.
The leader runs and we run.
He hops and we hop.
We do what he does.
That is the rule.
We follow the leader.
That's easy."

"Good," said Mac, "you've got it.

But there's more.
The leader jumps over a boy.
You jump over a boy.
If you can't do it, you are out of the game.
O-U-T out.
That's the other rule."

"I get it," said Chuck.
"We choose a leader.
"We follow him.
If we can't follow him, we are out."

Mac said, "Hurry up!
Let's go!"

All the words in that section are primer words except for well (1^2), follow (2^1), leader (3^1), and rules (3^2). My advice is to print those words on the board and ask who knows what they are. If someone knows, fine. If no one knows, you pronounce them and ask who knows what they mean.

Your purpose is not to make pupils guess at unknown words. Your purpose is to help the class build some meanings for the term *rules*.

The situation will be familiar to most children. The game will be known to many of them. The written words are mostly easy primer words. The language pattern approximates my tape recording of children's talk on a playground.

Now, after this has been read and discussed, what meanings might a child have in mind for the term rules?

Rules tell you how to play a game.

Rules tell you how not to play a game.

Rules tell you the penalty for breaking the rule.

Rules tell you what you can do.

Rules tell you what you can't do.

Rules tell you the penalty for not following the rules.

The child probably had some meanings for *rules* before he read the story. We hope that the story and the discussion that followed added more meanings to his cluster of meanings.

Has the pupil learned everything there is to understand about rules?

Of course not. The next excerpt of pupil text is intended to add more to a pupil's concept of rules.

(Chuck is at home with his brother, Mark, and his father.)

Mark said, "Dad, I need some money to. . . ."

"Dad," said Chuck, "I know a new game.

I know the rules for 'Follow the. . . .'"

"Don't butt in! I want to talk," Mark said.

"I want to talk about rules," said Chuck.

"Don't butt in, Chuck," said Mark.

"Don't you butt in!" said Chuck.

"Stop it," said Dad. "Stop talking!"

"Now we can talk," Dad said.

"Chuck, did you butt in on Mark?"

Chuck said, "I guess so."

"Did Mark let you talk?" said Dad.

"No," said Chuck, "he didn't.

Why did he butt in?

I wanted to tell you about rules."

"Is a rule a good thing?" said Dad.

"Yes," said Chuck, "a rule is a good thing.

Rules tell you how to play a game."

Dad said, "So you like rules?"

"Oh, oh," said Chuck.

"I know what you are going to talk about."

Of course Chuck knows. And so do your pupils. They now add another bit of meaning to their concept of rules:

Rules help solve problems that could cause trouble.

The next section deals with Chuck and Dad. Dad is working with some tools, and Chuck naturally wants to imitate him. Dad says Chuck can use the hammer, but he isn't to use the saw. When Dad's back is turned, Chuck grabs the saw and promptly cuts his fingers. Another bit of meaning is added:

Rules help keep us safe.

The next story situation deals with a first-grade class. The teacher is working with a small group when she spots a student out of his seat. She tells him to go back and sit down. He does, and then asks to say something.

The teacher asks what he has on his mind. He says he doesn't think the rule about staying in the seat is a good one.

The teacher asks why not. The boy says his work is done, he hasn't anything to do at his seat, and he wants to get a book to read. The other pupils back him up (naturally). The teacher asks what can be done about it. Someone suggests a new rule. It is discussed, voted on, and adopted. There is a bit more to the story, but out of it come three more meanings.

> Rules don't always work for the good.
>
> Rules that don't work can be changed.
>
> People who make rules, and agree to them, should try to follow them.

The last section is a set of pictures showing youngsters in situations where something is going wrong. There is no text, just three questions:

> What do you do if you don't know a rule?
>
> What do you do if there is no rule?
>
> What does it mean to try to do the right thing?

This last section provides no answers, and, in my judgment, neither should you. This is a place where discussion—among pupils, if possible, rather than between you and a pupil—brings out pupil understandings and values. Even if the class comes up with answers you agree with completely, the best thing you can do is say, "That was an interesting discussion."

If the class comes up with answers you don't agree with, this is not the time to try to change their attitudes. Instead, start planning how you will go about trying to begin changing their attitudes. Why wait? Because attitudes seldom change easily. You are going to have to introduce, over a long period of time, a series of situations for the class to consider and discuss. You may never change the attitudes of some children, but you will never help any of them change unless you let them do the changing as a result of their own reasoning.

What have these sections helped you do? They have been a springboard that helped your students dive into a pool of discussion and thought on an important topic. Pupils should be able to learn from these stories and from discussing them. The stories should lead to discussion of who makes rules (at home, in school, in the play group), of who has been helped by rules, of who has been hampered by rules, and of rules that needed changing and whether they were changed or not. If the stories remain just stories, if they don't get related to life, including life in *your* classroom and school, then the stories really were not worth writing or reading.

Almost all teachers teach something about rules. Many of them, unfortunately, do no more than say, "This is the rule, and you have to follow it. If you don't, I'll make you wish you had."

Some teachers have children memorize a definition of a rule, "A rule is a principle governing conduct." That definition comes straight out of any of half a dozen dictionaries. And it is neither very helpful nor very useful. A student must understand *principle, governing,* and *conduct* before the definition could possibly be helpful. And the only way it could be useful would be for showing off a pupil with a good memory in front of a visitor to the classroom.

Other teachers believe, and I'm with them, that a child should develop a cluster of meanings for the term *rule.* He should have a chance to build a concept of *rule* that will help him examine the behavior of people in a variety of situations. And he should have a concept of *rule* that will be useful to him when he asks himself, "What do I do now?"

The textbook, then, is a useful tool if it helps you help children think and value, if it deals with concepts important to their lives, and if it leads to positive changes in their behavior.

SUMMARY

No textbook will be perfectly suited to your purposes, but some textbooks can serve you well. There is no good reason to assume your pupils must read every part of a textbook. The same criteria you apply to selecting a text—accuracy, learnability, and usefulness—can be applied to chapters or stories in a text.

In planning a textbook lesson, you need to identify the key ideas, implied or explicitly stated, in a story. You then see how the text can contribute to the development of meanings for these ideas, and you plan the concrete activities you can add in building concepts and in helping pupils apply these ideas in their lives. The extent to which pupils think and value as the result of reading in social studies is partly a function of the questions you ask about the story.

Reading is not the basic activity in a good social-studies program, nor is the textbook the only source of learning. The text and reading are, however, valuable tools in some social-studies learning.

NOTE

1. Hanna, Paul R., et al., *Family Studies*. Glenview, Ill.: Scott, Foresman, 1970, p. 96ff.

SUGGESTED READINGS

Banks, James A. and William W. Joyce (eds.), *Teaching Social Studies to Culturally Different Children*. Reading, Mass.: Addison-Wesley, 1971. (Contains some excellent suggestions on reading in social studies, particularly for inner-city pupils.)

Chapin, June R. and Richard E. Gross, *Teaching Social Studies Skills*. Boston: Little, Brown, 1973. (A new book with a provocative chapter on reading and the development of reading skills in social studies.)

Cuban, Larry, *To Make a Difference: Teaching in the Inner City*. New York: Free Press, 1970. (A beautifully written book with great sections on stories dictated by pupils and on rewritten materials. If you will teach in an inner city, this book is a must!)

Howes, Virgil M. (ed.), *Individualizing Instruction in Reading and Social Studies*. New York: Macmillan, 1970. (A helpful selection of readings and programs for individualizing instruction; the editor stresses application to classroom practices as a criterion for selection of the articles.)

Huus, Helen, "Reading," in Helen McCracken Carpenter (ed.), *Skill Development in Social Studies*. Washington, D.C.: NCSS 33rd Yearbook, 1963, pp. 94–114. (A basic treatment of reading set in a social-studies context.)

Preston, Ralph, *Teaching Social Studies in the Elementary School*. New York: Holt, Rinehart & Winston, 1968. (This methods book contains an excellent chapter on reading; Preston is a reading specialist, as well as an expert in social studies.)

EXERCISES

1. For the grade you plan to teach, pick a story you like and draw up a lesson plan for its use. Get one or two of your classmates to criticize your plan.

2. Turn back to Chapter 4 and locate one of the references to valuing (I'd recommend Raths or Harmin). Pick a story or chapter from a pupil text, and see how it might be used as a springboard for *valuing*.

3. Identify a key term in any pupil text. Assume your pupils will not be familiar with it. What concrete experiences can you dream up and what questions would you ask to help pupils develop an initial operating concept for the term?

4. Copy a tough paragraph or two from some pupil text. Ask your classmates to role play with you. Some are poor readers; some can't read at all; only a few can actually read your sample paragraph. What do you do? (Remember the criterion of usefulness and the principle of transfer as you struggle with this.)

Units for Whom?

In the forties, when I began teaching, *units* was the hottest word in teaching. If you taught units, you were in. If you didn't teach units, you were in a class with teachers who taped kids' mouths and tied them in their seats.

For a year I was in doubt about what a unit really was, so I kept my mouth shut. The second year all teachers went to Lansing, Michigan, for Institute Day. Everyone got up at dawn, drove 90 miles, and attended the morning meetings. You attended in the morning because the principal had a check-off list. There was an unwritten agreement, however, that you weren't checked off in the afternoons. So, after lunch, the female teachers went shopping and the males gathered in a local hotel to drink beer and trade stories. The only people who attended the afternoon meetings were lower-echelon administrators, officials, speakers, and the speakers' friends. The following day my principal gave me a paper entitled *Units,* which he had picked up at an afternoon meeting. It was his way of letting me know he had been working while I had been wasting time. It was a fair trade. He got to feel morally superior, and I was able to discover that I taught units.

I still have that list of characteristics of a unit. There were 11 of them, which was one more characteristic than I had once memorized to become a tenderfoot scout. A unit:

1. Possesses cohesion
2. Is based on needs of children

3. Cuts across subject lines

4. Is based on modern psychology

5. Requires a large block of time

6. Is life-centered

7. Utilizes normal drives

8. Recognizes differences in maturation

9. Emphasizes problem solving

10. Provides for social development

11. Is planned cooperatively.

After puzzling my way through the list (I had never heard of maturation), I decided my teaching met 10 of the 11 characteristics. I knew that the mind couldn't be exercised like a muscle (the subject of a morning meeting), but that was the limit of my knowledge of modern psychology. One thing did bother me. I couldn't find anything specific on the list about ideas that just might be learned while my class was unit-ing.

Since my tenderfoot days, I've taught a great many units and I've read my share of books on the teaching of units. After all the jargon is stripped away and all the multisituation characteristics are factored out, just three characteristics remain: A unit demands a wide variety of learning activities; a unit takes from a couple of days to ten weeks of social-studies time; and a unit has a central, dominating topic.

In my judgment, there are two types of units. One is for teachers, and one is for pupils. The unit for the teacher insures that she knows her topic well enough to teach it. Some teachers refer to this as a *resource unit,* and they include lists of resource materials from which children may learn. This type of unit, to my knowledge, is always a written document. The two keys to the unit for teachers are ensuring that you understand the subject matter of your topic and ensuring that materials your pupils can learn from are readily available.

There is little point in teaching a unit if you don't know your subject matter. By this, I do *not* mean that you can't or won't learn about the topic as the unit is taught. But if you have to learn as you go, then the unit is going to lack direction, focus, and cohesion. For example, if your topic is *steel,* but you knew nothing about the roles of resources, capital, labor, and management, then you are bound to cheat your class.

Don't misunderstand. You don't have to know everything about steel.

And if a child asks you a question and you don't know the answer, don't crucify yourself. Say, "I don't know, but I'll find out." Or, "I don't know. How do you think we can find out?" Honesty keeps your conscience clean and keeps you square with your class. Why should you be expected to know *everything?* It should be more important that you know how to find the answer.

INDIVIDUALIZATION AND UNITS

To paraphrase Mark Twain's comment on the weather: Everyone talks about individual differences, but nobody does anything about them. It may be too strong to say *nobody* does anything, for some teachers surely do see children as individuals and try to get through to each one.

Many recent critics make it clear that they see uniformity and conformity as hallmarks of schooling. Part of this criticism grows from the everpresent practices of grouping primary-grade youngsters by reading ability and of forcing all upper-grade youngsters to "take" social studies through the medium of a single textbook. These two practices possess a certain utility: They permit teachers to view children in a given group or class as more alike than different.

To give one sound example, consider the general fate of the nongraded school. This seemingly excellent idea took a host of theoretical and practical variables into consideration. One of the brightest, most engaging, well-meaning men in elementary education spearheaded the movement. Articles began to blossom forth, speeches were given, institutes were held. The future looked rosy. School boards heard the news. Superintendents got the word. Principals passed it on. Teachers clasped the notion to their bosoms. Ungraded or nongraded schools cropped up all over the educational landscape.

And after all this, the idea flopped. Oh, it worked well here and there. But in general, the ungraded school was a crashing failure. Why? Because many principals did no more than put the label on their schools, and many teachers merely added some cosmetic touches to their previous practices. Conversations like this one gave the show away:

Visitor: "Gee, it looks funny with the walls torn out."

Teacher: "Well, we're nongraded now. You have to keep up with the times."

Visitor: "That group over there. (Points to a reading group.) What grade are they in?"

Teacher: (Condescendingly) "Oh, we don't have grades. They are at the seventh level in reading."

Visitor: "I see they're all reading from the same book. What book is it?"

Teacher: (She peers at the group.) "That's a Blank Company 3^2 Reader."

Visitor: "Things surely do change."

Behind a brand new façade, the same old basic readers operated in the same old ways.

In the social studies, unit teaching has something of this same flavor. Yet, just as there are some excellent nongraded schools, where individualization is king of the mountain, so are there schools where units permit individual interests, initiative, and learning to flourish.

Reading and arithmetic are supposedly developmental by nature. You need to know short vowels and long vowels before you learn *r*-controlled vowels. You need to know addition before you can multiply, and so forth. Except for a few things in geography, the developmental idea in social studies is based more on psychology than on logic. By this I mean you don't have to study all of European history before you can learn some U.S. history in fifth grade. That sequence of always moving from older to more recent history is logical, but it isn't psychologically sound to say you *must* teach history through adult logic. This lack of developmental logic means that social studies is a more-wide-open area of learning than, say, early arithmetic.

If social studies is an open area for study, this means that depth learning can vary from individual to individual on any particular topic. For example, say you and your second graders are studying transportation by air. Doubtlessly you and your pupils will agree on a few ideas that all should command, but the topic is so broad and so deep that beyond these essential learnings, an individual may proceed at his own pace, to his own drummer. Some may be interested in the operation of a jet engine, some in the history of planes, some in the varied uses of aviation, some in designing the air (or airless) ships of the future. There are occupations aplenty connected to flying. There are rules of the road to learn. There are stories to be read, films to be shown, pictures to be drawn, models to be glued, people to be interviewed. Some pupils will take this topic, some will take that one; some will learn a great deal, some will venture barely beyond the essentials. But each can plow his own field in the present and plant his own seeds for the future.

WRITING A RESOURCE UNIT

What follows is an example of a teacher, or resource, unit on the production of vegetables in the United States. I chose *vegetables* because it is a grubby, nonromantic topic that neither you nor I probably understand well.

I have written the unit as if I were going to use it. Vegetable production is a subtopic of agriculture, so I begin with some general information and ideas. The italics indicates what I feel are key ideas.

I could have written more—sections on canning, freezing, drying, juicing, and dehydrating are needed. But I should think the point about subject matter has been made.

What about fruit and grain and other agricultural products? There are two possibilities. I could follow the unit on vegetables with sequential units on all other farm and ranch products. Or I could say to the class, "Ok, you have these key ideas about production, harvesting, regional specialization, and so on. How would you like to divide into interest groups and use these ideas to analyze grain production, and the other key ideas?"

I prefer the second approach, mainly because my primary goal would be the development of concepts of *production* rather than the accumulation of information about vegetables. I want the pupils to pick up the information, but I know that, over time, they will forget much of it. However, I don't want them to forget about resources, specialization, and other key concepts, because I hope they will be used again and again.

USING THE RESOURCE UNIT

After my resource unit on vegetables is written, I have to decide what the key ideas in its content are. I go back to my italicized words and sentences. Aha, here's *comparative advantage*. I want them to develop a sound concept for that term. And here's a generalization: *When agriculture is mechanized, the proportion of the labor force in agriculture decreases*. I read my unit again and again until I have picked out all the concepts and generalizations I can find.

Resource Unit: Vegetables

General Content

In 1966, we harvested 200-million tons of grains, 200-million tons of hay and silage, 21-million tons of vegetables, 20-million tons of fruit, 62.5-million tons of milk, 3.7-million tons of cotton, 105,500-tons of wool, and large quantities of other agricultural products.

If all these products had been produced by hand labor, our entire population couldn't have done the job. Our use of mechanization in agriculture is largely responsible for the fact that only 5 percent of our labor force works in agriculture.

The basic elements of agriculture production are resources, capital, labor, and technology. Technology means the ability to plan and organize agricultural operations, and the level of technology (fertilizers, irrigation, special seeds, and so on) available to farmers for use in their work. The machines used represent the capital (money and equipment) used for the production of consumer goods; the work that machines, animals, and humans do represents labor; and resources include land, soil, rainfall, underground water, climate, and so on.

Man's first agricultural activities were the gathering of wild fruits and nuts, and the digging of roots. When man began to use grain, he had to harvest it by hand, stalk by stalk. Over the centuries, man developed a crude knife for lopping the head of grain from the stalk; then came the sickle, followed by the scythe.

In 1790, 90 percent of our population was occupied by agriculture. By 1890, only 43 percent of our people were farmers. The inventions most responsible for this shift were John Deere's steel plows, Cyrus McCormick's reaper, and John Applyby's grain binder. The trend continued with the development of the gasoline engine and its application to mass-production harvesting machines (the self-propelled wheat combine, the hay baler, the cotton and corn pickers). Because of these, our farm population dropped to 30 percent by 1915, and to 18 percent by 1940. Since 1945, the development of other harvesting devices (especially for perishable crops) has reduced our farm labor population to 5 percent.

The harvesting of crops (picking, winnowing, binding, and so on) usually makes up half the total cost of production. Thus, the concentration of mechanization is on the processes of harvesting. Today, efficiency demands that the harvesting machine be more than an accessory for human labor. Except for an operator, the machine should be able to do the whole task.

The harvester must be adapted to the crop and to the type of soil landform and climate where the crop is grown. For example, a grain combine that works perfectly on wheat grown on a Montana prairie won't work on rice grown in the wetlands of Louisiana.

Harvesting machines cost a great deal of money, but the comparative costs of land and machine harvesting favor the machine. Of course, the size of the farm has to be taken into account. For example, hand harvesting of snap beans grown on farms of about 200 acres costs $103 per acre, while machine harvesting costs $25 per acre. (This includes spreading the cost of the machine over a 5-year period.) On a small farm — say about 25 acres — the hand and the machine costs both run about $95 per acre. On a 500-acre farm, machine costs drop to $11 per acre. This business of harvesting costs explains why the average farm today is much larger than farms in any other period of our history.

Agricultural occupations tend to follow a certain sequence of activities. Depending on seasonal and climatic conditions in a given area, a field is plowed, harrowed, seeded, cultivated, and then harvested. Fertilization, spraying, and irrigation (if used) occur in varied orders, but always before harvesting. After harvesting, the crop is transported, sold, transported again, processed, transported yet again, and so on. Selling and transportation occur again and again from the time seeds are bought until we buy a loaf of bread and carry it home to eat.

There are a number of specialized jobs that workers perform in the process of getting food or fibers from the field to our homes. Division of labor is present and some jobs are highly specialized; thus, interdependence is necessary within agriculture as well as within society.

In agriculture, there is both occupational and regional specialization (and thus interdependence). For example, because of differences in climate, landform, soil, rainfall, and the number of frost-free growing days, there is regional specialization in fruit production. Washington and Oregon produce apples and pears; Florida, southern Texas and southern and central California produce citrus fruits; western Michigan produces cherries; Hawaii produces pineapples, and the northern-Atlantic-coast states produce cranberries. This regional specialization (and national interdependence) is built on our systems of rapid transportation and communication, upon the use of refrigerated carriers and containers for transporting perishable goods. In economics, the ability to specialize in regional production is called comparative advantage.

Vegetables

Vegetables, chock full of vitamins and minerals, are essential to a balanced diet. Some vegetables are perishable (tomatoes) and some are nonperishable (navy beans). That difference is a key to different problems in harvesting and shipping crops. Vegetables are sold fresh or processed (dried, frozen, canned).

California, Florida, Texas, and Arizona account for about 60 percent of our vegetable production. In these states, large-volume production is due to the large size of farms, level land, suitable rainfall or irrigation, climate that permits growing more than one crop per year, and the adaptability of machines to soil types and the lack of slope in landforms.

If most vegetables are grown in four states, then good communications (how are orders placed?) and transportation are required to get them to markets.

The steps in growing vegetables are:

1. Plowing and harrowing the soil — This involves turning over the soil and letting air into it, breaking up lumps, and smoothing out the field.

2. Planting the seeds — A drill set to a certain depth pokes a hole in the soil, drops in a seed, drops in a bit of fertilizer, and covers up the hole. (Most seeds today are bought from scientific seed breeders and growers, rather than saved by the farmer from previous crops.)

3. Cultivating — this amounts to loosening the soil around growing plants to let in air and water, and it kills off weeds that compete with plants for sun, air, and water.

4. Protecting plants from parasites and bad weather — Insects are kept away and diseases are prevented by treating seeds with chemicals before planting, picking seeds that resist parasites, and spraying growing plants with chemicals. (Irrigation can be a protection against drought, too much water can be handled by tilling and drainage ditches.)

5. Harvesting the crop when it is ready to be sold — The harvesting of perishable (watery) vegetables is difficult, because these crops must be handled gently. Lettuce and asparagus have always required hand labor, although equipment companies are now developing mechanical pickers for these crops.

The story of machine harvesting or tomatoes is instructive. In California, 125,000 acres are planted in tomatoes. Not long ago the farmers had to hire 40,000 workers to pick the tomato crop by hand. Then technology produced, after ten years of research, two things that were needed.

1. Biologists bred a tomato plant that would bear tomatoes of a uniform size. They ripened at the same time; the tomatoes were easy to pick off the vine; the skins were tough enough for mechanical handling; they would store well; and they looked and tasted good.

2. Engineers developed a harvester that cut the plant at ground level, lifted it into a combine, shook the tomatoes off the vine, discarded the vines, removed dirt from the tomatoes, and dropped them into containers. In 1966, farmers were using 800 of these machines to pick 80 percent of the crop; by now almost all tomatoes grown on large farms are picked by machines. (Note: Biologists are now working on a square tomato, whose slices will fit in a sandwich better.)

Vegetables are parts of plants. Carrots are roots, lettuce is leaves, beans are seeds, broccoli is fruit. Variations in the steps in growing vegetables depend on what plant a particular vegetable happens to be; this is especially true in harvesting: Potatoes must be dug, lettuce must be cut, beans must be picked, and so on.

After harvesting, vegetables are boxed or bagged. Some vegetables are sold by farmers at roadside stands. Some are taken by the farmer to stores or markets (retail or wholesale). Some are sold to processing plants. Some are shipped long distances to other parts of the country where there is a demand for them. Generally, vegetables are washed, graded, and then packed for sale or transportation. Refrigerated trucks and railroad cars are used to transport perishable vegetables long distances. In winter months some fresh vegetables are flown to northern cities by plane.

Do I understand those key ideas? Do I have a concept of *comparative advantage?* Can I give examples that support the generalization about mechanization and the labor force? If I do, I can move on. If I don't, back to the books I go. It's a tough job, but, at this point, a teacher bears the burden of scholarship.

I also suggest strongly that you record your sources. For example, here are the three major ones I used on vegetables:

Clarence F. Kelly, "Mechanical Harvesting," *Scientific American,* August, 1967, pp. 50–59.

Information Please Almanac, 1968.

Teachers edition, *Basic Social Studies—4,* Evanston: Harper & Row, 1964.

Your next step is to search for and record the resource materials that can be used by children. I expect you should always have at least nine categories of materials: (1) library books, (2) textbooks, (3) maps, (4) reference books, (5) giveaways, (6) films, (7) filmstrips, (8) study prints, and (9) pictures. (Reference books include encyclopedias, atlases, almanacs, and so on. Giveaways are free or inexpensive items that businesses, organizations, government agencies, and other groups will send you.)

These notes need not be extensive or fancy, but once done they save you time and trouble year after year. You can add to items, you can cross them out. For example:

LIBRARY BOOKS (General Content)

Johnson, Lois S., *What We Eat.* Scott, Foresman. (Origins and travels of foods round the world.)

~~Heady, Eleanor B., *Coat of the Earth.* Norton. (Story of grass.)~~ Does not apply —use with grains.

Helfman, Elizabeth, *This Hungry World.* Scott, Foresman. (Present and future utilization of food sources.)

Lewis, Alfred, *The New World of Food.* Dodd, Mead. (The sea as a future source of food.)

Etc.

As you can see, I used *Coat of the Earth* here and then decided it went best elsewhere. The last two books show I want the pupils to think about future sources of foods. I don't bother with complete citations in these lists—that sort of pickiness slows down my writing too much.

With this resource unit in hand, I am ready to begin thinking about the second type of unit—the one for pupils.

UNITS FOR PUPILS

The orthodox unit for pupils, the *teaching unit,* has four major parts: establishing purposes and objectives, initiating the unit, conducting the unit, and culminating the unit. In other words, the written unit answers the questions: What shall be learned? How shall we start? How shall we keep the unit moving? How shall we cut off the unit?

The business of reading statements of purpose and lists of objectives has kept many teachers from having anything to do with units. The preamble to the Constitution contains 53 words, but it seems as if no one who has written a unit has ever been that brief (nor thought that clearly). Statements of purpose run for two- or three-thousand words. A typical beginning would go something like this:

> This unit is a purposeful experience in learning highlighting the socially significant concept of "Mankind is a Brother to Nature." Objective intellectualization of contemporary phenomena compels the good citizen to involve himself in active inquiry into problem-solving procedures commensurate with his inherited ability to produce solutions compatible with the exhalted standards of Mom, Cherry Pie, and Naders Raiders.

From this ugly beginning the statement continues its crash dive into a sea of murky confusion. No one, certainly not the author of the statement, knows what is to be done or why it should be done.

I prefer something like the following:

---

1. Unit on Transportation

    Grade one: one week

    Purpose: to introduce children to the use of containers, carriers, and power in common forms of transportation found in their neighborhoods.

---

2. <u>Unit on Communication and Television</u>

   Grade three: two weeks

   The purpose is to develop concepts for <u>sender</u>, <u>message</u>, <u>channel</u>, and <u>receiver</u> through the study of our local television station.

3. <u>Unit on Development of American Cities</u>

   Grade five: seven days

   A study of the influence of steamboats and railroads on the location and development of what are now the 25 largest cities in the United States so predictions may be made about the relationships of future inventions and cities.

4. <u>Ecology</u>

   Grade seven: 16 class periods

   This unit serves to help pupils identify and propose solutions to environmental problems resulting from life in our urban, industrial, technological society.

These statements won't please everyone, but they are obviously clearer than the muck about being a "Brother to Nature." Number 3 isn't a complete sentence. Number 4 isn't clear about which of many environmental problems will be studied. But by and large, you can form an idea of what each unit is about.

This old plan which I found in my files gives you an idea of what can be added as a plan after the statement of purpose. It lists twelve items of subject matter that I used as guides for building understandings with pupils. It also lists five things I wanted to remember to do with this unit on transportation.

Unit on Transportation
Grade one: one week

Purpose: To introduce children to the use of <u>containers</u>, <u>carriers</u>, and <u>power</u> in common forms of transportation found in their neighborhoods.

Ideas

1. <u>Containers</u> are used for holding or storing.

2. Containers can be made to hold fluids, solids, or gases.

3. Containers can be made of different kinds of materials.

4. Containers can be made in many sizes and shapes.

5. Some containers can be carried by a person; some can be moved by a person; some can't be moved with muscle power. If a person carries or moves a container, then he is a carrier.

6. <u>Carriers</u> are things or people powered by nature, animal power, or fuel or electricity, and used to move things or people from place to place (sailboat, horse and cart, truck, elevator).

7. Sometimes part of a carrier is a container.

8. Sometimes carriers are connected to containers.

9. Carriers can be pushed or pulled, ridden on or ridden in. (Push: wheelbarrow, tugboat, bulldozer and dirt; pull: wagon, trailer, sled.)

10. Power means the strength or energy or force to do work.

11. Power can come from human muscles, animal muscles, the wind, the water, or from fuels that make motors or engines run.

12. Power can be applied to the carrier (wind on a sail or electric current to a motor powering an elevator) or power plant can be part of the carrier (automobile, airplane, steamship).

Things to Do

1. Grab attention of pupils.

2. Get pupils to give familiar examples.

3. Go exploring for other examples.

4. Use knowledge of containers, carriers, and power to solve problems pupils face.

5. Use three key concepts to examine influence of transportation on life outside classroom.

At this point, I imagine that some prospective teachers of first grade are saying, "I never heard of such ideas! Containers! Why, there aren't any first-grade books that use the word *container!* Why, *that* man is making up a unit that can't be taught. He ought to get out of his ivory tower and. . . ."

That unit was not, however, conceived in an ivory tower. It was birthed in the grubbiest inner city classroom you ever saw. And no one started out talking or reading about containers. It began with, "What have you got in your pocket? Why don't you carry those things in your ears? What's a pocket for?" Remember, the proper labels come after the meanings are developed!

"What else in this room works like a pocket?" (Note that with first graders, I am grouping by *usage* as a starting point.) The class finds the wastebasket, the fish tank, a balloon I hang up, the paint cans, a purse, the milk cartons, the box that holds the milk cartons. Whoops! We're off and running on ideas 1, 2, 3, and 4. After ten minutes or so of finding, examining, and discussing the many containers in the classroom, I ask, "Do you know the one word for the group of things all these things belong in?" I get a few guesses and a chorus of "No, what is it?" I tell them and we practice the word a few times.

The next day we talk about containers again. We go over our examples again. I throw in a few negative examples: "Is this blank paper a container? Can you make it into a container? Is this block of wood a container? Is the fish food a container? What about the fish-food box? What does it contain?"

After we locate all the containers we can out of our room, we go exploring. We check the kitchen, the gym, the boiler room (under supervision), and the bathrooms (the basins and toilets are containers). For reasons unknown to me, children love to discover that they are containers and that pipelines are a transportation system.

Out into the neighborhood we go. What do we see? Where are the containers? There and there and there! The carriers? Look, teacher, there they are! And power? Everywhere. Who says a word has to be written in a book before a concept can be learned?

Movies? Sure, McGraw-Hill has an award winner called "What's a Pocket For?" Run it twice. Leave the sound off the second time and let the kids do the narration.

Pictures? Tell the kids to find them. Then sort the pictures into groups: "Things That Push" and "Things That Pull"; "Muscles," "Nature," and "Fuel." What are the kids doing? They are grouping, classifying, categorizing. So, old Piaget was right! Six-year olds really can learn to do those things; they can think, can't they?

WRITING YOUR UNIT

I always end (culminate is the fancy word) the unit by sliding into the next logical unit or into some unit focused on a particularly strong interest of the pupils.

Are the units you see printed in methods books the ones teachers really use? Sometimes, but not often. Those printed units are used by some teachers in a few school districts, where units are standard procedure in social studies. Otherwise, the printed units are used mostly as rough models by first-year teachers and students in methods classes. The professor assigns the writing of a unit. The students, who don't have classroom experience, use those models in writing their units. This use of printed units as models is probably helpful to a prospective teacher. The printed units are usually well written and well edited. They are usually weakest in their lengthy statements of purpose and lists of objectives. They are usually strongest in their lists of activities and materials.

A teaching unit should be organized to suit the teacher who will use it. It shouldn't be organized to suit me or your methods professor. You may have to organize it to suit him for the purposes of your course, but for teaching, it must fit *you* and *your* pupils!

The unit that follows cannot be called a conventional unit, but it was a successful one. Included are the comments of the teacher who wrote and taught the unit. What you see is what she would have in front of her the second year she teaches the unit to her fifth graders.

UNIT TOPIC: Eli Whitney

CONCEPT: Standardization

TIME: 2-3 Weeks

Purposes

1. To build a concept of standardization

2. To apply known concepts of resources, labor, capital, and technology to production of cotton and muskets

3. To discover the advantages and disadvantages of standardization in production

Investigating and Building Background

1. Introduced term — Pupils had little knowledge of term and no useful meanings for it. Dictionary not much help; "make standard in size, shape, weight, . . ." Pupils can repeat definition, but don't really know what standard means.

2. Used school resources

   a. Basic text, New Ways in the New World, pp. 232-3. Brief introduction to times of Eli Whitney.

---

b. Read <u>Eli Whitney and the Machine Age</u>, pp. 1-13. Background of man and period.

c. Show film, Eli Whitney (EBF). (Film glamorizes Whitney and ignores his difficulties.)

d. Read pp. 14-21 of <u>E. W. and the Machine Age</u>. This helped get at:
   (1) Need for invention of cotton gin
   (2) Changes gin would bring
   (3) Roles of resources, capital, labor, and technology in cotton production
   (4) Patent (treated as minor idea)

e. Discussion of (a-d) — Whitney and cotton gin led to a series of predictions of how Whitney would solve problem of production of muskets. Predictions generally sound except that concept of standardization is not yet formed — they guess Whitney will "invent" something, but they don't know what!

f. Read <u>E. W. and Machine Age</u>, pp. 22-29, to see if predictions were correct or not. Discussion afterwards focused on:
   (1) Reasons for stress on muskets
   (2) Location of factory (land, source of power, labor pool)
   (3) Technology — they are amazed and delighted to discover that processes, as well as tools, are "invented." They now grasp idea that a <u>pattern</u> is used in production and that the pattern is the <u>standard</u> against which a product is measured.

g. Individual oral reports on Whitney, each to stress one important fact. Class then applied these facts to their own environment. They discovered their paper, their pencils, and so on are standardized.

h. <u>Test</u> — Pupils bring to class magazine pictures of standardized products. They distinguish between standardized parts and standardized products. (A shoelace is both.)

3. <u>Experiment</u> (concept of interchangeable parts gets more emphasis)

    a. Hypotheses made before experimenting:

        (1) The group using standardized parts will make more parts and products.

        (2) The standardized products will be better.

        (3) The standardized products will have interchangeable parts.

        (4) Each person in the standardized group will have a less complicated job.

    b. Class was divided into two equal groups.

        (1) One group made hand-crafted car (construction paper). Each car had four parts — body, 2 wheels, headlight and windows.

        (2) Other group used patterns for the four parts. Each person made only one part and others worked as assemblers.

    c. The hypotheses were "proven" correct (except for some confusion over the meaning of <u>better</u> in second hypothesis.)

4. <u>Generalizing</u> — Several days were spent making generalizations. The following were formulated by the children:

    a. Advantages of standardization

        (1) When using standardization, more work can usually be done in less time than when products are handcrafted.

        (2) With standardization the quality of the product is often better.

        (3) When standardization is used, the product will usually be cheaper.

        (4) Often when standardization is used, more workers can be employed.

(5) When using standardization, workers are usually skilled in making only one part of the product.

(6) With standardization more products are usually available.

(7) By using standardized parts, repairs usually will be easier, quicker, and cheaper.

(8) If you use standardized parts, the parts are interchangeable and the repairs are usually as good as new.

b. Disadvantages of standardization

(1) With standardization there may be less variety.

(2) With standardization you may lose time tooling up.

(3) With standardization workers may become bored because of doing the same thing over and over.

(4) With standardization a large investment is usually needed to begin.

c. Advantages of handcrafted products

(1) Usually less investment is needed when making products one at a time.

(2) A worker often takes greater pride in making a whole product than in making only part of it.

(3) There are individual marks of variety in handcrafted products.

d. Disadvantages of handcrafted products

(1) Handcrafted products usually take longer to build than machine-made products.

(2) Handcrafted products are usually more expensive.

(3) Handcrafted products do not have interchangeable parts and so usually take longer and are more expensive to repair.

(4) Usually more skill is needed to make a handcrafted product than a machinemade one.

(5) The quality of a handcrafted product usually depends upon the skill of the individual craftsman.

Questions

1. Why was the cotton gin so important to the southern farmers?

2. Why do some people say the cotton gin increased slavery?

3. Why did Eli Whitney build his cotton gin factory in Connecticut, when it was needed in the South?

4. Why did Whitney select a millsite for his musket factory?

5. Why was there a skilled labor shortage in Whitney's time? How did he hope to overcome it?

6. Why did Whitney select muskets for his factory to build?

7. How was Whitney's manufacturing process different from former processes?

8. What are the advantages of using standardization in manufacturing?

9. What must you consider if you are to begin your own factory?

References

Roger Burlingame, MACHINES THAT BUILT AMERICA, Harcourt, Brace, Jovanovich, 1953. (Teacher and best readers.)

S. C. Hirsch, THIS IS AUTOMATION, Viking Press, 1964. (Teacher and best readers.)

Jean Lee Latham, THE STORY OF ELI WHITNEY, Harper & Row, 1953. (6 copies.)

Wilma Pitchford Hays, ELI WHITNEY AND THE MACHINE AGE, Franklin Watts, 1959. (15 copies.)

Lewis P. Todd and others, NEW WAYS IN THE NEW WORLD, Silver Burdett, 1954. (Basic text)

Eli Whitney, EBF. (Film in curriculum library)
Assorted encyclopedias.

Main difficulties encountered

1. Finding suitable materials

2. Helping children hypothesize and generalize

USING SOMEONE ELSE'S UNIT

That unit didn't look typical, did it? I expect you could adapt it to your own use. If you were relatively ignorant about Whitney and standardization, you could correct that by reading Burlingame, Hirsch, and Hayes, and then drafting a brief resource unit.

Would you have to teach this the way it was written? Certainly not. Almost anything in here can be shifted around to suit what your pupils know or don't know. Could you work in another concept, say, assembly line? Why not? These fifth graders had been exposed to that idea earlier, so it was applied but not stressed by their teacher.

The teacher who loves music would work in the songs of the times and the rhythms of the factory. The teacher good at art would have had murals produced. Construction types would have built fabulous little machines with standardized parts. If the class doesn't read to grade level, then use more films. If you can't get films, make up more games. Every unit, in other words, can be shaped to the intellectual form of the teacher and to the interest contours of the class.

What's my intent? What goals do I seek? What materials are at hand? What activities can I handle? How do I know if they have learned? The unit is one way of handling time and space, ideas and people in the learning process.

SUMMARY

Teaching with units should guarantee two conditions: a solid knowledge of the subject matter of one topic, and some formal plan for teaching that subject matter. There are two types of written units: the *resource unit*, which provides for teacher background, and the *teaching unit,* which spells out a plan for teaching.

Most units have a central theme or topic, take from one to ten weeks of work, and involve an amazingly varied range of pupil activities. There are many models of units published in methods books and by enterprising school districts. My experience with teachers in the field, however, leads me to believe that once they are out of college, teachers adopt their written units to suit their individual purposes and temperaments.

Unit teaching suits itself nicely to developmental psychology, particularly the notion that any class exhibits a range of abilities and interests. Most units are loose enough to let you provide for these differences without calling undue attention to them. Units are more difficult to plan and teach than are day-to-day lesson plans. They are also more rewarding to you and your pupils.

SUGGESTED READINGS

Hanna, Lavona, Neva Hagaman, and Gladys Potter, *Unit Teaching in the Elementary School.* New York: Holt, Rinehart & Winston, 1963. (This is the classic on units, dramatic play, and construction in the elementary classroom. It is so good I can't keep a copy on an open office shelf for a year without it disappearing.)

Merritt, Edith, *Working With Children in Social Studies.* Belmont, Calif.: Wadsworth, 1961. (Another good book with plenty of information on units and dramatic play.)

EXERCISES

1. Pull Hanna, Hagaman, and Potter plus any two other social-studies methods books from the shelves. Compare the chapters on units. These give you a good notion of what formal units are. Take any one of them and try to reduce it to a three-page adaptation for your own use.

2. Go to your curriculum lab, and pick up three or four units stored there. Compare them to the units you examined in exercise one. Compare both to the units in this chapter. Ask a classroom teacher you like to show you a unit or two that she uses. What do you want for yourself in the future?

3. Take a topic of interest to you, but one you don't know well. Do your basic research, and draw up a short resource unit. (This will take you four or five hours.)

4. Take a topic you know well, and sketch out a resource unit on a single page. On a second page, list your initiating activities and some of the concrete activities you will use in the first two or three days.

Art, Music, and Literature

Children possess the lovely quality of seeing things whole. Their world isn't broken up into history and geography and the other social sciences. They develop an interest in something and never give a moment's thought to how differently an artist and a scientist might view the object or event. Children, in the primary grades at least, see nothing peculiar about blending art, music, and literature into the social studies.

Take the mundane example of machines. A machine is an arrangement of fixed and moving parts, each with some special thing to do. The function of the parts and of the machine as a whole is to apply power. The purpose of the machine is to do work that nature or muscle power cannot do as easily or effectively. Someone has a problem; someone invents a machine; someone works out a set of techniques for using the machine. The machine and the techniques affect our social, economic, and political lives; and we usually find out eventually that the use of the machine causes us some new and unforeseen problems. Thus, the scientist and the engineer develop the machine; the historian records the event; the geographer notes its effect on our use of space; the politician taxes it; someone makes a profit on it; the author writes a novel about it; the artist paints it into his scenes; and the songwriter sets it to music. If you think I'm exaggerating, consider the Model T, think of the sewing machine, remember the *Maine!*

The scholar, of course, can't study the whole world in depth, so he breaks it up into subjects. And like all the king's men, the scholars can't quite put the Humpty-Dumpty world back together again. Each scholar is proud of his subject and his efforts in its behalf; he fails to recognize that prejudice, discrimination, and stereotypes can be applied to more than people. Thus, our college curriculum is made up of courses; courses are grouped within subjects; and subjects are the province of sovereign departments. The high school, naturally, apes the college; and the elementary teacher, in a vain bid for respectability, divides up her day into subjects —struggling mightily so that nothing from one subject rubs off on another.

Well, not all elementary teachers are that hidebound. Some of them do seek out the natural relationships among subjects. This chapter is for those who want to take advantage of these connections.

ART AND THE SOCIAL STUDIES

Art means the efforts and products of pupils in art activities and the thoughtful examination of the products of those the world calls artists. The function of an art experience is the nurturing of personal creativity. The child who expresses his own view of an object or event in art is being creative; so is one who can synthesize a set of objects or events into a creation where the whole is more than the sum of the parts. I'm not talking here of budding Michelangelos or Rembrandts or even Winslow Homers. I'm talking about the child who knows enough about an Indian culture to tell a story on a simulated animal hide. I'm talking about the pupil who can make a clay contour map of Wisconsin to show why certain streams flow into the Mississippi, while others flow into the Great Lakes. I'm even talking about the kid who makes a diorama of 33 little fish who twist and turn together in response to the wind. In each case, the pupil can demonstrate the functional and aesthetic relationships between the social studies and art. In each case, the product reflects the creative insights of the individual.

For starters, let's take a simple and natural situation: Late Friday afternoon your fourth-grade students observe earth-moving machines being moved into the school courtyard. Questions concerning the machinery are asked, and a discussion gets rolling just as the bell rings for dismissal from school. As you sit in your empty classroom, your thoughts trace again the last 15 minutes of class. Your pupils were interested in the machinery; they asked questions; they wanted to learn. How can you exploit their curiosity?

Your class has studied simple machines (the lever, wedge, pulley, and so on) in science. You decide you want them to discover that modern machines combine simple machines and other parts into a system or arrangement for doing work.

With this as a general goal, your next question is how you can turn these outside observations into a classroom activity. What you want is an activity which all pupils can participate in and which will enhance their understanding of machines. You know the bulldozer outside is a combination of simple machines; you know that by carefully observing the bulldozer your pupils will spot refinements of these simple machines. Why not use a mural composed of three parts? The first part will show simple machines. The second will show parts of the bulldozer as they are actually seen. The third will show those real parts replaced by the simple machines from which those modern parts were evolved.

All you need in the way of materials are large 3-×-5-foot sheets of brown paper, black paint, a hand spray, three titles, construction paper, and scissors. The procedure is simple. Pupils draw pictures of simple machines on construction paper. The outlines are cut out, and the sheets are now templates. The templates are pinned to the brown paper. The holes in the templates are sprayed with black paint. The templates are removed. And the first mural is done, except for title and names of the machines. (Or, if you prefer, use the cutouts as templates and spray the whole paper —that gives you a black background and brown machines.) The next two murals are more complicated. The bulldozer must be examined carefully for the second mural, and reasoning must take place before the third one can begin.

This example began with the idea for an art activity enhancing the study of machines. Very often, the art experience comes after study is well under way. In terms of time it doesn't really matter where the art fits in; it does matter that art should somehow clarify an idea or call for some kind of reasoning. Here are five examples of good art activities for use in social studies.

Elevation Maps With Clay

The concept of *relief* is difficult for elementary-school children to understand without a concrete experience. One way to have the children become involved and understand this rather abstract concept is to have them actually manipulate materials which show the height and shape of land forms.

Materials

Plasticine clay, oak-tag paper, marking pen, water colors.

Procedure

1. Working in groups of three, have the pupils make a clay model representative of an island.

2. Be sure the bottom of the surface of the clay is flat.

3. Slice the clay island into layers. Each layer *must* be the same thickness. (See Figure 16.)

4. Take each layer, starting with the bottom one, and trace its outline on a piece of paper. (See Figure 17.)

5. Trace outline form of the clay on the oak-tag. The contour lines close together indicate steep slopes. Lines spaced far apart show gentle slope.

6. Research the altitude of the island and approximate the altitudes ac-

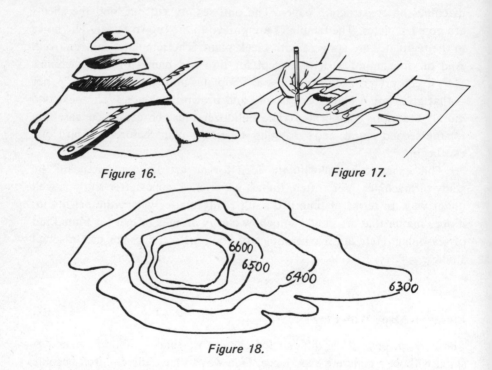

Figure 16.   Figure 17.

Figure 18.

cording to the contour lines on the drawing. Either write the height of each layer on the map, or have the students make a legend indicating the heights according to color.

Story Telling Using "Animal Hides"

This art experience is particularly relevant when teaching social studies to Indian children. It develops in them an appreciation and respect for their heritage. It is also advantageous to other children. Through this "animal hides" experience, pupils can develop skills in research, in socialization, and in the art technique of resist.

Materials

Tan wrapping paper (a 1½-×-2½-foot piece per student), earth-colored crayons, brown powdered tempera.

Procedure

1. Working in groups, students research Indian sign language. Each group should choose a particular Indian tribe and research their written symbols. In this research, students learn how and why Indians used animal hides as one of the materials for writing on. Others were sand, stone, cave walls and so on.

2. Tear from the tan paper a form that resembles an animal hide. Write an Indian symbol message on the hide with heavy crayon. Use earth and berry colors familiar to the early Indians.

3. When the message is completed, crumble the paper until it is well wrinkled. Smooth out the "hide" and place it under a water faucet or submerge it in a bowl of water until it is wet all over. Spread out the wet "hide" on newspaper.

4. While the "hide" is still wet, sprinkle brown powdered tempera over it. Smooth the paint out until the "hide" is covered. With a rag, rub excess water and paint to the edges, making the edges darker than the center. This is the *resist* technique. The paint is absorbed by the paper except where the heavy crayon was applied.

5. The "hides" are then hung on a clothesline strung across the room. When dry, they are displayed around the room. Each committee reports on its "hide," on what tribe made hides like it, on how that tribe lived, and on what the message says. (See Figure 19.)

"Friends journey by horse, day and night, for plentiful game."

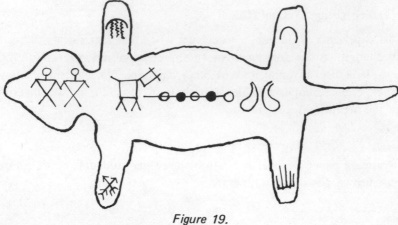

Figure 19.

Mobile Pictures

Combining the art technique of mobiles and a social-studies topic makes this experience valuable. Mobiles are a form of kinetic sculpture, which began long ago. The first application of kinetic sculpture was the Greek water clock. In modern times kinetic sculptures can be found in toys, advertising signs, fountains, and fireworks. Correlate this technique with concepts such as technology, natural resources, and so on. Students should research their subject and then plan the mobile picture.

Materials
Oak-tag, scissors, shoe box or a box similar in size, drinking straw, black thread, construction paper, water colors.

Procedure
1. Students should choose a social-studies topic. The topic is researched and a preliminary drawing is made. The teacher checks the plan for misconcepts. When the preliminary sketch has been approved, a background drawing is planned to correlate with the theme of the mobile picture.

2. Paint the background drawing (planned to fit the size of the box used) and glue it to the back of the box.

3. Next, fasten a short piece of drinking straw to the top of the background. (See *A* in Figure 20.)

4. Draw the mobile figure(s) on the construction paper. Apply details with a marking pen, cut out, and attach a black piece of thread to the top of the figure(s).

5. String the thread through the drinking straw and glue it to the back of the box.

6. To camouflage the straw, paint it to match the background. If the straw resists paint, rub soap on the brush, dip it in paint, and paint the straw again.

7. Display the finished mobile picture. Label the topic. (See Figure 20.)

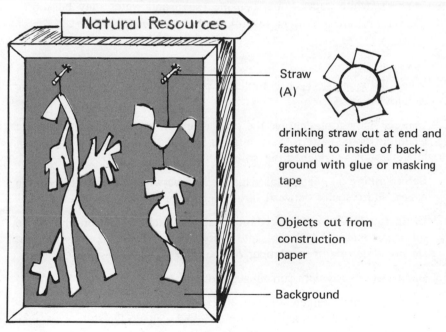

Natural Resources

Straw (A)

drinking straw cut at end and fastened to inside of background with glue or masking tape

Objects cut from construction paper

Background

Figure 20.

Etching Made Easy

When correlating this art experience with social studies, have pupils select and create linear drawings similar to Revere's *The Boston Massacre* etching. Pupils should create their own designs of political satire, cartoons depicting events of the times they are studying, and so on. Physical and rainfall maps also lend themselves well to the etching experience. Stress why etching was used as a form of art and communication. Problems pupils encounter can be paralleled with similar problems of years ago.

The drypoint technique in this experience makes etching less dangerous than when using acid as a means of etching the plate. The use of Celluloid and/or plastic enables pupils to cut directly on the plate.

Materials

Plastic Celluloid plates, pointed tools (such as, compass points, pins, and pen points), white paper, tape, benzine (soap and water may be substituted), vellum paper, blotters, felt ink dabber, and etching ink.

Procedure

1. When drawing has been completed, place and tape it underneath the celluloid plate.

2. Using a sharp tool, engrave the plate using the drawing underneath the Celluloid as the pattern to trace from. Hold the tool vertical for an even line. The lines scratched out will receive the ink.

3. Before inking the plate, soak white vellum paper in water and place the papers individually between large blotters or absorbent paper.

4. Using the felt-covered ink dabber, spread etching ink on the entire surface of plate. Dab the ink into every cut line. Use a dabbing motion. Do *not* slide or rub the dabber on the plate; it scratches the Celluloid.

5. Wipe plate lightly with soft muslin cloth.

6. Print only with dampened paper. Place etched plate on a press, if available, and place damp paper on top of inked etched plate. Place another sheet of dry paper on top of the damp paper.

7. Lower the press and print. (If a press is not available, follow same process as above, substituting hand pressure for the press.)

Footsteps into History

With the use of a social-studies theme, the teacher will be able to help her pupils understand where in time events took place. For example: for the theme of *events in American history,* the pupils make "footsteps" of an event and then place their footsteps in chronological order. This helps children visualize the concept of time in relation to when and where they are on the line of dates, past and present.

Materials
Oak-tag paper, crayons, scissors.

Procedure
1. Have each child trace his footprints on a piece of tag-board. Put in details and cut them out. (See Figure 21.)

2. On the chalkboard, list a group of ideas and events which pertain to a specific topic or time period in history. Example:
   Discovery of America 1492
   Magellan's voyage 1519
   Settlement of Jamestown 1607
   Treaty of Paris 1763
   Declaration of Independence 1776
   Inauguration of Washington 1789
   Louisiana purchase 1803
   Acquisition of Florida 1819
   Mexican secession 1848
   And so on

3. Each child chooses a topic, researches it, and reports about the subject on the footprint.

4. The positions of the footsteps are taped around the room, each child taking special care to place his footstep in the right time order.

5. Events should lead from early times to the present, so each child can personally relate to an event and also see where he stands in relation to the ʻpanorama of historical events.

Each of these five art activities can be used to meet these criteria:

1. The social-studies topic and the art activity are related.

2. The art activity affords the pupil an opportunity for self-expression.

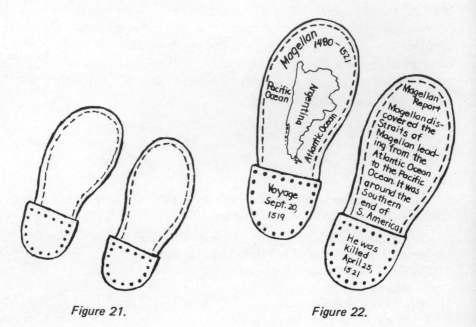

Figure 21.   Figure 22.

3. The art activity requires some form of thinking by each pupil.
4. The art activity allows for individual differences in the pupils' abilities to express themselves aesthetically.

These criteria help avoid the type of art activity many teachers dream up because someone told them to correlate social studies with other subjects. For example, I once watched a teacher scratch the bottom of her imaginative barrel by giving the pupils an outline map of South America and having them color in the countries. What a thrill! I wondered if she graded them down for going over the prescribed lines.

MUSIC AND THE SOCIAL STUDIES

Music in social studies—like literature, painting, and drama in social studies—helps pupils gain insights into peoples and cultures. Music provides a sound teaching medium, for it requires both a sensory and an intellectual commitment on the part of the pupil. By listening, he gets a feeling for the rhythm and melodies growing out of a certain life-style. A study of the lyrics tells him how people feel about the subject of the song. When he puts both together, he can draw conclusions about what the creators of the song believed and how those beliefs affected their behavior.

The variety of musical activities possible in a social-studies unit is as limitless as the variety of art activities. Music activities can range from song interpretation and pantomime to the composition of original songs. Songs can be used to introduce units. They can add depth and meaning to an event in history. They can reflect the thinking of people of a particular time in history. And they can stress similarities and differences among people all over the world. Music helps to reveal the relationships between nations and cultures. Once these relationships are realized, world understanding can be emphasized.

The interrelation of music activities and a social-studies topic should accomplish five ends. It should:

1. be directly related to the social-studies topic;

2. aid in the understanding of religions and other traditions of present and past civilizations;

3. offer a change of pace; be a release from tensions and alleviate fatigue;

4. increase the appeal of the social-studies topic;

5. provide a close and personal association with the event or period of time under study.

Music has the unique quality to "open hearts" to warm, friendly feelings and identification with all humanity. Children seem to delight in discovering the similarities between their lives and the lives of those in other societies. Everywhere in the world people sing about similar things: pets, toys, nature, buildings, construction, traveling, and life itself. Because it conveys this sense of the universality of human experiences, music can be used as a base line for the study of many cultures.

The difference between using music to enrich social-studies learning and using art activities for the same purpose is that the teacher has more resources at her fingertips when she uses music. Many school systems have music specialists, who go to the classroom once or twice a week. The specialist usually gives the children lessons in the fundamentals of music, leaving the classroom teacher with a large scope of enrichment. A great wealth of songs, books, and recordings are available for use. She usually has a music series for the grade she is teaching, and these books have a variety of songs, geared to the level of learning for her particular grade. Many record jackets include the history and stories of interest about the song and the composer. Two examples are Enrichment Records Company, which markets albums covering time periods in history from 1607 to the present, and Folkway Records in Music Education, which offers authentic folk music, ethnic music, and music history. Descriptive information accompanys each album.

Five Music Activities

When attempting to correlate and interrelate music in the social-studies curriculum, the teacher should be aware of the five basic areas of music activities: singing, rhythmic activities, creative activities, rhythm instruments, and listening.

Singing. Because singing is satisfying to most children, it is an excellent means for self-expression, for emotional release, and for the identification of one's self with people, places, things, and ideas all over the world. Too often teachers rely on gimmicks or tricks to sell a song to the children. The danger here is that, when the bag of tricks is empty, the teacher is left with nothing to use. It is not often necessary to "sell" a song. Interrelate the songs with the social-studies topic. Then, as the children sing these songs, they will tend to associate themselves with the people of the songs. The natural relationship between the song and the topic does its own selling! Many songs inspire worldwide regard for other peoples. Songs of our own people broaden appreciation of our country.

Peoples of the world have crystallized their deepest emotions and desires in songs. The song of a Russian peasant may mirror his despair or his hope. The hopes, fears, ambitions, and daily life of slaves have been portrayed in song. When singing, the children lose their own identity and become the character in the song. Singing is one way to learn the values and ideas held by other people.

Rhythmic Activities. Rhythmic activities are a combination of music and body movements based on that music. Walking like a bear and falling like a leaf to music that is "fit to the activity" are two examples. Just like dramatic play, rhythmic activities are a medium for self-expression. When accompanied by the appropriate music, the use of the body as a means of self-expression becomes a learning experience. Listening to the music and using the body to experience the feel of a song can give the pupils insight into other cultures. Folk dances (a rhythmic activity), are characteristic of many countries. Group planning, teamwork, and individual expression stimulated by this rhythmic activity help develop the ability to work with other pupils.

Creative Activities. Creative music activities encourage children to bring music into being. These music activities invite the study of other cultures besides our own, because they involve children in research into the values and ideas of other people. Creating their own song about someone else's life requires investigation and encourages thinking. To motivate children in creating their own songs, let them express their thoughts in words suitable for the melody and rhythm of a familiar song. This initial experience in song writing generally stimulates interest in the area of writing words and melody for an original piece of work. Children can work in groups on such a project, relying upon the child who has a musical background. In this situation the teacher should become a facilitator when a bit of research is needed.

Rhythmic Instruments. *Democracy in action* is the key phrase to describe children working together to make rhythm instruments to accompany an original song expressing social-studies topics. The characteristics of peoples are often revealed in the rhythms and the instruments that create the rhythms. Research into types of instruments used by a particular society leads to reproducing and using these instruments. Even though drums, tambourines, gongs, cymbals, triangles, wrist bells, and finger cymbals can be purchased, children enjoy making their own. In this way they experience the hardships, frustrations, and joys of accomplishments.

The type of rhythm instrument should be carefully chosen for the particular classroom. The instrument should be used only if the child has developed physical coordination for the instrument. Triangles and small cymbals, for example, are often frustrating to young children. The instrument should have a *musical sound*. This is especially important if the instruments are made by the children. Do not "over-use" rhythm instruments by employing a large variety of them with one song or by using them every time a song is sung or listened to in class.

Listening. Listening to the music composed and brought into being by others is a means by which most children gain an insight into the mores and folkways of many periods. Music reflects the times. Recordings can never take the place of firsthand experiences, but listening permits students to become acquainted with music of this and other countries.

Whenever possible, use the music of native composers, played on native instruments, sung in the native vocal style. For factual learning, all should be authentic. If authentic music is not available, then substitute quasi-authentic or idealized music. The children should realize, however, that while this type of music uses some of the characteristics of the authentic music it imitates, it is primarily a reflection of what an outsider feels. Never insist that a record is suited for only one grade level. The correlation of grade level with particular records should not concern the classroom teacher. Skillful motivation, correlation with the social-studies topic, and presentation should be the primary concerns.

Through the use of any of the arts children can understand how people everywhere have thought and felt about common problems. Music is a major contributor to these understandings. Good social-studies learning requires that music be studied in the context of the society and times it expresses.

Music and the Unit

Fifth- or eighth-grade pupils studying U.S. history often have a unit on the South and the institution of slavery. One of the more difficult aspects of teaching about slavery is determining the black man's response to his condition and to his new environment. As most slaves were illiterate, they left few written records of their feelings. Interestingly enough, an examination of their music offers some insights into how certain practices and values of their African homeland were transplanted into an alien environment and into how blacks survived and transcended the experience of slavery.

A bibliography of music and song follows. It is intended to aid teacher and pupil in a study of black folk music in the United States and in West and Central Africa. This list is not exhaustive, but it will serve as a start.

Music From the South. Folkways Records, FA 2650–2659. Recorded by Frederic Ramsey, Jr. (These ten volumes provide excellent source material; the collectors notes are included.)

American Folk Music, vols. II and III. Folkways Records, FA 2952, 2953. Compiled by Harry Smith. (A general collection with much you can use.)

Negro Religious Songs and Services. Library of Congress, AAFS–L10. Edited by B. A. Botkin. (Religious songs recorded in southern states.)

Negro Work Songs and Calls. Library of Congress, AAFS–L8. (You will like these for content; note the use of calls.)

The Rural Blues: A Study of the Vocal and Instrument Sources. RBF Records, RF2. Edited by Samuel B. Charters. (The subtitle tells the story.)

Music of the Ituri Forest. Ethnic Folkways Library, FE 4483. Recorded by Colin Turnbull and Francis S. Chapman with notes by C. Turnbull. (Turnbull is a superior writer on all African topics.)

Negro Music of Africa and America. Ethnic Folkways Library, FE 4500. Compiled by Harold Courlander, with notes by Richard A. Waterman and H. Courlander. (The advantage here is the built-in comparison between the two areas.)

African and Afro-American Drums. Ethnic Folkways Library, FE 4502. Compiled by Harold Courlander, who also did the notes. (Percussion is essential to a study of black music.)

To me, the three best teacher references for this study would be:

Courlander, Harold, *Negro Folk Music, U.S.A.* New York: Columbia University Press, 1963. (Contains words of songs.)

Hughes, Langston and Arna Bontemps, *The Book of Negro Folklore*. Dodd, Mead, 1966. (For ties between music and stories.)

Lomax, Alan, *Folk Songs of North America*. New York: Doubleday, 1960. (Words of songs are found here also.)

Listen carefully to some of the following songs that grew out of the slave experience:

1. "Who Built the Ark?"
2. "What Month Was Jesus Born?"
3. "Have You Got Good Religion?"
4. "You Got to Reap What You Sow"
5. "When the Saints Go Marching In"

6. "Soon I Will Be Done"
7. "My Lord, What a Mornin' "
8. "This Train"
9. "Many Thousand Gone"
10. "The Downward Road"

What can pupils say about the rhythm and musical aspects of slave songs based only on what they hear? They will probably note many of the following characteristics:

1. The voices that are doing the singing are rough and hoarse.
2. Sometimes the singers break away from the melody and sing very high sounds or make up sounds that are different from the melody.
3. There is a lot of humming, moaning, and groaning in the songs.
4. Sometimes the words are slurred or the endings of words are changed to make a humming sound.
5. In many of the songs a leader sings the main part and is answered by a chorus.
6. The songs are accented by hand clapping and thigh slapping.
7. There are buzzing and rattling sounds in the background.
8. The singers do not harmonize. Everyone either sings the melody or goes off into a kind of high part that has nothing to do with the melody.

Once pupils have identified these distinguishing characteristics of black music, they should be guided into researching both the African environment from which the slaves were taken and the new situations in which they were placed. This research period can be as short or as extensive as interest warrants, but it should be adequate to allow pupils to relate the special elements of black music to both the African and the slave experience.

Below are some of the insights into slavery and slave music that students should reach after having listened to that music and studied information about the slave's life in Africa. All of these learnings should come following a great deal of focus on the music itself. It would be best not to teach any of these points. If the students do not arrive at them on their own, provide additional musical and learning experiences that will produce them.

In Africa, music was very much a part of life. Black people sang when they worked; they sang when they worshiped; and they sang when they played. There were special songs used by young men to attract the girls they liked. There were songs used by the elders to initiate young men into adulthood. There were also songs that told how people felt about important events in their lives.

Even the tones black people used in their songs came from life experiences. They were hoarse, shrill, foggy, rough, . . . whatever the situation warranted. Africans had no interest in cultivated voices or instruments. Beauty in sound was like beauty in people: imprecise, uneven, irregular.

Then blacks were brought to a country where other people had very different ideas about music. Life and music were two different things in America, and Americans preferred pretty voices that made pleasant sounds. Still, the slaves did not abandon their old practices. They did not care for the smooth, sweet qualities that they heard in Western music. They continued to sing, pray, preach, and tell stories in the style they considered beautiful. This style carried over into their blues music and into jazz. It was very noticeable in the music of the late, great Louis (Satchmo) Armstrong, who was famous for his gravelly tones and choppy phrasing.

When slaves sang, it seemed as though they were singing out of key. In fact, they were quite on key. But it was a different key, one to which Western ears were not accustomed. In Africa, black people used a musical scale corresponding closely to the sounds they heard in life: the drum beat, the rush or the tumble of the river, the sounds of the birds and animals. When they sang or made music in this country, they included those types of sounds.

African music placed more emphasis on rhythm than on melody or harmony. This rhythm grew out of the drums that they used for communication. In Africa, most singing was accompanied by drums. Africans produced a very subtle harmony from the use of different kinds of percussion instruments: membranes attached to xylophones, pieces of metal on sticks, and drums with different ranges and sounds.

When black people were brought to this country as slaves, they were not allowed to use their drums when they sang or made music. Therefore, they tried to reproduce the sounds of the drums in their singing. Eventually, they found drum substitutes that were acceptable to white masters: empty containers, old wash basins, clapping, and thigh slapping. This accounts for the rattling and clapping sounds heard in the background of many slave songs.

Black people did not rely solely on harmony to make the melody more interesting. They got different sounds through a singer's interpretation of the notes. Sometimes a singer would take the melody and sing it higher. Sometimes he would make up a musical line in a very high voice (falsetto). Then again, he might just start humming, moaning, or groaning. Slave songs were filled with falsetto passages, moans, and groans. The moans did not mean sadness, just different ideas and feelings. For example, I remember hearing these lines:

> When you feel like moanin',
> It ain't nuthin' but love.
> It must be the Holy Ghost
> Comin' down from above.

Many of the words in slave songs sounded as though they were slurred or mispronounced; as though the songs had been made up by people who knew nothing about grammar. Slaves had been brought into a strange place where they did not know the language in any formal way. Slaves merely picked up words and put them into a grammatical patterns they had used in Africa. Many people believe that what is called a southern accent today is really the accent of foreigners (slaves) speaking an unfamiliar language. White children who were raised by black house servants naturally picked up that accent.

Africans attached great value to a kind of singing and speaking where a leader developed a theme and was answered by a chorus. The answers were often comments on the leader's line or on the replies of the chorus. There were many patterns developed for the leader-response type of song. The chorus sometimes repeated a line sung by the leader. On some occasions the leader sang the entire verse, and the group joined in at the end of a line or phrase. Often, the leader made a statement and the group answered or added to it. In many cases, the part of the leader and that of the group overlapped. Usually, there was no set pattern; it just developed according to the feelings of the leader and the chorus.

Much of the interplay between the leader and the chorus was improvised. The amount of improvisation depended on how long the chorus wanted to continue the song. Improvisation continued in the slave songs of the ante-bellum South. Work songs and spirituals were sung in the leader-response tradition, and words and rhythms were made up by the singers to suit their moods. It is said that jazz developed from improvised answers on a given theme or melody.

It is probably fair to say that all of the distinguishing characteristics of slave music contain elements of the African background of black people. As best they could, blacks tried to keep their values, their customs, and their musical forms in a new land that did not understand or appreciate them. Wherever possible, they merged the old with the new, so that their heritage would not die. These forms survived and became some of the most outstanding contributions to the history of music. Blues and jazz forms are recognized and admired by music lovers the world over.

Much of what we know about the black man's response to the condition of slavery and to his new environment comes from a study of the spirituals and work songs in which he expressed himself. We do know that the slave responded in a very positive manner to Christianity. He had come from a strong religious tradition in Africa and wanted to continue it. Christianity was the one element of the white man's culture that was open to the slave. It offered him the promise of a better life in the hereafter, and it gave him an inner strength with which to bear the grief and the hardships of slavery.

A study of the lyrics of many spirituals offers pupils important insights into the slave's attitudes toward Christianity and his life in this world. Any grouping of spirituals might be used. See Courlander or Lomax for suggestions. After listening to them to determine rhythmic patterns and studying words for meaning, students can be led to draw conclusions similar to those gained after a consideration of the musical elements of the previous songs.

The same kind of study in a unit can be built around the development of country-and-western music, rock music, or cowboy music. To do that, keep these questions in mind:

1. What kind of cultural and societal conditions produced this music?
2. Who were its leaders?
3. What musical tradition formed its background?
4. Where does it fit in the pattern of American social and musical history?

A very interesting study can be made around the musical experience of the Puritans. How did their music serve as an expression of their religious and social views? What were its origins? What needs did it meet in the New World situation?

It is not necessary to create an entire unit based on the music of a group of people or of a particular era. Certain key pieces of music can be analyzed and placed into the more general study of social and cultural history. Whatever method is employed, it would be advisable to gather music that will tell pupils something about the area of study and to present it along with such background material as will give the pupils some insight into what the music tells about the people and the time.

TRADE BOOKS AND SOCIAL STUDIES

Books provide a place to meet new friends and to find out about new places. In addition to all the good reasons listed by authors and editors for reading library books, there is a special reason for using the trade (or library) book in social studies. The child who reads it feels it is his book. Everybody reads the textbook. Everbody looks in the encyclopedia. But with a trade book, somebody gets to read it first. That makes it his to hold to his heart, to share, to brag about, to entice a friend to read it.

If trade books are that special, then teachers who have read them and who are shrewd observers of pupils can often get the right book into the right hands and the right mind. Then what do you do? Ask for a book report? Boo on book reports! Imagine this conversation:

Teacher: "Hold it! What started this punching match?"

Jimmy: "He's buggin' me. He's always buggin' me."

Johnny: "I just wanted to see what he was doin'."

Jimmy: "You're a chicken grip. You always butt in."

Johnny: "I don't either."

Jimmy: "You're a nuisance!"

Johnny: "Don't you swear at me! You swore!"

Teacher: "Jimmy, I want you to read this book and then tell me if you still think Johnny's a nuisance."

Johnny: (In a whisper to a third pupil.) "Gee, Mrs. King swore at Jimmy."

No, that sort of too-clever technique won't work. Let's try again.

Jimmy: "You're a nuisance!"

Johnny: "Don't you swear at me! You swore!"

Teacher: "A nuisance? Oh, dear, mercy me, isn't that the end of the world? What do you think we ought to do with a nuisance, Jimmy?"

Jimmy: "Flush him down the toilet!"

Teacher: "Send them down to the minors. Take away their batting helmets. Call them out on the second strike. What do you think, Mary Ann?"

Mary Ann: "I dunno."

Teacher: "What about you, Jake? You have any views on this hot topic of being a nuisance?"

Now, you know Jake read the story of *Stevie,* a boy who was an expert nuisance. Yet, when Stevie left the family he was staying with, the boy who found him such a nuisance missed him the most. What Jake has to say may or may not help calm down Jimmy and Johnny. That depends on how much they respect Jake. But your question gives Jake a chance to distill the wisdom of *Stevie* in a remark or two. If he makes the point and the two boys accept his idea, then you cool off a situation and know Jake got what you hoped he would from reading *Stevie.* If Jake blows it, then you've got two problems: Jimmy and Johnny are still mad, and you have to wonder if Jake can do more than pronounce words.

I used to depend on the school librarian and the city librarian for help in selecting trade books. I'd let them know the general topic I wanted—and the range of reading abilities in my class—and they would load me down. I tried to read everything, but I must admit that I skimmed about 50 percent the first year. On the basis of my reading and skimming, I would annotate my list of books. Each year, I would add a few books and drop one or two. My lists saved me all sorts of time and grief.

The last list I drew up was for a third-grade class in which about half the pupils were blacks. We were studying our local community. I wanted some books that would give every pupil some insights into the lives of blacks.

What Color Is Love? Joan Walsh Auglund. Harcourt, 1966. (Great pictures; basic idea of love as a feeling.) (K–1)

Swimming Hole. Jerrold Beim. Morrow Junior Books, 1950. (New boy wants to join gang but not to play with black in it; he learns his prejudice is unacceptable.) (1–2)

The Dragon Takes a Wife. Walter Dean Myers. Bobbs-Merrill, 1972. (A lonely dragon seeks a wife; to get one he must defeat a knight. His helpful fairy is Mabel Mae Jones, a black swinger and the hippest good fairy of all.) (1–3, but may be harder?)

A Place to Live. Jeanne Bendick. Parents Magazine Press. (Stresses interdependence of all living things.) (3)

All About Us. Eva Knox Evans. Golden Press. (Endorsed by Einstein. Best early resource on human commonalities and differences. Conclusion: prejudice is dysfunctional.) (2–5, but I wonder about 2nd and 3rd grades.)

Faces. Barbara Brenner. Dutton. (Pictures of faces and parts of faces; all races. Great.) (1–3)

The Africans Knew. Tillie Pine and Joseph Levine. McGraw-Hill. (Directions for reproducing tools and artifacts of ancient African cultures.) (3?)

They Lived This Way in Ancient Africa. Marie Neurath. Franklin Watts. (Survey of achievements and heritage of ancient cultures and empires of Sub-Saharan Africa.) (3)

Atu the Silent One. Frank Jupo. Holiday House. (Great one! Kung Bushmen.)

Frederick Douglass, Freedom Fighter. Lillie G. Patterson. Garrard Press, 1965. (Vivid action but great for young readers.) (2)

George Washington Carver. Sam and Beryl Epstein. Garrard Press, 1960. (Best of all biographies of Carver for primary.) (2)

My Dog Rinty. Ellen Tarry and Marie Hall Ets. Viking, 1949. (Photographs are old but great. It's a grabber.) (2)

Five Friends at School. P. Buckley and H. Jones. Holt, Rinehart & Winston. Textbook. (Shows urban classroom; pupils build model of their community; dramatic play of economic life. Good textbook for this.)

The Picture Life of Ralph J. Bunche. Margaret B. Young. Franklin Watts. (The career of a Nobel Prize winner.) (3)

Frederick Douglass. Arna Bontemps. Alfred A. Knopf, 1959. (Good details on black hero.) (3)

Melindy's Medal. Georgene Faulkner and John Becker. Julian Messner, 1945. (Old but good. Set in Boston housing project. Girl wins medal for bravery.) (3)

A Sundae With Judy. Frieda Friedman. Morrow Junior Books, 1949. (Old. Setting is New York City. Hokey but kids like it.) (3)

Stevie. John Steptoe. Harper & Row. (The benefits of brothers; the original nuisance.) (3)

Goggles. Ezra Jack Keats. Macmillan. (An award winner. Two kids outwit a gang.) (3)

Rosie's Walk. Pat Hutchins. Macmillan. (Barnyard animals as city dwellers. Violent individuals hurt themselves.) (3)

Little Boy Who Lives Up High. John and Lucy Hawkinson. Albert Whitman. (Balances loneliness of high-rise living with variety of people in the city.) (3)

Beautiful Junk. Jon Madian. Little, Brown. (Art in Watts.) (3)

Famous American Negro Poets. Carlemae Hill Robbins. Dodd, 1965. (Warmth and sincere pride; a moving book.) (4)

Ladycake Farm. Mabel L. Hunt. Lippincott, 1952. (Black family moves to a farm; good switch and good story.) (4)

Skid. Florence Hayes. Houghton Mifflin, 1948. (Black boy moves north from Georgia. Great "adjustment" story.) (4)

Art of Africa. Shirley Glubok. Harper, 1965. (Sculpture, pottery, pictures, carvings.) (5—but try it out.)

Musical Instruments of Africa. Betty W. Dietz. Day, 1965. (Fascinating! Instruments used by different tribes.) (5—but try it.)

This list includes 27 books ranging from first to fifth grade in readability. Some are fiction, some are nonfiction, some are biographies, one is a wacky fairy tale. You will note that I forgot the dates on some of them— no matter, I'll fill those in next year. The important thing is that I have enough information to find the books again. In some cases, I have question marks after the readability figure. That means I'm guessing; as pupils read them I should get more accurate information.

Would this list carry a unit by itself? I doubt it. The list is useful in a general way, but it doesn't have a sharp focus. Some of the stories deal with the stresses and problems of city life. Some touch on the matter of black pride. Some present the lives of others as models. Some are largely informational.

If I had a single purpose in mind, say, an inquiry into interpersonal stress of life in the city, I would have to hone and then expand my list. *Skid* would stay on the new list, *Art of Africa* would be dropped. Because the school library I'm drawing on has a limited selection, I would work out an arrangement with the city library to borrow 10 or 15 of their books. I'd arrange for plenty of free reading time during social studies. I'd use a lot of role-playing with the books. I'd use some of the great new filmstrips (for example, the guidance series from Imperial Films in Lakeland, Florida, or the Learning About Me series from QED Productions in Burbank, California). Although the trade books are essential to what I want to do, the content of the filmstrips and the potential content of role-playing are excellent. And both activities provide variation in classroom activities.

This last point is an important one. Some children don't learn much from reading; some learn a great deal. The principle involved in my suggestion is based on some 20 years of observation and participation: Different children learn in different ways at different rates from different materials and activities. Art, music, and literature offer means for adapting to these differences. They should not control the social-studies experience, but they can enrich that experience in subtle and profound ways.

SUMMARY

Art is used in the social studies as a visual, emotional, and expressive means of organizing and visually representing ideas related to social-studies concepts. It is also used as a cultural link with the many peoples of the world, past and present. Art lets the students play the role of the creator, and it deals directly with their appreciations, creative abilities, feelings, concepts of self, and emotions. With preplanning by the teacher and the correlation of the art activities to the social-studies topics, many desirable outcomes associated with creativity and reasoning strengthen the teaching of the social studies.

Music is used as a means of self-expression and of gaining insights into the values and ideas of any society, past or present, in this nation or in other nations. Not being able to sing very well, many teachers dread teaching music as part of any classroom activity. For that reason, the music activities suggested were presented with the teachers playing dominant roles only as motivators and facilitators. As was the case with art, music in social studies should require students to investigate and to reason—two skills which can easily be applied to music and lyrics, as well as to types of instruments and cultural rhythms. All major cultures have their music, and to a great extent all societies sing of the same things.

Trade books can be used as the major vehicle for a unit or as supplements to other activities. One key to their successful use means selecting enough books of varying readability to accommodate individual differences. Trade books can be informational, inspirational, or entertaining—and sometimes all three. Whatever else they may be, they should contribute to understanding a topic and stimulate reasoning about the problems involved in that topic.

Art, music, and trade books also function to break up a steady dose of textbooks or any other materials used constantly in your classroom. Even the most successful of approaches can become boring if it is never varied. The approaches discussed here are valuable in themselves and as peanut butter and jelly to be spread on the staff of life.

Special thanks to Professor Sue Hart of Carthage College, Professor Roger Berg of the University of Nebraska at Omaha, and Dr. Shirley Baugher of the Law in American Society Foundation. They taught me what I know about these topics.

SUGGESTED READINGS

Art

Bareford, George, *Clay in the Classroom*. Worcester, Mass.: Davis Publications, 1971. (A good basic book on types of techniques involving the use of clay. Includes how to fire a kiln, use of glazes, molds, and so on.)

Betts, Victoria Bedford, *Exploring Papier-Mâché*. Worcester, Mass.: Davis Publications, 1970. (Tells how to use papier-mâché in illustrated step-by-step, easy-to-follow directions.)

Hart, Annette Sue, *Intermediate Art Activities*. Inglewood, Calif.: Education Insights, 1973. (Art activities with easy-to-follow directions. Many activities are correlated with social-studies concepts.)

Knudsen, Estelle and Ethel Christensen, *Children's Art Education*. Peoria, Ill.: Bennett, 1971. (Gives art activities on a grade basis, K–6, and art media for children ages 5 through 12.)

Quick, John, *Artists' and Illustrators' Encyclopedia*. New York: McGraw-Hill, 1969. (A must if you want to understand the meanings of materials for art activities!)

Music

Green, Carroll, E., *Notes, Time, Terms: A Reference Book*. Peoria, Ill.: Byerly Co., 1970. (A very basic pamphlet on fundamentals of music. Many ideas for bulletin boards, etc., or for children to refer to when composing their own songs.

Hawkinson, John and Martha Faulhaber, *Music and Instruments for Children to Make*. New York: Scholastic Book Services, 1970. (A must for elementary-school teachers! The book is filled with musical experiences and the making of rhythm instruments.)

Hughes, William O., *A Concise Introduction to Teaching Elementary School Music*. Belmont, Calif.: Wadsworth Publishing Co., 1973. (This book is an introduction and a reference. It gives the teacher a free hand to superimpose her own ideas.)

Lyons, John H., *Stories of Our American Patriotic Songs*. New York: Vanguard Press, 1942. (Although this book is old, it's one of the good ones. Great stories correlated with songs and record suggestions.)

Nye, Vernice T., Robert E. Nye, and H. Virginia Nye, *Toward World Understanding With Song*. Belmont, Calif.: Wadsworth Publishing Co., 1967. (The book provides a foundation for the approach of song with generalizations about world understanding. Includes extensive reference lists. Folkways Album FD 5720 is available for use with the book.)

Trade Books

Berg, Roger M., "Resources for Teaching International Education in the Elementary School Social Studies Curriculum." Unpublished Ph.D. dissertation, Northwestern University, August, 1972. (Contains 400 annotated references, many of them trade books, suitable for your use.)

Gast, David K., "Minority Americans in Children's Literature." *Elementary English,* vol. 44, January, 1967, pp. 12–23. (A burning article on a burning topic; well worth the half hour it takes to find and read it.)

EXERCISES

1. Research a topic from a magazine like *National Geographic* or *National Geographic School Bulletin*. Write up at least two art activities that would enhance learning a social-studies concept gleaned from the topic.

2. Discuss or list all the information you can obtain from a picture by a famous artist. Do not do research. This should be your own interpretation. How many social-studies concepts can you find? Correlate your findings with an art activity.

3. Look through music books used by elementary-school children. Choose a grade level and pick a song to correlate with a social-studies topic. Use all five basic areas of music activities with the song.

4. How would you use a music activity for the introduction of a social-studies unit on cowboys? Explain.

5. Visit the children's section of your local library and select 15 or 20 trade books for use with a social-studies topic (you choose it). Remember, readability of most books should range well below and of a few books somewhat above the grade you teach.

PART FOUR

The Swingers

IN my first year of teaching I ran into the usual discipline problems. "Spank them," the principal said.

I wasn't sure spanking eleven-year-olds was right, so the next time I had trouble I asked the kid what I should do. "Spank me," he said, "what else?"

So I spanked him, one hard whack across the rear. He blinked pretty hard, but he didn't cry.

Over the next few weeks I spanked one or two boys a week. I never had to spank anyone twice, but I began to notice a pattern. A kid would be going along fine and then, for no reason I could see, he would deliberately provoke me. When he knew he had made me angry, he'd walk up to the front of the room, lean over, and take his punishment. I began to notice the class wasn't really interested in anything but the kid's reaction after he'd been whacked.

It took awhile—too long actually—to catch on. When I figured out the game, I waited for the next incident. When it came, I asked the class, "This is something you have to do, isn't it? Once the first guy got hit and didn't cry, you all had to pass the test, didn't you?"

They allowed that I was right. Whenever things got too boring, one of them would gulp up his nerve and get my goat. "Boring?" I asked, "Has it been that bad?"

Just like every other grade, they told me. Read and recite, read and recite. Some of the questions were better than usual, and I was good about recess, but generally it was pretty boring.

"What would liven it up?" I asked.

The spankings liven it up, they said, but maybe if they could put on a play? "Why not?" I said, "Who's going to write it?"

In 15 minutes they had themselves organized into committees and the rest of the afternoon was pure pleasure, as they worked hard at their own goals. Just before the last bell, I was reminded that I still had to deliver a spanking. "Ok," I said, "Everyone who has to pass the manhood test yet, line up here."

Eight boys and one girl lined up, and I hit each a good whack. It really hurt me more than it did them. But I never laid a hand on a kid again.

Moral: The teacher who finds ways to make a class swing
doesn't have to swing at pupils.

Dramatic Play

I was born within sound of the high, winter waves of Lake Michigan. I have never lived farther than a mile or so from a lake or an ocean, except for a few poor years in the desert. Naturally, then, one of my favorite units has to do with ships and ports.

My preferred method of teaching primary grade units is through *dramatic play*. What a name: dramatic play! Almost as misleading as the meaning of social studies. Thinking about it makes me write in incomplete sentences.

A drama is a story written to be acted out by actors on a stage. But dramatic play has no script, no lines to commit to memory. It has actors— every child in the class. It has a stage of sorts—any place in the classroom or on the school ground that can be used for learning.

The *play* in dramatic play has no theatrical implications; rather, it indicates fun. Fun, of course, is frowned on by those who don't teach children or who can't teach well. The fun in dramatic play refers to the fun in playing and the fun in learning something you want to know.

Four small examples:

The first grader reads, "Look at the horse walk. Clomp, clomp, clomp! Now look at the horse run. Clippity, clippity, clippity!" The teacher says, "Show me how the horse walks. Show me how the horse runs."

The third grader says, "Watch me, I'll show you how they get into the lunar module."

The fifth grader says, "I got a dead fish and some corn. This is what the Indians showed the Pilgrims."

The seventh grader puts on his wig and says, "The delegates from the colonies, assembled here in Continental Congress, will put out their pipes and come to order. Stop selling insurance, Hancock, and take your place!"

Five short episodes:

The kindergarten teacher has a kitchen and living room set up in a corner of her room. Two kids are dressed up as adults; three kids are the children in the family. The mother is cooking; the daughters are setting the table; the son is taking out the garbage; and the father snores on the couch.

The second-grade west wall has been turned into a store. Empty, washed cans line the shelves. A lady wheels her load up to the cashier. An eager boy waits to cram the purchases into the sack. The friendly neighborhood grocer says, "Come back soon."

The fourth-grade room is a cave. Eight Cro-Magnon hunters are chipping at spearheads. Six more are working on a cave drawing. Beyond the desks comes a plaintive cry, "We're tired of waiting. Come on and hunt us."

Two sixth-grade boys tear down a model they had built. "That smart-aleck Mary Jane," says one, "how'd she know the Egyptians didn't build Roman arches?"

The eighth-grade girl stood and looked coolly at the council. "As prime minister of my nation, I would point out that our conduct during this cease-fire has been characterized by restraint."

In these examples, the students obviously had a topic of study, they were dealing with subject matter; they were using special settings and props; they were acting out the roles of some characters; their products and their behavior reflected what they knew and understood; and the quality of their dramatizing told the teacher exactly what they did not know or had failed to understand.

Dramatic play is a device for studying a topic, for demonstrating what is known or not known about that topic, and for creating situations where the child asks to learn because he wants to know.

Dramatic play is a learning activity in which pupils state their own goals, conduct their own research, and test themselves in play. Yet, the teacher really gives up no authority. She can see that her goals are being sought; she can see that learning is taking place; and she can evaluate progress every day. In the hands of a good teacher, dramatic play is one of the most cooperative, most intense, most profitable learning experiences possible.

ARRANGING THE ENVIRONMENT

On a Friday afternoon, you have the class strip the bulletin boards, put away all old displays, and take all used books back to the library. The class leaves for home. You are about to create an arranged room environment.

Everything in this new environment will have some relationship to ships and ports. One bulletin board is filled with pictures of ships. Underneath goes a strip of tagboard on which you have printed "What do these ships carry?"

Another, but smaller, bulletin board is covered with a chart showing signal flags. Across the bottom of the chart hang four or five flags you have made from scraps of cloth. On a small table below the flags are small heaps of scrap cloth.

You cover the library table with books. In each are two or three colored markers, each inserted at a colorful picture or an exciting passage.

You set a large fish tank on the sink counter and fill it with water. You toss in a small wooden ship. Next to it you leave two metal ships (one must be large enough so that its displacement of water can be observed). You add a sign, "Why do metal boats float?" You drop a ruler and grease pencil next to the sign.

In one corner of the room you pin up, just above floor level, 6 feet of paper that will take tempera paint. Cans of paint and brushes sit nearby. Above the paper is an accurate picture of a port. In front of the paper you drop enough scraps of lumber so breakwaters and docks can be built.

Above the science table goes a picture of a lighthouse. On the table goes a set of instructions on how to build a lighthouse. Next to the instructions are batteries, wire, wood, tacks, bulbs—everything needed to build a lighthouse.

You use masking tape to hang a display. It shows men and women at work on ships and around the port. The caption asks, "What are these workers doing?"

You drop some more scraps of wood in the construction corner. Next to them go three small, dull saws, three small hammers, and an assortment of nails. You also leave a small ship that you made.

You put a song of the sea on the record player, slip on your coat, and head for home. The trap has been baited. The quarry is the interest of your pupils.

PLAY, DISCUSSION, AND RESEARCH

On Monday morning your class can't miss the changes in the classroom. When school begins, tell the class they may spend a little time wandering around the room, looking at things, and playing with the objects.

Give them enough time to prowl, but not enough time to satisfy their curiosity. (The interrupted pleasure is sure to be returned to eagerly.) Then ask, "Well, what do you think this is all about?"

"Boats!"

"Sailing!"

"The ocean!"

"Etc.!"

You ask, "What did you see that you liked most?"

"The boats!"

"The lighthouse!"

"The tools!"

"Etc.!"

Pick out from one-third to one-half of the class (depending on the size of the class, the amount of free space you have, and the number of toy ships available). Say, "Ok, each of you get a ship or boat, and you can play with it."

They play. You watch. The other pupils watch. You circulate among the watchers and ask quiet questions.

"What is Billy doing?"

"Why is Mary running her boat up the wall?"

"How would you do that?"

Then you shift the groups until everyone has had his chance to play with the toy ships. The class has finished its first session of *dramatic play*.

The next step is discussion of what went on during play. You will probably pursue several ideas that occurred to you as you observed the play, but I'll just use one example.

"Billy, why were you and Kathy hitting your ships together?"

"Because. I was sailing along, and she ran into me."

"Why'd you run into his ship, Kathy?"

"Because he was in my way. He should have let me by. He's a boy and I'm a girl, and boys are supposed to be polite to girls."

"What happens if two ships smash into each other out in the ocean?"

"They sink."

"The policeman comes out in a rowboat and gives them a ticket."

"What policeman?"

"Oh, you know. It was a joke."

"Do ships smash into each other on the ocean?"

"Sure, and some of them smash into ice cubes . . . uh, icebergers and sink."

"Do all the ships that are on the ocean smash into each other all the time?"

"No."

"Why not?"

"I dunno."

"How can you find out?"

"Look it up."

"Where?"

"In the books."

"How else?"

"Ask somebody."

"Who?"

"My dad."

"A sailor."

"A sixth grader."

"The principal. He thinks he knows everything."

"Ok. Who wants to work with Billy and Kathy on this question?"

And so it goes. A small research group is formed. You move on to another mistake or question or problem.

"Now, about that policeman in a rowboat. Do you really believe? . . ."

And so on.

When children play, they reflect what they know. They do some things correctly, and they make some mistakes. The mistakes are used to stimulate discussion that leads to questions that can be researched.

You do *not* say, "Billy, you are doing that wrong. Someone show him the right way." What you want is for the pupil to *find* the right way by his own (or his research group's) efforts.

You keep at these questions until everyone has elected a research group. The next day, you begin the period by asking each group to get together. Then you review, with each group, what they are trying to find out. Don't tell them! Ask them.

"Everybody set? Ok, how much time do you want?"

And off they go, some to the library table, some to the library. They will waste time this first time. Why not? They have to become acquainted with many new books. They have to find what will be useful. They skim and finger and look at pictures. You visit each group, praising and prodding. Research takes time. And you must be willing to let them take time.

Your responsibility is to be certain that they can find out. You have to be sure the answers are in materials available to them. Why else did you do your research and write that resource unit?

Of course, someone always comes up with a question you didn't, and couldn't anticipate. Then you have to dig out the answer. If third graders can't read your source, then you rewrite the source as simply as you can. I don't think I ever taught a unit of any kind where I didn't have to do some rewriting for the class.

Then, after one day or three days—however long it takes to find answers or partial answers—each group makes its report. When all are armed with this new knowledge, you go back to a play session.

Let's review for a moment. You create an environment. The class explores that environment. You let the class play with the ships. You observe the mistakes in the play. The class discusses the mistakes. Research groups are formed. Research takes place. The results of research are reported. The class plays again.

"LEARNING" TO PLAY

In these early stages, you are not working on developing any major concepts. That comes later. Right now you are working to lead the class to find enough information—simple factual information—so that while they play they will learn with some degree of accuracy.

You are also guiding your pupils into developing the abilities needed to play together, work together, and discuss together. If other teachers in earlier grades have not used dramatic play or some equally active method, then your pupils have to learn how to conduct themselves in a freer learning situation. They aren't born with a sense of responsibility to others. Consideration of others is not genetically transmitted. Courtesy and civility are learned behaviors. And if they haven't learned that before, they have to learn it now, or dramatic play won't work for them, or for you.

The first time I tried dramatic play was with a fifth grade. We were studying life on the Kentucky-Ohio frontier. Everything was fine until the first time we used research groups. Then everything went wrong. I didn't realize that these pupils had been taught that social studies was *always* learned from a basic text and that pupils *always* stayed in their seats in social studies. I gave them the freedom of groups, of multiple resources, and of leaving their seats. The room was so noisy that the principal came up to see if I had disappeared. The teachers in rooms anywhere near me sent their classes to recess.

I learned that children have to learn how to learn in different ways. If I wanted to use research groups, my pupils had to learn to work in groups. Some people refer to this as learning human-relations skills. To me, it was learning to work together without doing anything that keeps others from learning. Group work requires some noise, but it doesn't require shouting. Group work requires some movement, but it doesn't require running or kicking or hitting. I also found that a record player helps.

The other major type of learning in dramatic play has to do with learning to research. Pupils need to know what they are trying to find out. They need to know where the likely places are for finding out. They need to learn to read at different speeds for different purposes. They need to learn to interview. They need to learn to observe. They need to learn to separate fact from opinion. In simple ways, appropriate to their need to know and their ability to learn, they need to learn to do what you do when you do your research.

So, in the beginning, you are concentrating on four categories of outcomes: information, thinking, group skills, and research skills. And all four are needed to perform well in dramatic play.

PLAYING AND REPLAYING

Out of the second or third session of play is bound to come a request for more ships or docks or lighthouses. The answer is a period or two for construction.

"We need more ships. We don't have enough ships for all of us."

"What kind of ships?"

"I need a freighter."

"I need an oil tanker."

"I need a fishing boat."

"I'm in the Coast Guard."

"Do you know what those ships look like?"

"Sure, and if we don't, we'll find pictures of them."

"What will you build them with?"

"That wood over there."

"There aren't enough tools for everyone. How do you think the class can handle that?"

And so it goes. From play comes a need to construct. To construct, they must solve the problem of too few tools for everyone to be building at one time. They must build ships that look like the real ships, hence they must research. And when they have measured and sawed and nailed and painted, they are ready to play again.

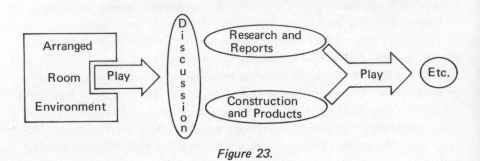

Figure 23.

New needs arise. The need for a harbor, docks, breakwaters, buoys, a lighthouse. The need to know what is shipped from and into the harbor. They need a harbor master, a Coast Guard, a communications system. And somewhere in here you work in your key ideas—transportation, systems, harbors, products, cargo, wholesalers, and so on.

And the questions! You can't keep them down. What harbor is this? Why did a city grow up here? What is produced in this area? Why do we need railroads, roads, an airport? Why are most of our major cities located on waterways? Why don't iron ships sink? Why do sailors have unions? Why do people like beaches? What pays for the beaches and the lifeguards? Where do taxes come from? And on and on it goes. Every question leads to research. Research leads to answers. And the answers lead to improved dramatic play.

When do you stop all this? When the outcomes you sought have been achieved. When interest wanes. When you begin to deal with trivia. When the play has become sophisticated and refined. When you have exhausted the resources your class can research. Any of those moments is a good time to stop.

When you stop, do you give them a big test? I don't see why. Haven't you been asking questions everyday? Isn't your observation of their play a test situation? You still want to give a test? Ok, but keep it short and focus on key ideas. Why? Because on Friday you want the class to strip the bulletin boards, put away all old displays, and take all used books back to the library. You've got something up your sleeve for them to see and do on Monday morning.

THE FIELD TRIP

Field trips? What have field trips to do with dramatic play? Plenty. To begin with, one of the functions of dramatic play is imitation of adult occupations and activities. Obviously, there are multiple opportunities for children to observe adults at work during a field trip. If you want to know what goes on at a harbor, visit a harbor, observe everything you can, ask plenty of questions. The second reason for a field trip is to find out something about the tools and settings in which men and women carry out their basic human activities. Go and see! There's no reason to confine yourselves to books and films unless you have no harbor in your community.

The usual field trip amounts to a telephone call for setting a time and day, arranging for the school bus, getting legal permission slips from parents, finding four or five parents who will come along, visiting the place in question, counting the pupils *before* the return trip, thanking the parents, and answering a few questions the next day. These are all essential to a field trip but there are a few essential steps left out. *You* should visit the site of the field trip before you even consider taking the class. You should take your camera, loaded with slide film. You should find out the route the bus will take and drive the route between the school and the site.

Visiting the place beforehand gives you some prior knowledge of what children will see, gives you a chance to note any dangerous situations, and gives you information about the tour guide's (if there is one) understanding of children.

Taking your camera lets you make slides for use in motivating pupils to be alert for certain interesting machines or situations. The slides also provide a continuing resource for use as references in later class discussions. Your own observations will provide a basis for deciding whether or not to encourage your pupils to take their own cameras (be careful on this point not to embarrass pupils if few of them own cameras).

Driving the bus route lets you see what pupils might see *on* the trip. Pupils can become rowdy on any trip taking more than ten minutes. Give them a choice of research questions to consider as they travel. What sorts of neighborhoods did we go through? Where are gas stations located? How many police cars were there? What kind of traffic did we see? What kinds of stores did we pass? You can dream up 20 legitimate questions for the trip. If pupils are busy talking and looking and pointing and sketching, they won't be too tempted to shout and hit and pull hair.

If you have been using dramatic play, then your pupils have surely raised questions. If the field trip grows out of a need to answer these questions, then they will have plenty to research when they arrive at the site. They should get ideas about activities to imitate, items to construct, and processes to follow. Among other benefits of field trips, children learn they will someday be doing, as work and for money, some of the jobs they observed. Oh, yes, learning can be useful.

THE SCROUNGING FUNCTION

One by-product of dramatic play is the collection of articles useful in arranging the environment and in facilitating play. Teachers always ask how to store "all that stuff." In the old days we used heavy cardboard beer cartons (painted over nicely) or wooden orange crates. Today, these are rare items. Any moving company sells tough cardboard boxes for a reasonable price; so do Sears and Wards. Two bits of advice. Label each box and keep the items for each unit separate.

Collecting materials for dramatic play is easy for a natural-born scrounger. Every lumberyard and plumbing shop always has odds and ends to give away or sell at a reasonable price. Appliance and music stores often have scrap lumber, big boxes, cardboard, and insulating foam to throw away. The cardboard rolls used as a center for linoleum flooring make great logs or pipes. The wooden boxes that coffins are shipped in make great counters for stores or airplane bodies. If nothing else works, appeal to the local Rotary or Lions club; the businessmen who belong will help you out.

Garage and rummage sales are sources of all sorts of useful junk. So are second-hand stores, antique shops, and flea markets. If you need a few tools for construction or if you need games for an interest center, it's better to spend $2 or $3 on used, dull tools than several bucks on new, sharp things.

The local community possesses many other resources you can tap, among them the human resources of skill and knowledge. Parents possess some amazing skills, and I have persuaded some to enter into dramatic play. Parents often hesitate to give little lectures to pupils, and I support their reluctance. Let's say, however, that a mother can make jewelry; why not let her set up shop in the room and proceed to do her thing? She'll get plenty of attention and answer plenty of questions. I once had a plumber-father come in for an afternoon and thread pipe; he was a great success. The other obvious source of help is the senior citizen; for one thing they know about the old days and ways. Have you ever seen ice cream handmade in the back of the class? It's an attention grabber.

The local community is a gold mine for dramatic play—things, places, and people are available for the polite asking.

SUMMARY

One of the basic approaches to primary-grade social studies is dramatic play, and this technique works well as a now-and-then activity for upper grades. Dramatic play involves every pupil, and the involvement usually permits a pupil to follow his own interests within a broad topic of study. Pupils act out the roles of real-life characters; they use special settings and props; and their overt behavior reflects what they know and feel.

The beauty of dramatic play is its clear dependence upon intellectual development. The pupil states his own goals, conducts his own research, and tests what he has learned. The first few times dramatic play is used, the teacher may be a rather constant guide to learning; but as the pupil relaxes in the positive reinforcement of success, the teacher becomes largely a facilitator of learning. At the same time, the teacher gives up nothing professionally, because she still chooses the major topic, sets up the environment, and can step in to help any child who is struggling without much success.

The local community provides many resources for dramatic play, particularly field trips, sources of construction materials, and human models for pupils to observe and question.

SUGGESTED READINGS

Hanna, Lavona, Neva Hagaman, and Gladys Potter, *Unit Teaching in the Elementary School*. New York: Holt, Rinehart & Winston, 1963. (*The* text on dramatic play; if you like the idea, you should read much of this book.)

Merritt, Edith, *Working With Children in Social Studies*. Belmont, Calif.: Wadsworth Publishing Co., 1961. (Another good book on dramatic play.)

Siks, G. B., *Creative Dramatics, An Art for Children*. New York: Harper & Row, 1958. (Check this one out to identify the differences between dramatic play and creative dramatics.)

Inexpensive Materials

Big Rock Candy Mountain: Resources of Our Education ($4.00)
Dell Publishing Company, Inc.
750 Third Avenue
New York, N.Y. 10017
(The offspring of *The Whole Earth Catalog*.)

Elementary Teachers Guide to Free Curriculum Materials (c. $11.00)
Educators Guide to Free Social Studies Materials (c. $11.00)
Educators Progress Service, Inc.
Randolph, Wis. 53956
(Should be in your school or district library.)

Materials List: A Useful List of Classroom Items That Can Be Scrounged or Purchased ($.72)
EDC
55 Chapel St.
Newton, Mass. 02160
(Good breakdown by subject areas.)

Yellow Pages of Learning Resources ($1.95), Richard S. Wurman (ed.)
The MIT Press, MIT
Cambridge, Mass. 02142
(Invaluable for teaching, fun to read.)

EXERCISES

1. Take a topic of your own choosing and plan, on paper, what you would do to arrange a room environment to stimulate interest in that topic. Remember, there must be enough items so at least one-third of the class can play with them the first day.

2. Use your imagination to create a dialogue following the initial dramatic play on a topic of study. Be sure to direct the dialogue so it ends up leading to research or construction.

3. Plan a field trip, including an on-site visit and activities for the enroute trips.

4. Be sure you or someone else reads and reports on the chapters on dramatic play in Merritt and Hanna, Hagaman and Potter. These are essential if you want to extend your knowledge of dramatic play.

Games and Simulations

I once taught a sixth grade in a room with a rubber-tiled floor. For some forgotten reason we had gotten interested in squaring numbers. The brightest boys and girls had no trouble, but much of the class was slow to grasp the notion. One day, with my head hung in despair, I saw the answer beneath my feet.

"You know what a square is?" I asked my slow-to-learn young friend.

"Sure," he answered.

"Show me one. No, don't get out of your chair. Find one right where you are." He found an 8-x-8-inch floor tile in front of his toe. I gave him some chalk and had him outline it. Then I said, "Draw another square and make it two tiles wide."

He drew across the bottom of two tiles, up the side of one tile, hesitated, went up one more tile, and then completed the square.

"What shape is that?" I asked.

"A square."

"How wide is it?"

"Two tiles."

"How many tiles in your square?"

"Four."

"Ok. Now draw a square three tiles wide."

He did. And he told me it was three tiles wide, three tiles high, and contained nine tiles.

We moved some desks, which got us an audience, and moved on to a four-tile square.

"I got it," he yelled, "a five square would be 25 and a six would be. . . ."

Later we got some blocks from the kindergarten and discovered cubing. Two high, two wide, two deep—hey, there are eight blocks here!

At the end of the week a boy in the other sixth-grade class complained to his teacher, "Even Mr. Lee's dummies can square and cube."

"Read your book," she replied.

In social studies, my class was studying the influence of specialization on American industry. The book was a dull one. The author kept using the term *specialization,* but he never gave any examples.

"I wonder," I asked on a Friday afternoon as I had a beer with the coach, "if what works in arithmetic would work in social studies?"

"You can't use a football play in a basketball game," he replied.

It was lucky for me that I didn't believe him.

All day Saturday and Sunday were spent trying to work out a game that would give meaning to the written word, specialization. On Monday we played a game. It worked. Specialization was no longer just a five-syllable word. Now it had meaning. We could use it, apply it, and solve other problems with it. The class had discovered specialization, and I had discovered transfer of learning.

SIMULATING WITH WIDGETS

First, I told a little story. "Once upon a time, when most of the people in the United States lived along the Atlantic Ocean, most industry was called cottage industry. A lady sat in her cottage with her wool and her spinning wheel and. . . ."

My story wasn't completely accurate, but we established the idea of cottage industries. Then I told the class about widgets. There was a craze for widgets in those days. Anybody who was somebody had a widget. Anybody who wanted to become somebody had to own a widget. The market for widgets was a hot market. Naturally, in their little cottages, men and women began to make widgets.

Widgets are easy to make. You take three sheets of plain paper (I always swiped the paper out of the ditto machine). Stack the three sheets neatly.

Next, you mark three dots along one side of the paper. From either end, you put a dot at 1″, 5¼″, and 9½″.

Next, you punch a hole at each of the three dots.

Next, you slip a paper clip through the middle hole. This holds the widget sheets together.

Then, for decoration, you draw a star around each of the other two holes.

There, you now hold a finished widget in your hands. And believe me, the market for widgets is great. You can make more money on widgets than you can on Davy Crockett hats.

To play the game, put three desks and three chairs in front of the room. Move all other furniture, so everyone can see what will go on at the three front desks.

On each desk, put a stack of paper, a pile of paper clips, a one-hole paper punch, a ruler, and a pencil.

Pick three pupils to make widgets. Let them each make one for practice. Then let them make widgets for three minutes. Stop! Count the widgets for each pupil. Record the number of widgets on the chalkboard. Send the widgets to market.

Pick three more pupils. Let them make widgets for three minutes. Stop. Count. Record. Send to market.

Pick three more students. Ask if they can think of anyway they might make more widgets in the same amount of time. They shove the three desks together. The cottages become a factory, and they invent the assembly line—although they don't call it that. One pupil stacks and measures. One punches holes. One clips and draws stars. Let them make widgets for three minutes. Stop, count, and so on.

Now three more pupils come forward. They have analyzed the situation. The big job really is a matter of several small jobs:

1. counting out stacks of three sheets

2. measuring and marking the dots

3. punching the holes

4. clipping the center hole

5. starring the other two holes.

Those are the jobs to be done. They want five workers, not three. Each worker will do one special job. What? What was that word? *Special!* Where have we heard that word before? In *specialization?* You smile. They grin.

The five workers specialize. They turn out widgets like crazy. Stop, count, record, compare. The factory has produced slightly more widgets per man than did cottage industry.

Four more pupils come up. Why four, you ask? Because they have a new idea! They will punch out one sheet and use that sheet instead of marking holes. They will lay it on a stack of three sheets and punch through the holes in their special sheet. What was that word? *Special?* They have invented a special tool—a pattern—to help a *specialist* do his special job. The four make widgets, and the special tool proves its worth. The four have turned out more widgets per worker. And their total is even greater than that of the five-man group. They specialized. They invented and used a new tool. They cut a five-step job down to four steps.

What else can they do? The idea of invention grips them. Invent more new machines they shout! What? you shout back! A three-hole paper punch, they cry! I have one in my desk, you admit. So the three-hole punch is introduced and production goes up. The class demands a stapler and a rubber stamp. The stamp won't make stars, but they don't care. The new machines are thrown into the assembly line. What did you say? *Assembly line?* What's an assembly line? Patiently, as if to a younger child, the class explains an assembly line to you. You act surprised. Production skyrockets.

Then you discuss what they have been doing. *Specialization, invention, assembly line,* and other economic terms tumble out of their mouths. What are the advantages of specialization? What are the disadvantages? Of inventions? Of assembly lines?

Time to go home. The game is over. Taps. But look at all the stuff to put away. "Easy," says a pupil. "We'll specialize and have the room cleaned up in no time."

THE PRODUCTS OF SIMULATION

Does the game really work that well? It does, although you won't handle it as well the first time as you will the third or fourth time. And it works as low as grade three and as high as graduate seminars.

Is the game a real-life situation? No, but it is realistic. It simulates reality. In some ways the game is a better learning device than real life. It is neater, it can be shaped and handled to fit the abilities and temperament of any given group of students. Life is demanding, harsh, and inefficient. And most pupils approach life in a tentative, trial-and-error manner. Errors in a game don't make you bleed; life often does.

Nevertheless, games such as this produce learnings that apply to the outside world. What is learned in the simulated and arranged environment of the game can be transferred to the solution of problems that face the child alone or that he shares with adults in out-of-school life. How do we clean up our yard? How do we take care of ourselves until mother gets home from work? How do we get ready for our picnic trip? How do we get a clubhouse for our gang?

You don't have to play the game in one session, although that's the way I like best. If you can't get an hour and a half or two hours worked into your schedule, the game can be played over a three- or four-day period. Some teachers tell me that their pupils can't stay interested in anything for 90 minutes. Mine could, although I don't really know why. If yours can't, then break up the game over a number of days.

The game also has the advantage of spin-off learnings. The game leads to new games and other ideas and concepts. Gaming is used to discover meanings; that is to say, it is a device for the development of concepts. As I described this game, we focused on the concepts of *specialization, invention,* and *assembly line.* The activities built meanings for those concepts, and you will note carefully that the meanings developed *before* we put the name on the idea. Labeling something as *specialization* was not the key to learning. Building meanings was important; the name gave us a handle to use in our thinking and our talking. The name was shorthand for many bits of meaning that were clustered into a concept. Each pupil had his own concept, his own cluster of meanings. What they shared was some commonality of meaning and a label—*specialization*—that could be used in referring to those meanings. Concepts do not exist on paper, they live in a person's mind. Words exist on paper, they are symbols that refer to concepts that exist only when an individual has meanings for them.

What other ideas could be explored within the context of this game? How about *resources, labor, capital,* and *technology* as factors in *production?* The paper and paper clips were resources needed for production. The pupils were workers who provided labor. The ruler, pencil, and paper punch were capital goods used to produce consumer goods (widgets). The ideas of specialization and the assembly line were technological decisions.

How about *production, product, producing,* or *producer?* These terms, and the concepts behind them, are useful terms for analyzing any local business. Let's take the corner candy shop. What resources are needed? What labor? What technology? What capital? What are the products? Who is the producer? Are goods or services produced?

The game also spins off other games. How about a game on *standardization* and *interchangeability* of parts? (See Chapter 14.) How about a game on *discrimination* and *prejudice?* (All blue-eyed children are inferior.) How about a game on *legislative log-rolling?* (Some senators must compromise their votes to stay in office.) When you are done with this chapter, why don't you make up a game? Colonial smuggling can be done for U.S. history. Pass a law. Run a court. Operate a store.

MAKING UP A GAME

Games are fun, and sophisticated games are reasonable models of believable situations and events. Almost any actual social, political, or economic variable can be simulated. Admittedly, widgets aren't Fords and cigar bands aren't dollars, but widgets and scraps of paper can function as if they were real. In making the widget, the resources, labor, capital, and technology used aren't "real," but the players act as if they are. The roles of laborer, foreman, and time-and-motion specialist aren't "real," but they are realistic. The learnings, however, are real. Behaviors change during the game, and pupils have a chance to reflect on what they learned and why their behaviors changed.

Remember Miss Shepherd and her approach to slavery? In a sense, she was using a game. We got into her game because of a conflict of opinion and a too-ready acceptance of the validity of the printed word. We played unfamiliar roles and suffered unfamiliar emotions. We learned, and our behavior changed. After the game, we had a chance to reflect upon and talk about our experiences. And, in time, we had the opportunity to apply what we had learned in the case of the farm boy who had no shoes.

When I first used simulation and games in teaching my social-studies methods class, I worried that I wouldn't be covering as much material as I might have covered in a combination lecture and discussion. I mentioned this fear to a class one day after they had produced widgets. To my pleasant surprise, they disabused me about my concerns. They went over the list of subject-matter ideas built into the experience; they talked about the concepts (*capital,* in particular) they had extended; and they pointed out that the assembly line was a notion they had read about but never before experienced. Further, they hammered home the point that *all* of them had been involved *most* of the time; they patiently explained that, for the first time, they felt confident that they could run a game like the widget game in their own classrooms.

Building your own classroom games begins with the decision to emphasize a particular topic. I got into widgets simply because I found my students weren't developing reasonable meanings for the word *specialization,* even though they were reading about it constantly.

The second step is to analyze the actual operations of specialization. This calls for a bit of research and for a paring down of steps and activities. It would be too much to simulate specialization in the assembling of an actual car, so something simpler had to be found that would be a model requiring the use of prepared materials (a paper clip instead of a fender), of a processing skill (drawing a star instead of welding a seam), of preparing materials (punching holes instead of grinding down a weld), and of assembling the constituent parts. This second step is the one that bewilders some teachers. "Oh, I could never think of things like that!" they say. Actually, most of them can; they have just never tried.

The third step is asking yourself what concepts are related to the concept of specialization. That's easy: *assembly line, production, capital, labor, resources, technology, cooperation, invention, job analysis*—you can add to the list.

The fourth step is figuring out what materials are needed to play the game. These should be readily available, inexpensive, safe, and easily handled.

The fifth step is to play the game yourself. As you play each of the roles, talk aloud about what you are doing, and try to act as if you were an eight-year-old. This provides you with the chance to smooth out rough spots in the process and to think of questions you can ask if pupils seem stymied when they play the game.

The sixth step is to write down the rules for the game. Keep the rules to a minimum; keep each rule short but clear; and write for the proper readability level. In the case of widgets, the only rules had to do with the original construction of the widget and that a group couldn't stop during the assembly process and say, "We could do better if. . . ." The "better if" suggestion had to come from the next group to make widgets. Then each following group builds its performance on what they learned by watching.

The seventh step is to field test and revise your game. Try it out on a class, and note what goes right and what goes wrong. Keep what is right, and change the things that are wrong.

I am assuming that there is an eighth step. You will probably want to anticipate the nature of the discussion that follows the game and to plan for applying what has been learned to future situations.

Want to try your hand at games? Try these for size:

1. the need and origin of money
2. why families are needed
3. the value of interchangeable parts for machines
4. the buying and selling of food
5. preparing and delivering the six o'clock news on television.

SIMULATIONS AND GAMES

Technically, clear differences exist between simulations and games. Simulations are used for theory building, experimentation, and teaching. Simulations involve sound theory, adequate data, mathematical rules, and scientifically defined external variables. Simulations often require the use of desk calculators or computers. Games are used for learning and entertainment. The translation of real variables into game variables is loose (for example, the widget producers never resist the introduction of inventions to speed up production). Games require only a minimum of equipment, and the equipment is usually easy to operate.

Operationally, there isn't much difference between games and simulations for elementary-school use. The widget learners were experimenting and producing theory, but the variables were quite loosely defined. The major problem in using games as an educational term is its connotation of fun. In an uptight community, I'd ignore any real distinctions and use the term simulation, thus implying a connection between a school activity and science or business.

Computer Simulations

There are simulations (as opposed to games) for elementary-school pupils. The Massachusetts Institute of Technology's Artificial Intelligence Laboratory has developed a number of computer-controlled devices. One, called the Turtle, lets children draw geometric figures on the floor of their room. A computer-controlled music box lets children write music, listen to what they have written, and then vary its timing, pitch, and structure.

I can hear some teachers now, "My God, I don't believe him. Children can't use computers." Sorry, madam, but indeed they can. And so can you.

The usual image of the computer involves a series of large metal boxes with whirring tapes and a set of consoles with twinkling lights, all serviced by mathematical geniuses in pure-white smocks. This image is a compound of fear-inspired imagination and countless memories of NASA control centers during trips to the moon. Actually, if you use a computer at school, you will be miles from the computer, and your connection to it will be through a telephone line.

Come with me into your future:

We are in your classroom, or in a small room in your school. On a small desk is a telephone and a teletype. The teletype looks like a standard typewriter. You pick up the phone and dial the computer's number. When the connection is made, you hear an "answering" tone. You then place the telephone in a special coupler box on the side of your teletype. You now type out a message on the keyboard; the message passes through the telephone line to the computer: the computer responds, and its message is typed out on a print-out sheet that rolls out above the keyboard on your teletype. Is that difficult?

You do have to use a particular language, but humans and computers have several languages they share. One, called Basic, goes like this:

Comments on what you and the computer do	WHAT YOU READ ON PRINTOUT SHEET
To begin your conversation, you type	SIGN ON 1331,4
<u>Sign</u> <u>on</u> is like saying "hello"; 1331,4 is a budget code.	
The computer asks . . . . and you type in your codeword so the computer knows who to bill for its use	PASSWORD? PASSWORD? JONLEE

You want to use a simulation called MARKET, so you type . . .	FIND MARKET
The computer searches its memory, finds the program, and your teletype types	MARKET FOUND
You then type . . . . and the game begins.	RUN

Market is a simulation played by two people or two groups, each representing the decision makers of one of two competing bicycle companies. As the simulation begins, the computer states the fixed and variable production and marketing costs. A fixed cost would be the cost of making a bicycle, say, $20.00 per bike. A variable cost would be the amount you decide to spend on advertising, say, $300,000 for the first quarter of the year. The computer also states the number of bicycles you can expect to sell at a specific price with no advertising. Then the computer states how many bikes you have stored in inventory, how much cash you have on hand, and your total assets.

Each player (or group) then makes three decisions. How many bikes will they produce during the next year? How much will they spend on advertising? What will be the sale price of a bike? This information is typed in and the computer reports the results of the quarter in question.

The beauty of computer simulation is the extent of pupil involvement. If a pupil doesn't make a decision, nothing happens. Reflection on what has happened leads to a new set of decisions. The simulation is structured to encourage the pupil to ask a question: "What happens if I spend twice as much on advertising as my competitor does?" The pupil simply doubles his competitor's budget and finds out. If both manufacturers are selling bikes for about the same price, the effect of advertising is significant. But what if the pupil raises the advertising budget, while his competitor drops his sale price $15.00 per bike? Our pupil suddenly discovers the sets of connected relationships in the market. He now has the freedom to experiment actively, to use his knowledge of consequences to make new choices,

MARKET (Sample Output)*

PROFIT	% MARKET	CASH ON HAND	# SOLD	INVENTORY	ASSETS
641	50.61	8371	41	44	9251
605	49.39	7970	40	45	8870

UNITS AND DOLLARS BELOW ARE IN THOUSANDS

QUARTER 4

NEW LABOR CONTRACT – PRODUCTION COST NOW = $21/UNIT

*The MARKET simulation and these figures are from the work of Dr. Daniel L. Klassen of the Huntington II Computer Project at SUNY, Stony Brook, N.Y.

and to judge the utility of his choices by using the computer feedback as a record of his progress.

There are clear similarities between the widget game and the market simulation. The activity is visible, so pupils can observe and learn from each other. In both cases, the teacher is more of a coach than a transmitter of information. In both, a pupil can be wrong and try again without being "punished." And, in both, playing the game is a reward in itself.

Today, there are simulations for computer use by fifth through eighth grades. You can rerun any presidential election from 1828 to the present. You can try to eliminate malaria in India or flies in Nigeria. You can predict population growth for the next 50 years. In the next few years, the number of programs suitable for elementary-school use should grow steadily.

There is another use for computers in social studies. The computer is the fastest, most efficient data bank known. Facts—millions of facts—can be stored in the computer and retrieved whenever you wish and in whatever subject area you desire. For example, let's say you hypothesize that the ten leading corn-producing states are also the leading hog-producing states.

Corn	Order	Hogs
Illinois	1	Iowa
Iowa	2	Illinois
Indiana	3	Indiana
Minnesota	4	Missouri
Nebraska	5	Minnesota
Ohio	6	Nebraska
Missouri	7	Ohio
Wisconsin	8	Wisconsin
N. Carolina	9	S. Dakota
Kentucky	10	Kansas

The computer will rank-order the two sets of data for you in the time it takes to type out the answers on your print-out sheets.

Except for 9 and 10, the same states are on both lists. The computer can give you the number of bushels and number of hogs for each state. It can also, if you wish, calculate a correlation between corn and hog production and draw a graph of the correlation. You can sit and explore any sort of social, political, and economic relationships for which data are available. These data, of course, must be programmed for the computer, but that is no big problem. In fact, all that stands in the way of computer use in elementary schools is a few thousand dollars for the teletype and for your share of some computer's time.

My hunch is that you will use computers sometime in your near future. Don't be afraid to try them. They are one of the handiest tools we ever invented.

Board Games

Most of you have played Monopoly. The market today offers any number of board games for use with two or more pupils. Some of these are *zero-sum* games; that is, the winner's gains equal the loser's mistakes (as in tennis, chess, and other competitive games). The idea is to force or fool your opponent into an error. *Non-zero-sum* games are those that reward a player for his accomplishments rather than for the errors of others. As school is a form of zero-sum game itself, you should be careful about using too many zero-sum board games; there is no point in hammering some pupils deeper into a rut of failure.

Most board games are clearly competitive, certainly more so than Widgets or Market. Those two simulations had elements of competition, but the emphasis in each was in discovering the effects of making decisions and applying courses of action. ABT Associates produces a game called Neighborhood. Four teams compete in creating an ideal community in a period of urban-suburban growth. If the game is played merely to see which team "wins," then its use is virtually worthless. If, however, the game is played and replayed as a means of understanding the placement of residential, commercial, and industrial areas as forms of relationships, then the game is highly worthwhile.

Bibliographical Sampler

Baldicer. John Knox Press, P.O. Box 1176, Richmond, VA, 23209. ($20.) Grade 5+. Feeding the world's population.

Ghetto. Western Publishing Company, Inc., 150 Parish Dr., Wayne, NJ, 07470. ($24.) Grade 5+. Life in a ghetto.

Market. Benefic Press, 10300 W. Roosevelt Rd., Westchester, IL, 60153. ($15.) Grade 5+. Buying and selling food.

Neighborhood. ABT Associates, Inc., 55 Wheeler St., Cambridge, MA, 02138. ($16.) Grade 3+.

Pink Pebbles. Education Ventures, Inc., 209 Court St., Middleton, CT, 06457. ($8.) Grade 5+. Origin and need for money.

Starpower. Simile II, P.O. Box 1023, La Jolla, CA, 92037. ($25.) Grade 5+. Building a society and the uses of power.

Supreme Court. Leswing Communications, 150 Adrian Way, San Rafael, CA, 94903. ($7.) Grade 5+. Appealing a court case.

System I. I.S.I., 2147 University Ave., St. Paul, MN, 55114. ($10.) Grade K+. Learning to classify.

S/G/N. Simulation/Gaming/News, Box 8899, Stanford University, Stanford, CA, 94305. ($4 for five issues.) For teachers. A newspaper on simulation and gaming; well worth the money!

PLAY AND LEARNING

There are teachers who believe learning to be such a serious academic business that play can have no possible value for learning. They didn't play when they were in school. They sat up straight, kept both feet on the floor, and never, never smiled except in response to praise from their teacher.

Good teachers, good parents, and children know better. The basic process of early learning is a mixture of observation and imitation. How does a child learn to talk? By reading about talking? By being told about talking? By attending formal lessons about talking? Of course not. The child listens and imitates what he hears. The pattern is heavily trial and error, but out of many trials comes progress. The child imitates pronunciation, inflection, vocabulary, word order—the whole verbal bag.

The growing child observes many activities and he imitates most of them. A child imitates his father, his mother, and any older brothers and sisters. When he begins to have frequent contact with other people—adult or child—he begins to learn from them.

When groups of children are together, they play. They explore their environment and the objects in their environment. They explore each other. They act and react. They play games, and in many of those games they play at imitating adults. They dress up and act the way they have seen adults act. They play house and store and school. They play astronaut and fireman and sometimes doctor. They play with older children and they learn certain rules for games and they learn the penalties for breaking the rules. They learn about strength and weakness, about kind people and bullies, about being part of the group and being an isolate.

The plain fact of the matter is that people learn by playing. Play is not a waste of time, but an effective means of learning. Of course, play is like ice cream. You can get too much of a good thing. School shouldn't be all play, because there are other ways human beings learn. But play is a useful tool for the elementary teacher. Play simulates adult activities. Games simulate adult situations. The teacher who fails to utilize games and play is an incomplete teacher—and probably a crab, as well.

Johan Huizinga has written a book claiming that, among other things, man is *homo ludens,* a playing animal. Human beings like to play. Play brings pleasure. Play is its own reward. Play is also a means to any number of ends, and one of them is learning.

SUMMARY

Simulations and games are models of actual or hypothetical events and settings. As models they are simpler than the real thing, but they resemble reality enough to produce valid, reliable results. Games call for decision making by the participants; educational games go one step further and ask the learner to reason out why certain consequences flow from certain decisions.

Games can be used to reach any sort of legitimate goal from simple skill building to valuing. Concepts can be formed; generalizations can be drawn; hypotheses can be tested. Games also lead to further research in other sources and they require some degree of cooperation and self-discipline among pupils.

Games can be purchased from commercial sources or they can be made up by teachers. In the elementary grades, teacher-made games require a minimum of equipment and expense. Computer simulations are still relatively unknown in elementary schools, but the next decade should see rather widespread use of computer simulations.

Play is a natural human activity, one of the natural ways we have for learning. The experience of learning through a form of play has any number of attractions for pupils, including the fact that you learn as much "subject matter" as you do in far less interesting methods.

SUGGESTED READINGS

Inbar, Michael and Clarice S. Stall, *Simulation and Gaming in Social Science.* New York: The Free Press, 1972. (Case studies demonstrating methods for designing and using simulations for teaching, experimentation, and theory-building.)

Nesbitt, William A., *Simulation Games for the Social Studies Classroom.* New York: Crowell, 1971. (Introduction to simulations; good but old bibliography.)

Raser, John R., *Simulation and Society.* Boston: Allyn & Bacon, 1969. (Excellent little paperback; a reasoned examination of simulation.)

Zuckerman, David W. and Robert E. Horn, *The Guide to Simulations/Games for Education and Training.* Information Resources, P.O. Box 417, Lexington, MA 02173. ($15.00. Annotated bibliography of simulations in all fields; excellent information on each game. This book should be in every library.)

"Abbreviated Games and Simulation Guide." *Social Education,* November, 1972. Write the Social Science Education Consortium, Inc., Boulder, CO 80302 for a copy. (Very helpful and detailed information on games.)

EXERCISES

1. Take an idea like specialization, which can be demonstrated as a process, and work out a simple game for developing meaning for the idea. Imitate the specialization example in this chapter.

2. Go back to Chapter 14, and review the unit on standardization. Work out the details of the standardization game mentioned there.

3. Make a brief list of possible simulations for use in the elementary grades. For example:

Social	*Political*	*Economic*
Planning a home	Constitutional	Bartering
Communicating accurately	Convention	Banking
Etc.	Passing a law	Etc.
	Etc.	

4. Use the library to build a bibliography of journal articles on computer simulation for the elementary grades. (This is a small group activity and the product should be shared with the class.)

5. Locate someone on your campus who uses digital computers. Get that person to show the class how easy it is to use a teletype.

Case Studies and Mock Trials

The law deals with three major questions. Who is to decide? To whom does it belong? Who is to blame? If you examine the courses offered in law schools, you discover that the question of *deciding* is the province of politics and procedure. The question of *ownership* is the province of property and contracts. The question of *blame* is the province of torts and criminal law.

Behind these questions and courses lies a more basic question: What is right and just? Each of the questions, including the basic question, is answered differently by different persons. These are questions of conflict, and the parties who argue different answers are adversaries. The purpose of law is dealing with the resolution of conflict in a reasonable manner, so that people may live in peace with one another.

The law deals with conflict, because men and women can and do disagree over things of value to them. Two men can want, and then claim, the same land or car or woman. The two men can fight over the object of value, and each will blame the other for the fight. If no one interferes in the fight and if the two are equally persistent, one will die and the other will try to hold the object against others who come to cherish it. The intent of the law is to resolve such conflicts, so that the two parties will no longer dispute the question in a manner threatening to them or disturbing to others in the community. The dispute must be settled in a reasonable manner, so that the decision can be accepted by the disputing parties and can be approved of by the community. To ensure these conditions of acceptance and approval, the law must be seen as legitimately authoritative and coercively powerful. If the two parties see the law as authority, they will obey it voluntarily; if they do not, then the political community has the power to compel obedience.

Even when the law is obeyed, the decision by law is not always acceptable to one party and it is not always approved by members of the community. In such cases, the questions of rightness and justice arise. People may agree that a decision was legal but may disagree as to whether justice prevailed or the right thing was done. Fortunately, the law, like all human endeavors, changes. An examination of split-decision cases and reversed cases by the Supreme Court indicates clearly that law is the product of changes in human opinion and reasoning. The law may change for better or for worse, but over time and in the main, people seek right and just laws and right and just decisions by law.

In law schools, especially in the first year, instruction in case studies is dealt with in a manner known as the *case method*. The professor asks, "In your own words, Ms. Dye, state the rule in *Gibbons* v. *Ogden*." From Ms. Dye's response, the professor then leads her through a Socratic dialogue in analyzing the Supreme Court decision.

Before Ms. Dye came to class, she had read and analyzed a number of appellate-court decisions on the regulation of commerce. Among them was *Gibbons* v. *Ogden*. The notes below are those made by Ms. Dye in briefing the case.

Parties:

> *Gibbons* v. *Ogden*
> 9 Wheaton 1: 6 L.Ed 23 (1824)

Facts:

1. Exclusive *navigation* rights to all water in New York State given by state statute to Livingston and Fulton.

2. Livingston and Fulton assigned Ogden the rights to navigation between New York City and New Jersey ports.

3. Gibbons had two steamships operating between N.Y.C. and Elizabethtown, N.J.

4. Gibbons licensed to do this under act of Congress.

5. Ogden got an injunction to make Gibbons stop. Gibbons appealed.

6. Ogden's argument: The State of New York had right to regulate navigation, no matter who has right to regulate commerce.

7. Gibbons' argument: Congress, under Art. I, Sec. 8, U.S. Constitution, has the *sole* power to regulate commerce among states.

Issue:

Whether state regulations on commerce violate Art. I Sec. 8 of the U.S. Constitution.

Decision:

No. Gibbons win. Ogden loses.

Reasoning:

(Chief Justice Marshall)

1. Commerce means buying, selling, or exchanging goods or services.

2. Commerce includes the acts and instruments of exchange.

3. Navigation is an instrument of commerce.

4. The right of Congress to regulate commerce among states includes right to regulate navigation.

5. The New York statute conflicts with the commerce clause of the Constitution and thus is unconstitutional.

Ms. Dye is now prepared to identify the case, specify the issue, and report the decision. The professor who asks her about *Gibbons* v. *Ogden* uses her response to force her to argue through a number of legal problems. Here, her memory of the facts of the case, of the arguments of the attorneys, and of the reasoning of the court permit her to think and talk like a lawyer.

What has all this comment about law to do with elementary social studies? Simple. Jurisprudence is the latest social science to contribute to social-studies content, and the use of cases has spread through the upper elementary grades with great rapidity.

CASES IN THE ELEMENTARY SCHOOL

The case study provides the teacher with a classroom activity combining orthodox and progressive elements of instruction. My observations over the past half-dozen years indicate that cases are probably the single most effective new teaching new teaching procedure with fourth through eighth graders. Pupils clearly build understandings from cases, and there is considerable evidence that cases influence attitudes and overt behaviors in highly favorable ways.

A case can be short or long, it can be historical or contemporary. It can deal with a grand principle or with the most fleeting of relevant problems. But the real beauty of a case is that pupils must respond to it by reasoning rather than by memorizing or identifying an answer. The pupil must infer his or her answer from a variety of facts and from his or her own ideas about right and wrong. Consider this short case:

> Tom Faraday lives in a neighborhood zoned for residential housing. Each house sits on a half-acre lot, and the houses are expensive. Tom, who owns a junkyard, begins storing junk behind his garage. His neighbors complain to him. Tom says he isn't selling the junk at his home, he is just storing it there.
>
> 1. Do you think Tom has a right to do this? Why or why not?

This obviously isn't a case apt to get to the Supreme Court, but note the similarities between it and the case Ms. Dye briefed. The *parties* are Tom and his neighbors. The *facts* are: (1) the neighborhood is zoned for residential use; (2) Tom is storing junk in a residential neighborhood; (3) the neighbors want Tom to move the junk; (4) Tom says he has a right to store but not sell junk at his home.

If the class is free to express any opinion (and they should be!) you will find some arguing for Tom and some for the neighbors. Before long, the class will identify the *issue* as whether storing junk is a commercial or residential function. Those favoring the neighbors will point out that warehouse or outdoor storage is a part of business and business is commerce, so Tom is wrong. These pupils will then seek evidence to back up their argument. They will look at what can be seen in their residential area. They will phone an uncle in business to ask his opinion. They will ask their parents. Some bright pupil may call the zoning board.

What is important here is that pupils are identifying facts, separating relevant from irrelevant facts, stating an issue, and reasoning with facts about the issue. They are doing this in an atmosphere where the teacher is *not* saying "Good" or "Yes, I agree" or even nodding her head. It is not important that a pupil please his teacher with his answer. It is important for the pupil to support his own views with logic and facts, and to do this in the face of a spirited attack against his position by others.

When cases are first introduced into the classroom, the shock is sometimes too great for the teacher and some pupils. The rigid authoritarian has a terrible time with situations where the answer isn't fixed, where closure doesn't occur, and where her dogmas aren't accepted as truth. Some pupils have never thought actively and independently; they prefer being told what to think. Unfortunately, the authoritarian teacher is apt to remain authoritarian unless she gets outside help. The pupil who has accepted being dominated by authority, however, can overcome his anxiety over divergent thinking if a teacher brings him along through skillful questioning and rewards him for taking an independent stand.

Some cases are moral dilemmas. Consider this one.

> Bill Ping lived on the frontier before his area was made a territory. When he found two of his three horses had been stolen, he set out to catch the rustler. It took him two days to catch and capture the rustler.
>
> It was a three-day ride to the nearest small town. There was no lawman or jail in the town. The rustler told Bill, "You'll never get me to town. You'll have to sleep sometime. When you do, I'll kill you and get away."
>
> Bill tied a short rope to a branch of a big cottonwood tree. The rustler was still on his horse, which was eating grass under the tree.
>
> Bill made a loop in the end of the rope and put it over the rustler's head. Then Bill laid down and went to sleep.
>
> When Bill woke up the rustler was hanging dead from the tree. To get to more grass, the horse had walked out from under the rustler.
>
> 1. Who hanged the rustler, Bill or the horse?
>
> 2. Did Bill have a right to do what he did? Why or why not?
>
> 3. What would you have done?

This case leads pupils to discover the multiple meanings of the word *right*. There is the legally right, the morally right, and the practically right.

In this case, there was no territorial or state law to consider. Pupils have to debate the morality of killing and the right of an individual to kill as a practical solution to a difficult problem. (This is the same sort of dilemma you find in *Billy Budd* or *The Oxbow Incident*.) The case also requires some research to set it in an historical context.

The zoning case was adapted for fourth graders from an actual municipal case. The Bill Ping case is imaginary and taken from an old western anecdote. A case can deal with legal procedure, as well as with ownership rights and questions of blame. For example:

> Richard Carlisle published a paper in the 1800's in England. His paper backed up some workers who stood for their rights. He was arrested and tried for writing the article.
>
> The jury did not think he was guilty. The judge did. The judge wouldn't let the jury have anything to eat or drink. He wouldn't let them out to sleep. He said he would keep things that way until the jury found Mr. Carlisle guilty.
>
> The jury finally gave in and said Carlisle was guilty. The judge sentenced Mr. Carlisle to pay a big fine and to spend two years in prison.
>
> 1. Was this a fair trial? Why or why not?
> 2. What is a judge supposed to do?
> 3. What is a jury supposed to do?
> 4. On what should a jury base its decision?
> 5. How is a jury a third party to a dispute?

In this case, what Carlisle did isn't as important as the behavior of the judge. He ignored the evidence and the law of the land, and wanted Carlisle judged on the basis of personal prejudice. The last question is useful because it makes three points. The two parties to the case are adversaries presenting their positions and arguments to an impartial third party, the jury. The jury, to be impartial, must base its decision only on the evidence presented and on existing law. A jury is supposed to be a sample of the adult population of a community; as humans, the members believe in the norms of their society and therefore may bring these norms into their decision.

Most of us agree that our court system isn't working well at this moment. Some people therefore argue there is no good reason to teach about law and the courts. My own position is contrary to the defeatist view. Neither our law nor our courts have ever been perfect. History clearly reveals that both have been used more ruthlessly against the common welfare in the past than they are used today. The youngster growing up today with a sound knowledge of the purpose of the law may as an adult be concerned to move the law away from imperfection. In the recent Watergate affair, the Department of Justice and the courts performed far better than the executive or legislative branches of our government. The law may be a burden to be borne, but our backs would be bent even more without any law.

To my knowledge, the recent interest in legal cases for elementary pupils began with Charles Quigley and Robert Ratcliffe. Quigley, an elementary teacher, churned out a number of cases on an old duplicating machine in his garage. The cases became widely used with great success in California, and then were published commercially. I have used his casebook with fourth- through eighth-grade pupils and can recommend it highly. The reference is:

Quigley, Charles N., *Your Rights and Responsibilities as an American Citizen: A Civics Casebook*. Boston: Ginn, 1967. (An excellent teacher's guide is also available.)

Professor Robert Ratcliffe, as director of the Law in American Society Foundation, led a group of lawyers, law professors, historians, political scientists, educators, and master teachers in producing two series of casebooks. The first is the Trailmarks of Liberty, the second is Urban Justice. The Trailmark series includes *Law in a New Land* (upper-elementary grades), *Great Cases of the Supreme Court* (junior-high grades), and *Vital Issues of the Constitution* (senior-high grades). Urban Justice can be used anywhere from eighth through twelfth grades. All are available, with teacher's guides, from the Houghton Mifflin Company, 110 Tremont Street, Boston, MA 02107.

Another highly useful resource is *Law in American Society,* the journal of the National Center for Law-Focused Education. It is free and it is great! Write to the Law in American Society Foundation, Suite 1700, 33 N. La Salle St., Chicago, IL 60602. The May, 1973, special issue on children was a gem—they may still have some in stock.

There are all sorts of reasons why teachers should consider using cases with elementary pupils. My reasons focus on what happens to the youngsters. First, the procedure recognizes the pupil as a social being—as one who does and will spend his life among others. The procedure offers opportunities to learn how to live among others who seek ends in conflict with those of the pupil. Second, the pupil learns to form his own ideas, to make his own decisions, and to express both in his own words. Third, the cases require a pupil to examine his values constantly—he must keep asking what would be best for all of us. Fourth, the pupil realizes that knowledge is a form of power. The abilities to tackle a problem, break it down, sort out the facts, reason on what is known, arrive at a decision, and be willing to act on it, all require knowledge and effort. Fifth, the pupil becomes capable of transforming data and ideas into intelligent action.

THE MOCK TRIAL

A mock trial usually consists of three sequential segments. They are preparation, simulation, and evaluation; sometimes these are called briefing, trying, and debriefing the case.

Preparation begins when you decide on a case to be played out in a mock trial. Certain characters are specified in the case, and someone must play each part. You will also need certain court personnel. Some of the pupils playing these roles will need a day or two to prepare themselves. For a civil trial, you will need:

Plaintiff
> The person who accuses a second party of doing or not doing something; the plaintiff is the person who asked the court to hear the case. (In a criminal trial a prosecutor brings the case to court for the government.)

Defendant
> The person accused by the plaintiff; in a sense, he is in court against his will.

Plaintiff's Attorney
> He tries to prove the accusation is true. He makes an opening statement to the jury; in this opening, he describes the case and summarizes the relevant facts from the plaintiff's point of view.

Defendant's Attorney
> He makes the second opening statement in which he denies the plaintiff's accusation or tries to show the defendant had

good reason to do what he did. He summarizes the relevant facts from the defendant's point of view.

Witnesses

They may be called by the defendant or the plaintiff. They may testify only to what they perceived directly; they cannot discuss their beliefs or what they heard others say they heard or saw. In a mock trial, they must stick to the facts laid out in the case.

Judge

The judge keeps order in the courtroom, gives instructions to the jury, and explains the law to the jury.

Jury

Usually 6 to 12 persons; in most states the jury's decision must be unanimous, but this varies by type of case and by state. Their task is to determine who the facts favor under the law.

The two attorneys need time to get their facts and arguments arranged. The judge needs time to check on the law involved. And the parties to the case and the witnesses need time to get their stories straight. These people are contacted privately and are asked not to discuss the case with the class until the trial. I usually draw a jury randomly on the day of the trial.

The simulation follows a set, but simplified, procedure. There are nine steps:

1. Opening the court

2. Swearing in the jury

3. Opening statement by plaintiff's attorney

4. Opening statement by defendant's attorney

5. Direct examination of witnesses

6. Cross-examination of witnesses

7. Closing argument by defendant's attorney

8. Closing argument by plaintiff's attorney

9. Instructions to the jury; deliberation; verdict.

For more information on procedure, a good source is the teacher's guide for *Law in a New Land* (Boston: Houghton Mifflin, 1972), pp. 29–36. Another helpful item is *Twice the Price and Oog and Ugh,* a carrousel slide presentation with narration on a cassette tape. This presents two stories intended for use in mock trials and spends some time on the actors and their roles. (Order from the Law in American Society Foundation, Suite 1700, 33 N. La Salle St., Chicago, IL 60602.)

Evaluation, or debriefing, is perhaps the most important part of the mock-trial technique. Strangely enough, some teachers skip this segment. The intent of debriefing is the clarification of ideas and actions. Certainly, pupils will have some questions about the substantive and procedural matters making up the trial. These lead to research, and the answers found lead to more sophisticated and accurate mock trials in the future. Debriefing also provides the opportunity to organize what has been learned and to predict when these new learnings will be useful. Some helpful debriefing questions are:

1. Which roles were played convincingly? What made them convincing?

2. Which roles would you have played differently? Why?

3. Of what was the defendant accused? What law was said to have been broken?

4. What was the issue? For what reasons do you believe this to be the issue?

5. Did either side fail to present facts that should have helped them?

6. How sound were the arguments for the defense? For the plaintiff? How could you improve on them?

7. Do you agree or disagree with the decision? Why?

8. Are there grounds for an appeal?

In considering the last question, remember that there are both trial and appeals courts. In a trial court (civil or criminal) someone is accused of breaking a law; the decision must be related to some law. In an appeals court, no one is on trial, but the decision handed down in a trial court is being appealed. In a sense, the law or courtroom procedure are on trial in an appeals court. One judge, or a panel of judges, hear the appeals; they decide whether the law involved was constitutionally correct.

If you doubt your ability to handle a mock trial of the sort described, you might try a pro se mock trial. The pro se (pro-say) court is held for the person who can't afford an attorney and who can't spend days in court. The pro se (or small claims) court deals only with civil cases involving $300 or less. The trial date is set for six weeks after you file a suit. No party to the trial needs a lawyer, although either party can bring one if the state law permits. Actually, a lawyer can be a liability, because these judges like to hear a person tell his own story in his own words. Most cases are heard by the judge, although the defendant can ask for a jury trial—and if he asks for a jury, he gets one immediately.

The best preparation for a pro se mock trial is for you alone or for you and your class to visit a pro se court. Chances are you will be amazed and delighted at what you see and hear. There are only four steps to this type of mock trial:

1. The plaintiff presents his case.

2. The defendant presents his case.

3. The judge asks questions.

4. The judge makes a decision and explains his reasoning.

The babysitting case that follows will give you an idea of the simplicity of the pro se mock trial.[1]

Facts:

1. The plaintiff is a babysitter.

2. The defendant is a parent.

3. The plaintiff agreed to babysit for the defendant's two children for 50¢ per hour. When the babysitter arrived, there was a third child, a cousin, present. The plaintiff said nothing about an increased rate at that time. But, when the defendant returned home two hours later, the plaintiff demanded 75¢ per hour, claiming the rate to be 25¢ per hour per child. The defendant refused to pay the additional 25¢ per hour. The plaintiff sued.

Issue:

Is the plaintiff entitled to the additional 25¢ per hour?

Decision:

From the facts, it appears the plaintiff had agreed to babysit for 50¢ per hour. When the plaintiff arrived on the job and saw an additional child, he did not say he wanted more money. The plaintiff had never told the defendant that he expected 25¢ per child when they made the agreement. It was, therefore, unfair for the plaintiff to demand this amount after the fact. The defendant understood that the charge was 50¢ per hour and not 25¢ per child per hour. To give the 25¢ additional fee per hour would be unfair to the defendant. Judgment for the defendant.

For a mock trial, you can divide the class up into groups of four—plaintiff, defendant, judge, and an observer-reporter. Each group of four holds its own pro se trial, then the reporters discuss the reasoning and decision of the judges with the entire class.

The debriefing of the pro se court shouldn't take long. Still, it is important. The basic questions are:

1. What was the issue in the case?

2. What new or different facts would be needed to change the decision?

3. Was the decision fair?

4. Was the judge's reasoning clear?

If you begin with the pro se mock trial, it makes it somewhat easier for pupils (and for you) to shift to a regular civil or criminal court procedure. The difficulty in beginning with the pro se court rests with our lack of familiarity with it. It is worth your looking into—who knows, you might want to have your own day in court with some heartless landlord.

The advantages in using the mock trial are multiple. Trials deal with interesting subject matter, and participation in a trial calls for keen thinking and clear valuing. Everyone participates, everyone gets involved, everyone learns. Each pupil, in the trial and in the debriefing, must form his own opinions and conclusions. Watch how they fare in the give and take of open discussion. Each pupil must listen to and think about the opinion of others. Each must identify points of agreement and disagreement with his own views. In all of this intellectual and emotional rough and tumble, you can identify what a pupil really thinks and feels. Knowing this, you can plan how you want to attempt to influence a pupil's reasoning and valuing processes.

USING A CASE OR A MOCK TRIAL

Teachers always say they wish they knew more law, but the elementary teacher can use cases without too much apprehension. For one thing, local bar associations will always help the teacher if a sticky point arises in the discussion of cases. For another, there is usually a lawyer on the school board, and if there isn't, every school board retains legal counsel. So, advice and help are generally only a phone call away.

To be effective in the elementary school, cases must be presented and discussed in an open-ended manner. Each pupil must be free—completely free—to arrive at his own conclusion. This frightens some teachers, for teachers tend to believe every question (every school question, at least) has one correct answer. In the law, there is always an answer—but that answer is always subject to two limitations. First, not all judges agree that the answer given to a legal problem is *the* right answer. If they did all believe alike, then there would be no "split decision" or dissenting opinions by Supreme Court justices. Second, judges die or retire and are replaced from time to time. A new court may well reverse the findings of an earlier court. If judges can't always agree, why should we expect all the pupils in a classroom to always agree?

The teacher can expect pupils to get their facts straight, to cite any known precedents, to reason with accuracy. But the teacher can't expect every pupil to arrive at the same conclusion at the same time. In great part, that's the way cases excite and interest children—because *they* get to do the reasoning, to arrive at the conclusions, and to take their own positions on important matters.

Quite often, the use of cases and mock trials leads to an interest in pupil-developed and pupil-enforced classroom rules. There is no good reason why pupils shouldn't make and enforce most of the rules they live by, but you must remember one axiom: rule making is not transmitted genetically. Children have to learn to make rules in the same way they learn other elements of our culture. I have seen many well-intentioned teachers tell kids to make rules. The kids do, and many of their rules fail. Then the teacher says, "Too bad! I guess I'll just have to make the rules myself."

To begin with, you should expect some pupil-made rules to be bad and to work badly. Why not? Are all adult-made rules good? Do all your rules function perfectly? Making some bad rules should be a first-rate learning experience. Why doesn't the rule work? What went wrong? How can we change the rule so it will work? Are there any standards for judging the worth and utility of a rule?

This last question usually poses the greatest problem for the teacher. There is a set of standards, derived originally by the law profession. These have been used with great success in many elementary classrooms. These standards are:

1. Pupils who are supposed to live by the rule should know the rule exists.
2. Rules should be understandable to the pupils who are expected to follow them.
3. Rules should not be changed so much that pupils can't keep up with the changes.
4. Rules should not say to do something and also not to do it.
5. Rules should not tell pupils to do something they cannot do.
6. Rules should not make something done in the past a crime if it was not a crime before the rule was passed.

And there are certain standards for those who enforce rules:

1. People who enforce rules should obey the rules.
2. People who enforce rules should only enforce the rules they were chosen to enforce.

Two of the best sources for help with this general topic are Robert H. Ratcliffe, "Trial on the Moon," pages 1–25 of *Law in a New Land,* and Charles N. Quigley, "A Children's Island," pages 2–7 of *Your Rights and Responsibilities as an American Citizen.* Both of these materials for pupils adopted the ideas of Lon Fuller's *Morality and the Law.*

There are usually a few pupils who seem to take antisocial positions. They say, "It's ok to steal." At least their attitude is now out in the open. It's my experience that the other pupils now begin to work on these characters. If robbery and theft cases pop up from time to time during the year, it's my observation that the antisocial views begin to be modified. The arguments of the peer group begin to have a positive effect. The "it's ok to steal" pupil has to defend his position; he usually has to agree that if it's right for him to steal, it's also right for others to steal from him. That is a difficult position to defend, so there is a tendency for change.

Don't misunderstand me, I'm not saying that thieves reform if you use cases. I am saying that thieves have to think about reasons for stealing, and some of them probably do stop. The chances are you never got anyone to stop stealing by just saying, "Stealing is bad, so don't steal." The chances are, on the other hand, that pupils do influence pupils—and with cases, pupils are supposed to do the discussing and arguing. Your jobs are picking good cases, asking good questions, and looking inscrutable.

Some teachers look at a book of cases and say, "Great, but my kids can't read them." Well, you can read can't you? Or you can have five or six pupils read to small groups. Cases for pupils are usually brief, so they can sit through the oral reading. Anyway the bulk of the time ought to go to thinking and discussing. Enough said?

Teachers often like to write their own cases, particularly because they can thus stress issues they feel their pupils ought to be considering. If you write your own cases, be sure to include the background material necessary for the pupils to understand the case. This can be historical, geographical, or sociological. The important thing is that the pupil be able to put the case into some meaningful framework.

Whatever the structure of your case (drama, narrative, and so on), try to keep it short and well-paced, so that it will hold your pupils' attention. Try to be as unbiased as possible in your presentation of materials. Do not lead the pupils to a desired conclusion.

Be sure to give the arguments that form the basis for making a decision in the case. If the case culminates in a court trial, you will want to give the arguments for both the plaintiff and the defendant. If there is no court trial, as in some literary cases, you may only be able to present the arguments of the plaintiff. Keep the vocabulary at the class reading level—the simpler the better. If new terms are necessary to the case, be sure these terms are defined either in an introduction or in explanatory phrases. Limit the questions at the end of the case to four or five which will provoke a good discussion. Be sure to include a question requiring a statement of the issue involved in the case and a question requiring the student to tell how he would have decided the case on the basis of the issue and the facts.

SUMMARY

Who is to blame? To whom does it belong? Who is to decide? These are the basic questions of law. They rest on the more fundamental questions of what is right and just. Thus, the law deals with conflicts between people and between ideas. As opinion and reasoning in the society change, so will the law change. All change is not progress, but the historical thrust of the law has been progressively in favor of the general welfare.

The case study and the Socratic dialogue are favored methods in law schools. Over the past few years cases have been used in more and more elementary schools. Cases obviously contain subject matter; reasoning about issues requires both facts and logic; and the adversary flavor of cases influences attitudes and values. Pupils find themselves caught up in arguing point of view in cases—the case seems to be self-motivating for many pupils. The cases are social activities. They deal with people and their problems, and pupils must deal with other pupils in using case materials. There are no set answers to cases, so pupils must make up their own minds about issues. And pupils learn to express themselves clearly and convincingly if they want their ideas to influence others.

The mock trial is a simulated court scene where a case is tried and a decision is reached. It is even more active than the simple use of a case. The discussion following a mock trial has all the advantages of case discussion. Research may grow out of debriefing as pupils feel a need for more information about laws or courtroom procedures. The actively engaged pupil reveals his most deeply held ideas and feelings in discussing a case or a trial. You can gain insights into pupils in ways you would never touch on in ordinary reading and reciting. Even though your roles are those of the guide, the clarifier, and the prod, you will be amazed at what you learn about your ideas and feelings when you use cases.

NOTE

1.   Arlene Gallagher and Elliot Hartstein, "Pro Se Court: A Simulation Game." *Law in American Society,* vol. II, no. 2, May, 1973, p. 29. By permission of the Law in American Society Foundation.

SUGGESTED READINGS

Black, Henry C., *Black's Law Dictionary*. St. Paul, Minn.: West Publishing Co., 1968. (Find it in your library, it will clear up many questions.)

Fuller, Lon L., *The Morality of Law*. New Haven, Conn.: Yale University Press, 1969. (This book gives you a great set of criteria for judging the worth of laws. Most writers of elementary law cases borrow from Fuller.)

Sanders, Norris M., *Classroom Questions: What Kind?* New York: Harper &

Row, 1966. (The techniques of asking questions are beautifully laid out in this paperback; you ought to own this book.)

Wormser, Rene A., *The Story of the Law*. New York: Simon & Schuster, 1962. (A paperback overview of the law throughout history.)

Zelemeyer, William, *Process of Legal Reasoning*. Englewood Cliffs, N.J.: Prentice-Hall, 1963. (This paperback describes, in detail, legal reasoning from a trial through a final appeal.)

EXERCISES

1. Visit a pro se courtroom and bring back three or four cases for a mock trial with your classmates.

2. Get a copy of Quigley's *Civics Casebook* or Ratcliffe's *Law in a New Land*. Let someone role-play a teacher while five or six of your classmates role-play fifth graders. Use two or three cases.

3. Read Robert M. O'Neil, "An Approach to Teaching the Bill of Rights," *Teachers College Record,* vol. 65, no. 3, December, 1963, pp. 272–79. This article is excellent background for your own use of cases. Type up an abstract for your classmates.

4. Try your hand at writing a case or two. Use the *Civics Casebook* or *Law in a New Land* as a model for length, structure, and readability. Try the cases out on your classmates or friends. It's a great change of pace from bridge.

Role Playing

Bob:	"Come on, let's play ball!"
Tom:	"Bill and Chico can choose up teams. Flip for first pick."
Bill:	"I take heads."
Chuck:	"It's my ball. I get to be a captain, or I go home. No ball, no ball game."
Bill:	"Ok, you can take my place as captain."
Tom:	"No, he can't. He's always pulling that stuff. Let's just take his ball. He can play, but he can't go home until the game is over."
Chuck:	"I'll tell my mom on you. And she'll call your mom."
Tom:	"How'd you like a punch in the nose? How'd you like that, you sissy?"

The scene and dialogue above have been acted out on a thousand playgrounds by tens of thousands of boys. Sometimes conflict is avoided, and the game goes on. Sometimes Chuck gets his punch in the nose, and his mother calls Tom's mother. Sometimes the mothers get into such a verbal battle that the two boys are forbidden to play with each other long after the basis for the original dispute is forgotten.

THE NATURE OF ROLE PLAYING

Each of us has played our little roles in similar mini-dramas. Each of us has learned or failed to learn from our confrontations. We learned when we reflected on what we did and said and on the effect of our words or acts on others. We learned when we reflected on how we felt about the words and acts of others. We failed to learn when we failed to reflect.

When you take a part in a play, you act out a role that contributes to a sense of drama. This drama centers on nature or on the differences between individuals and ideas. At some point in the drama, conflict erupts during a confrontation of opposing forces. The conflict heightens with the reactions of individuals to each other during the confrontation. The purpose of drama is clarification of an individual's relationship with himself, his society, or his environment.

Role playing, as a means of learning, also has its actors and roles, its dramatic situations and confrontations. But there are differences between acting and role playing. In role playing, the participant must always improvise, for he has no set lines to speak. In role playing, the audience can always rewrite the final scene to its own satisfaction.

If you wanted to have pupils role-play the earlier scenario on softball, you would go about it in roughly this way. *You would construct a dramatic situation setting the scene for conflict.*

"You've been talking about the problem of having a softball game when there isn't enough equipment. Let's see if we can show what could happen if the only boy with a softball wanted some special privileges.

"Let's pretend this part of our room is a place where you could play ball. Our scene begins with someone suggesting two names for captains, who will choose up sides. At this point, the boy who owns the ball says he will take his ball and go home if he can't be one of the captains."

Next, you would select some pupils to play the roles and you would give the audience their instructions.

"Who wants to play one of the roles? Jack, you want to be one captain? Ok. Dave wants to be the other captain. Rod wants to be the boy who names the captains. All right, Who wants to be the boy with the softball? Ralph says he will play that role. Now, let's have three more boys who will be team members.

"The rest of the class will be the audience. You watch what the actors do and say. Think of how the actors must feel when certain things are said and done. And think of other ways this problem might be solved."

Then, you would review the situation and have the actors begin.

"Each of you pick an actor's name for yourself. Tell each other who you are. You are on the field. You want to get the game started. Go, team, go!"

Bob: "Come on, let's play ball!"

And off they go. Within moments the confrontation occurs, a solution is proposed, and the solution is challenged with a threat. Several things may now occur. The boys may take the ball away from Chuck. There may be a fight. Or, some compromise may be worked out. In any event, words are spoken and acts are performed.

Role playing provides pupils with an opportunity to learn to reflect on interpersonal experiences. The primary value in role playing lies in drawing conclusions about the relationships between certain acts and their consequences. This being the case, *reflection takes place in the discussion that follows the role playing.* Through discussion, the teacher and pupils try to get at cause-and-effect relationships, reasons and motives, standards for judging behavior, and alternative solutions for solving interpersonal conflicts.

Some teachers fail to use role playing because of two fears. They are afraid that the audience will associate the role with the actor to the extent that discussion will focus on the child rather than on the role he played. They also fear that they will be stuck with an unfortunate solution—that perhaps the players will beat up Chuck and steal his ball. The answers to these fears lie in two elements of role playing.

First, improvisation mirrors what a child knows or believes he feels. But the teacher can counter this by stressing explicitly that a child's acting is not to be viewed as his own behavior. She may do this by introducing role-playing situations in which certain characterizations are required. "We need two girls to play roles. One will be a tease, a girl who loves to pick on other girls and make them appear dumb. Who wants to try to be a tease? Carla? Thank you, Carla, it's a hard role to play." The actor must be freed from worry about appearing mean or foolish. The character he portrays may be heartless or a clown, but the viewers should realize the actor is "just acting." Thus, without demeaning the actor, the classroom audience can later comment objectively about the role played and the confrontation.

Second, if the role playing has produced a highly undesirable solution, the audience can suggest other solutions. Members of the audience can assume the roles and work out their alternative solution. A theater audience may be restricted to seeing only one author's solution to a conflict, but a role-playing audience can replay a scene and thus explore any number of possible endings.

HUMAN INTERACTION AND LEARNING

The lives of pupils are filled with conflicts, some minor and some major, arising from contact with other pupils and with adults. Because one source of content for the social studies is the actual lives of children, role playing becomes a useful tool for learning how to resolve some interpersonal conflicts. The conflict may be as simple as reducing conflict over who should clean up the art corner after a map has been painted. Or it may be as complex as reducing conflict over the use of playground equipment when second and fifth graders go to recess at the same time. The role-playing situation may also deal with out-of-school situations. How does Billy keep from stealing candy when all his friends raid a drugstore? How does Mary Jane avoid the gang of older boys who like to pull her braids? For example:

> Two ten-year-old girls are watching eight boys playing work-up in softball. The girls want to play but aren't sure how the boys will react. How do they get into the game?

> Stan, Pete, and Sam are good friends. Stan has no pencil so when Pete goes to talk to the teacher, Stan takes a pencil from Pete's desk. Sam sees this happen. When Pete gets back to his desk, he says, "Someone took one of my pencils. Who took it?" Stan says, "Not me. I've got a pencil of my own. See." What does Sam do?

> Carla and Tina are talking quietly. Tina says, "Aren't you happy we're both going to Mary's birthday party?" Mitzi breaks into the group, "Did you two hear about Mary's party? I'd sure like to go. Did you get invited?" What do Carla and Tina say?

Another area of human interaction open to role playing lies in learning history or literature through dramatization. Who did what at the Constitutional Convention, and why did he do it? What else could Tom Sawyer have done when he fell for Becky? What could Senators A and B say to President C about the undeclared war with XYZ? How would the chairman of Super Steel react to Ralph Nader if both were on a television show discussing ecology?

There is an old cliché about the number of people who actually take part in a two-person conversation. There are Carol and Alice and what each thinks she is saying, what each thinks the other is saying, and what each thinks the other thinks she is saying. Make it a four-way conversation by adding Bob and Ted, and the whole thing may become so complex that nothing will really happen. The same is true of pupils. How a pupil interacts with others depends on how he feels toward others, how he views the feelings and acts of others toward him, and how he feels about himself in light of his perception of how the others view him.

Teachers can help children explore this maze of feelings and perceptions by getting them to analyze their answers to such questions as these:

"What did he mean by that?"

"What would I mean if I had said that?"

"What would he think I meant if I had said that?"

"How do I feel about what he did?"

"How does he think I feel about what he did?"

"How would he feel if I did to him what he did to me?"

There is always the danger of challenging a pupil's sense of worth if such questions are put directly to him. There are times when direct questioning is called for, but role playing often offers the possibility of freer discussion. The main advantage of role playing is that the pupil can reflect objectively on role behavior rather than on his own behavior. Of course the teacher seeks to change his behavior from undesirable to desirable, but the indirect approach may be the more profitable means to this end.

TOOLING UP FOR ROLE PLAYING

To state the obvious, you ought to begin by reading some of the literature on role playing, by thinking out how you want to use it with your class, and by practicing it with some of your friends. A number of books and articles are listed for you at the end of this chapter. They treat the theory behind role playing and provide enough illustrations to be helpful in planning experiences for your pupils. The suggestion to try role playing with some friends will give you a feel for the reactions of the role player and will alert you to some of the hidden problems that can suddenly emerge from a role-playing situation.

Depending on who you read, there are from three to seven steps in a role playing sequence. Reduced to a minimum, the steps are the warm-up, the action, and the discussion. The *warm-up* involves the identification of a problem situation, the assignment of specific roles to be played, and instructions to the observers. It is important for the actor to know whether he is just any second grader or one with certain feelings and ideas. The observers need to know whether they are to pay attention to specific actors and events or to watch the general interaction.

Action covers the time from when the teacher says to begin to the time when she calls a halt (for whatever reason) to the role playing. Primary graders may be active for only a few minutes, although they may go on for 10 or 15 minutes if the confrontation feeds on itself. Upper-grade pupils may also exhaust their ideas in a few minutes, but they often can carry role playing for as long as a half hour. During the action, the teacher must pay close attention to what is said and done, to emotional reactions, and to cause-and-effect exchanges. Generally, she shouldn't interrupt unless the actors get completely away from the problem or seem likely to become violent.

The evaluation should begin with the teacher helping the pupils shed their roles. There should be no comments about Jimmy being nasty, only about Jimmy's ability to act the role of a nasty boy so realistically that Mary reacted to his projected nastiness just as she might have in a nonacting situation. The point is that discussion should focus on role behavior as it was acted out, not on Jimmy as a person. Next, the class analyzes the content of the session. How did so and so feel? Why did she react the way she did? What did her action lead to? What else might she have done? What might the consequences have been if she had? The actors can tell how they felt during the session and can discuss the motives they had in mind for the ways they acted.

During discussion, the teacher must be open-minded about comments. She must avoid direct criticism of pupils' opinions. It is better for the teacher to bite her tongue than to bite off a pupil's head by making him feel wrong or inadequate. There are several alternatives for solving the question of Chuck and his softball. If someone insists Tom really should punch Chuck in the nose, the teacher kills the discussion if she says, "That's not the right thing to do!" She should try to get the class to state and explore other alternatives, but she won't be successful with role playing if she gives the class the idea that she has *the* right answer. If they see you believe you do have the answer, they will guess until they hit on it. When they do that, they are back to playing word games with you. If you can't lead them to find a better answer than Tom slugging Chuck, then you face a problem that can't be solved in one role-playing session.

Next, you need to guide the discussion so pupils attempt to apply any ideas generated by the role playing to problems they have faced or to problems they think they might face. This refocusing of discussion helps provide for the transfer of their conclusions to something other than role-playing situations. Last, the class can consider the value, or lack of value, in this type of classroom experience. Did they enjoy playing roles? Did they enjoy watching others play roles? Did they learn something they can use in their daily lives? Do they want to use role playing again? Why?

ROLE PLAYING AND SOCIOLOGY

Role playing and sociology are paired in this chapter primarily because sociology provides so many concepts that can be explored through role playing. In fact, role playing can be utilized with ideas and situations from any of the social sciences. Concomitantly, sociology can be studied through the use of any of the other methods discussed in this book.

Sociologists study the way humans interact with each other. The sociologist is not as interested in production as the economist is. He is not as interested in power as the political scientist is. The sociologist does, however, manage to poke his scholarly nose into every form of man-to-man, man-to-group, and group-to-group relationship. In his pursuit of truth, the sociologist tends to work with specific analytical ideas within four general areas of ideas: social organization, social interaction, socialization, and social change.

Social Organization

Every human has basic *physiological needs* that must be met if he or she is to survive. Everyone needs food, water, rest, and shelter; without them, hunger, thirst, exhaustion, or exposure leads to death. The human child cannot meet its basic needs without help, so the child must be raised as a member of a *group,* usually the family.

The human adult could live alone and meet most needs, but the life of the dependent child conditions most persons to live in groups. Life in a group leads to the acquisition of a set of *social needs.* A person's needs for security, for love, for recognition, and for response are met within group life. A person's happiness is partly dependent upon the reactions of others to his or her attempts to satisfy social needs.

Because humans have needs and because needs are met within group life, humans form and live in groups. Because of such differences as age, sex, ability, and responsibility, a person plays different roles in different groups at different times in his or her life. A male child, for example, plays the roles of son, brother, and playmate with his parents, siblings, and friends, respectively. As an adult, he plays the roles of father to his sons and daughters, of husband to his wife, of son to his father and mother, of son-in-law to his wife's father and mother. He plays other roles in relationship to his grandparents, brothers, sisters, cousins, nephews, nieces, and so on. He also plays different roles within each of the other groups to which he belongs—in his job, in his poker club, in his circle of family friends.

Partly because of the group to which he belongs, partly because of the roles he plays, and partly because of such other criteria as birth, race, wealth, and education, he is seen by others as belonging to a particular socio-economic *class.* His class is part of a set of classes, arranged in some rank order. The members of each class have certain socioeconomic expectations for themselves and for the members of each other class. A person may move from one class to another, but the result of such *mobility* is that he takes on the distinctly characteristic behavior and beliefs of his new class.

Humans also organize themselves in certain ways to solve economic and political problems. In our society, for example, it is easier for an individual to meet his needs through a *division of labor* than through his or her own efforts alone. Each of us may work, but our work tends to be *specialized.* Some of us grow food; others transport food; others sell groceries; still others manufacture farm machines, trucks, and store fixtures; still others keep records, handle money, or manage the activities of others. Because we specialize in what we produce, we are *interdependent;* each of us must do his work or the complex *system* we have for getting food from the farm to the table breaks down.

Whenever a group fails to help people satisfy their needs, people create a new group in an attempt to solve the problem. Each of us belongs to a number of *communities of men*—the family, the neighborhood, the local community, the state, the region of states, and the nation. We have also created a network of larger-than-national relationships with the people of other nations in other parts of the world.

Social Interaction

Group life implies social interaction with others. The four commonest forms of interaction are *cooperation, accommodation, competition,* and *conflict.* The nature of any of these forms of interaction is determined by a person's feelings toward other people and the task or situation involved. For example, a person might cooperate with six other people he hates if the task is to rescue a child who has fallen into icy water. Or, two sisters who love each other can compete for the affection of a parent. Accommodation is a matter of accepting working arrangements with others in a particular situation even though these persons have little in common with each other in other circumstances. Conflict implies ill-feelings and the possible use of force. Day in and day out, every person interacts with others in these ways.

Face-to-face interactions that occur in small groups or among individuals are called *primary relationships.* The individuals in primary relationships directly affect each other, get to evaluate each other's beliefs and behaviors, and have the satisfaction of participating with other. *Secondary relationships* are those where someone represents a large number of people. The mayor, the senator, and the school-board member represent large groups of people. They know few of their constituents; they seldom meet them face to face, but they act (or purport to act) for the benefit of those they represent. Our society, particularly in economic and political affairs, is characterized by a dependence on secondary relationships, and thus an individual often finds himself disturbed by his inability to influence directly those who make important decisions affecting his life.

All groups have some form of *social control.* The commonest form of social control is based on *norms* derived from custom or tradition. Through these informal rules of behavior, the group brings pressure to bear on a member who violates its norms. Pressure to ensure conformity to norms takes many forms—ranging from praise, rewards, and acceptance to gossip, shunning, or banishment. Formal rules of behavior are called *laws,* and laws are always paired with formal penalties of some sort. Laws function to reduce conflict and to increase conformity.

Socialization

By socialization, the sociologist means the ways a society teaches its members, as children and adults, to be members of an organized group. The *family* socializes the child as he grows, by teaching the limits of acceptable and nonacceptable behavior. Speech patterns, manners, and modes of dress are established in the early years. Interests, beliefs, and concerns are also developed within the family. Socialization is both formal and informal. The child is taught to use a fork in a formal way, but he learns how boys act or don't act through both formal and informal means. As soon as the child begins to interact with *neighborhood* children and their parents, he comes under their socializing influences. The *school* then adds its efforts to mold him in certain ways. The *communication media,* from comic books to television, fill his mind with ideas about which behaviors bring which rewards. In our society, socialization goes on until death. Old timers, or senior citizens, learn patterns of behavior appropriate to living together in retirement centers.

The members of a group learn specific behaviors commonly accepted by that group. Within our society there are many groups based on differences in class, religion, money, and ethnic heritage. A society has its subsocieties and each subsociety has its own mores and behavior patterns. Each subsociety socializes its own members, and to some extent influences the socialization of members of other subsocieties.

Social Change

Every society and every culture change with time. The rate and magnitude of change depends on attitudes toward change, on contact with other societies, and on the ability of the society and the culture to support the economics of change. The rate of change in a culture depends partly on *invention* and *technology*. If invention is encouraged, the possibilities for change are high. If a people actively seek technological applications of their inventions, then change is enhanced. *Migration* and *borrowing* influence change. These two ideas are especially useful in history. Explorers brought corn, the white potato, and tobacco (among other things) to Europe. Settlers from Europe and Africa brought their ideas and tools to the Americas. Today, migration may not play too great a role in inducing change, but borrowing still occurs. An American physicist reads an article published in an Italian journal and borrows an idea; in time that idea influences some new invention or discovery. Modern *communications* play a fundamental role in bringing about change. Most people in the world today have either radio or television or both, and they learn to desire new products from what they hear or see.

Social Problems

The literature of sociology abounds with unsolved social problems. How do we resolve differences among our social classes. How do we handle poverty in the midst of plenty. How do we handle the problem of population growth. How do we feel we influence our government in an age of increasing secondary relationships. How do we get justice from our laws and our courts. How are adults to learn to adjust to such rapidity of change that their work skills become obsolete every five years. How do we become inventive in our political and social affairs in order to narrow the gap between our material and our human achievements. How do we control pollution without eliminating industry.

You need to be a student of sociology if you wish to help pupils develop concepts for needs, roles, norms, groups, division of labor, and other ideas used by sociologists. You need to be able to pick certain social problems from life and from the literature of sociology—and to be able to pick those that influence the lives of your pupils. The subject matter of sociology holds great potential for use as content in the social studies. The choices are yours to make.

Role playing and sociological ideas have a sort of natural affinity, but case studies, simulations, source materials, and other means of learning are equally effective. Again, the choices are yours to make.

INFLUENCING CHANGES IN ATTITUDES

The topics of role playing, sociology, and changes in attitudes are mutually reinforcing. Attitudes are always a source of concern to teachers, for attitudes predispose a pupil to behave in particular ways. Further, the moral question regarding the right to attempt to change attitudes always worries the conscientious teacher. And the teacher feels baffled because attitudes seem to change with glacial slowness.

The elementary teacher is more fortunate than her high-school counterpart, for the elementary pupil seems to hold fewer attitudes and to hold them somewhat less tightly than the high-school student. This difference may be an illusion, but I suspect it holds some water. The elementary pupil is introduced to more wholly new topics than the high schooler. The young pupil has not been subject to as many years of reinforcement of existing attitudes. And the young pupil tends to trust his teacher more than the high-school student.

If these differences are true, what are the implications for you? First, you can affect some pupil attitudes to some extent. You can influence attitudes toward new things and events more than you can influence already existing attitudes. You can influence weakly held attitudes more than you can influence those the pupil hold dearly. There is one more factor you must consider: attitudes are changed in the same ways they were originally learned—over a goodly period of time and with a goodly amount of satisfying reinforcement.

A fairly common experiment on attitudes goes something like this:

1. A group of pupils, all from the same grade, are divided randomly into three groups.

2. Each group is pretested for certain prejudices.

3. Each group is exposed to a different set of experiences.
   a. Control group A is merely tested.
   b. Experimental group X sees a film on prejudice.
   c. Experimental group Y sees a film on prejudice and discusses it.

4. Each group is posttested for prejudice.

The results usually show a number of things:

1. The pretesting will show there are people in *each* group with high, low, and intermediate degrees of prejudice.

2. The control group will show little or no change between the pretest and the posttest.

3. Both experimental groups will show a significant reduction of prejudice.

4. Experimental group Y will show the greatest reduction of prejudice.

5. The amount of information learned is related to the initial degree of prejudice; people low in prejudice will learn more than those high in prejudice.

If a retention test is given again, six or more weeks after the film was seen, two results may be observed:

1. The film and discussion group will maintain the greatest amount of change.
2. But, there will be a gradual shift back toward the initial attitudes in both experimental groups.

There are a number of factors influencing any methodology you might devise for attempting to change attitudes. The strength of the initial attitude of a pupil influences the amount of factual content he will learn and the extent of change in attitude. A pupil with a negative attitude may ignore or distort certain unpalatable facts. Discussion helps pupils clarify facts, feelings, and ideas, and gets all three out in the open where a variety of positions may be examined. The extent to which a pupil participates actively in a discussion is tied to the amount of change in his attitudes. Lastly, the change in attitude learned from the classroom experience will be maintained only if there is some sort of continual reinforcement.

Is the teacher a prestigious enough figure to cause changes in attitudes? My observations lead to three conclusions. The primary teacher can produce some attitude change simply because "she says so!" In the upper grades, very few teachers have the prestige to influence changes in attitudes just because they are who they are. When teachers lead pupils to find facts for themselves or to solve a problem by their own efforts, then there is more attitude change than when a teacher merely rewards a pupil for agreeing with him.

Some teachers attempt to cause change and to influence its direction by arousing fear. This was a common approach when I was a child, and it still shows up today. "If you kiss girls, you will catch a horrible disease that will make your nose rot off!" But such appeals have limited influence. I noted with great interest that girls' noses never rotted off, so a seed of doubt was planted through observation and thought. This seed of doubt, in time, demanded experimentation—so experiment I did. The primary product of the whole experience was my consequent distrust of *that* teacher's information.

Actually, a minimal emotional appeal is more effective than a strong, fear-inducing appeal. There is an interesting reason for this. Fear arouses strong tensions that must be reduced in some way. Some pupils stop listening and ignore the content of the message. Other pupils turn their anxiety toward the person delivering the message.

Some teachers stay away from emotional appeals and attempt to influence change through the use of logical argument. Assuming you know the facts on both sides of an issue, there are three approaches you can take: (1) You can present the facts on only one side of the issue. (2) You can present the facts favoring a position first, and then present the facts opposing that position. (3) You can present the opposing facts first and the favoring facts second. The procedure you choose should depend on what you perceive as the initial attitude of the pupils you most want to influence. If those pupils are opposed to your position, then they are most apt to respond favorably by any presentation using both sides of an argument. If this is a reasonably new topic, use the favorable argument last; if it is a topic of review, use the favorable argument first. If the pupils are initially favorable to your position, then they are likely to respond to a presentation of favorable arguments. Using both sides of an issue works best with the better educated, no matter what their initial position is on the issue.

If a pupil belongs to a tightly united group, then neither he nor his friends will be influenced much by direct attempts to change attitudes set by group standards. Attacking a dominant attitude of a group has little desired effect on pupils who value membership in the group. Indeed, a direct attack usually strengthens the attitude held. The tough part of group influence is that you get change only if you discredit the leaders in the eyes of their group or if you can get the leaders to change their attitudes. With groups, you must work on the leaders; you must be reasonably indirect; you must avoid fear-arousing appeals; and you must try to tie a change to some outside behavior model that the group admires.

One of the easiest influences a teacher can bring to bear on attitude change is personal involvement in a psychologically fair classroom climate. By psychologically fair, I mean a pupil is free to express an opinion without you or the class attacking that person's sense of worth. You can't say, or imply, that he is a bad person or has bad ideas. You can attack the form or content of his argument, or his sources, or his illustrations of consequences. But you don't depreciate the individual—brainwashing is not cricket. What counts, in a most effective way, is the active participation of the pupil in the process used to influence change in attitude. For example, you might ask three groups to read a message on the origins of prejudice: "Prejudice is Infectious." One group simply reads the message. One group reads the message and then reads a television script based on the message. One group reads the message, then tapes the message for a television program, and then makes a speech on the message. The pupil in the third group tends to change most. Why? Because in the taping and the speech, he was playing roles. As he tried for realism, he began to think and feel as a person who wanted to get his message across would think and feel. By playing a role, the pupil begins to understand how a person living the role would think and his attitudes begin to change in the direction implied by the role. Note carefully, please, I said "begin to change." One role-playing experience does not bring about sudden, complete, and lasting changes in attitude.

Role playing has its advantages for influencing attitudes. You can concentrate on group leaders. You can evoke prestigious models. You can get free, open, rational discussion, in which everyone participates, of the content of the roles played. You can use role playing frequently and thus work for reinforcement of earlier changes.

Role playing takes a certain amount of courage and imagination on your part. You have to suspend judgment for long periods of time in the hopes of seeing changes you desire become established. You have to be able to live with openness and freedom. You have to recognize when a child's sense of integrity is unduly threatened. You have to work your creative faculties overtime to dream up role-playing situations and scenarios. But, if you can handle these difficulties, your reward is seeing decent, rational, humane behavior develop in your pupils.

SUMMARY

Role playing is a means of learning facts, influencing attitudes, and changing behavior in the elementary classroom. Role playing demands improvisation of dialogue, the realistic taking of roles, and reasoned discussion of the action involved. In almost every case there is a dramatic situation setting the scene for some form of conflict. As this conflict is resolved or heightened, pupils begin to see the content of role playing as cause-and-effect relationships, as reasons and motives, as standards and judgments —all open to discussion and examination.

Role playing must occur in an open, free, and fair atmosphere intended to protect each pupil's dignity and integrity. Viewers should realize the participants are just acting; actors are not to be discussed except in the sense that their acting was realistic. The content of their dialogue is subject to discussion, as are whatever attitudes, beliefs, and ideas seem to lie behind the actors' acting. To repeat, discussion focuses on role behavior as it was acted out, not on the actor as a person. If a teacher can't accept this dictum, her pupils would be better off if she would avoid role playing as a means of learning.

Sociology provides an unusual amount of potential subject matter for role playing. The major areas of sociology suited to role playing are social organization, social interaction, socialization, and social change. Each of these areas abounds with social problems ripe for conflict and conflict resolution.

One major social problem is that of changing undesirable attitudes. The use of the term *undesirable* implies philosophical considerations, but such questions as poverty, peace, discrimination, and justice demand concern, whereas problems of hair length, playing cards on Sunday, and the daily eating of green vegetables are not likely to bring our world down around our ears. Attitudes are learned early and are highly persistent. Thus, changes in established attitudes are difficult to effect. Probably the most useful procedure is to enlist the pupil in an active consideration of changing himself. Leaders are the key to change in group members, but it seldom helps to attack the group directly. Mild emotional appeals are far superior to fear-arousing attacks on individuals or groups. Role playing helps bring about changes in attitudes if everyone participates in open and rational discussion of concrete content of the roles played. Frequent role playing provides the reinforcement to stabilize changes in beliefs, attitudes, and behaviors.

SUGGESTED READINGS

Atkinson, Gretchen, "The Sociogram as an Instrument in Social Studies Teaching and Evaluation." *The Elementary School Journal,* October, 1944, pp. 74–85. (This article provides, in the clearest possible terms, a sound example of how to test for attitude changes in social studies.)

Berelson, Bernard and Gary A. Steiner, *Human Behavior: An Inventory of Scientific Findings.* New York: Harcourt, Brace & World, 1964. (Jam-packed with conclusions of experiments with human behavior. Not much discussion, but one finding piled on another. Very helpful on attitude change.)

Chesler, Mark and Robert Fox, *Role Playing Methods in the Classroom.* Chicago: Science Research Associates, 1966. (An excellent source for beginners; first-rate annotations of earlier articles.)

Gayer, Nancy, "On Making Morality Operational." *Phi Delta Kappan,* vol. 46, no. 2, October, 1964, pp. 42–47. (More help in here for you than in most books; beautiful discussion of mandatory and permissive language. Great discussion on how differences arise within general standards accepted by all sides to an issue.)

Learning, vol. 1, no. 2, December, 1972. (This issue deals with values; it is not directly applicable to role playing, but you ought to become familiar with the journal.)

Shaftel, Fannie R. and George Shaftel, *Role Playing for Social Values.* Englewood Cliffs, N.J.: Prentice-Hall, 1967. (*The* classic work. Enough said?)

EXERCISES

1. The single, most worthwhile activity would be for you to read Shaftel and Shaftel, and then, with some classmates, role play a few of their selections.

2. Try your hand at creating a role-playing situation; don't hesitate to imitate the Shaftels, you won't go wrong with their model. Then make your own notes for conducting the warm-up, action, and discussion sequences.

3. Find the Atkinson article in the dusty part of your library. After reading it, set up a similar project for social studies with some imaginary class divided along some lines you hope can be overcome.

4. Read the Gayer article, reduce it to a tape recording, and present the tape to your class. Her position is debatable, so you should get some spirited discussion.

Film and the Study of Other Peoples

Most teachers recognize that films provide an interesting interlude for a heavily textbook-oriented course of study. The film used in this situation provides relief, as well as an opportunity to learn. Most teachers also know that films sometimes help keep pupils quiet during the last part of a Friday afternoon. In this case, the film is merely less obnoxious than most other school activities. Films are misused more often than other types of material for learning. Consequently, many good teachers assume that any use of film reflects poor planning or poor learning situations.

Nothing could be further from the truth, for as with any approach to learning, the usefulness of the tool is limited by the teachers' technique. In the hands of the skillful teacher, film provides a basis for excellent learning experiences. If a film is well conceived, if it meets high technical standards, and if it deals with events and conditions within a pupil's comprehension, then the use of film can provide for concept development and reasoning of several kinds.

USING FILMS

The first comment about using film must be tied to purposes. Why did you want to use *a* film in this situation? Why did you want to use *this* film?

Films are not selected out of thin air, except as a crutch on days when nothing seems to be going right. Usually, the teacher and the class have selected a topic and thus know they will be dealing with, say, families of the world, or life in the city, or the geography of the Northeast. When a general topic is known, the role of film is to provide the basis for an experience that substitutes for interaction with the real thing or situation. If you want something on family life in Japan, it would be nice to fly to the land of chrysanthemums and observe a family or two. Barring that possibility, a film may be a great substitute.

The reason for using a particular film rests on your judgment, after previewing the film, that it will serve a set of purposes for your pupils. You know your class has interests about the food, clothing, games, work, and other activities of people. You like the film because it shows the relationship between a natural environment and the ways people do things. You believe your class will be attracted to the humor, or plot, or problem, or slice of life around which the film was shot. You see the possibility of pupils expanding their concepts by reflecting on what they see and hear in the film. Whatever they may be, you should have some clear and direct reasons for electing one film (or a set of films) rather than other films available to you.

Once you have decided to use a film, you have three questions to answer. How will you introduce the film? What will you do while the film is running? What will you do after the film has been viewed? There are a number of ways to introduce the film. You can tell the story of the film part way through and get the class to anticipate the remainder. You can ask the class what they think they will see. You can tell an outrageous lie, see if anyone challenges you, and then run the film to see who is correct. You can locate the area, make some predictions about the people and their lives, and then check out the predictions. Anything that will help motivate children will serve as an introduction.

Some films are meant to be stopped so the pupils can discuss or argue a point or make a prediction. Most films are meant to be run completely through. Unless a film specifies an interruption, it probably works best to run it completely through the first time it is shown to a class.

After the film has been viewed, the key activity is discussion. What did they see? What interested them? How was the Japanese family like their own? How was it different? Were their predictions correct? No one can predict all that might be discussed about a film, but you should work to involve every pupil in the discussion. Then, consider whether or not the film should be run again. Are there areas of argument among the pupils? Are there questions that might be answered by viewing the film again? Are there details that were missed? A rerun can often help with such questions.

I also used to rerun a film with the sound off and let pupils take turns narrating the film.

In wondering how I might give you an idea of how to use films, I began to think about the ideas an advisor, an editor, and a producer work with in making a film. I dug around in my files and found three sets of old notes. The first was a memo on a proposed series of films on children living in various societies around the world. The second was a memo to me from the producer, which amounted to a rough shooting script; the third were some notes I used in writing a teacher's guide for the film.

The Original Idea

Memo

Subject: Family Film Series

To: Chris Hansen, Authentic Pictures
              Ed Meell, Editor in Chief, McGraw-Hill Text-Films

From: John Lee

Audience

Kindergarten through sixth grade. Keep narration to a minimum so teacher can adapt use of film with any age group.

Focus of Film

Emphasis must be on children in a family, although the viewer must see relationships of children to adults. Enough shots must show natural environment, so viewer can relate activities to surroundings.

General Idea

Every society is composed of families, and all families engage in certain common activities. The way an activity is carried out, however, depends on the resources available and on the customs and traditions of the society. All families must provide themselves with food, but the kind of food, source,

---

means of preparation, and manner of eating vary from society to society. What we are after is enough visual detail about activities within a society that our viewing audience can imagine what is is like to belong to the society shown in the film.

Basic Human Activities

We need to include the following activities in each film:

1. Producing and consuming goods and services — Types of shelters, food grown or purchased, clothing worn.

2. Transporting people and goods — Types of vehicles used by children and families; also public and commercial transport can be shown in backgroun shots.

3. Communicating ideas and feelings — How does family get its news? How do they communicate with others? With each other?

4. Organizing and planning — Who makes the rules for the family? Who makes plans for the family? Who makes plans for the family and who carries them out?

5. Protecting and conserving — How does the family keep children safe and healthy? How do they care for animals and property?

6. Educating — Who in the family teaches what to whom? How? What other ways are available to help a child learn?

7. Playing — What games do the children commonly play? How does the family have fun as a family?

8. Traditions — What ceremonies does the family observe? How is a birthday celebrated? How does the family express itself religiously?

9. Aesthetics — What does the family do to make the home or articles attractive? Do any members play instruments, dance, or produce works of art?

Story Line

Vary this from film to film. Use small plots or slice of life technique.
Show problems to be solved. Use humor wherever possible. What we want
is a day in the life of a family; thus the story line will depend mostly on the
natural activities of the particular family you are permitted to film.
Remember, we need enough realistic details so the viewer will (1) gain
enough accurate information about life in a society so that he can (2)
compare and contrast his life with that of other youngsters.

The Shooting Script

Memo

Dear John:

Enclosed is the script for family life in Malaya, We Live in a Kampong.
You will see the rushes on this film next Tuesday afternoon. Hope we hit all
the points you wanted.

Cordially,

Ed Meell

Family Life in Malaya

We Live in a Kampong

(13 Minutes)

Credits pan over green rice fields to village. Rice growing in water-flooded
fields.
MS [a medium distance shot] Mr. Bint Kasim (father) leaves with buffalo.
In the back his house on stilts, wooden house with roof that is partly gated

iron and partly thatch. His two daughters, 8- and 11-years-old, come out of house—leaving for school.

CU [a close up shot] They put shoes on at the foot of stairs.

MS Girls leaving with school bags. Aslan (name of boy) sits on stairs putting his shoes on. Mother comes from inside house, sits down and combs his hair.

Aslan leaves house, joins Munah on road, while father, with buffalo, passes and talks to them in Malay: "Make sure you learn a lot in school today."

Aslan's friend, Munah, also with school bag, cones down village road. Waves Aslan on. (Both girls and boys in school uniforms.)

Father walks down road with buffalo, while old woman with basket on head passes.

Pan with the two boys and girls across green rice fields, walking to school.

CU Small wooden bridge across little stream on which older boy is standing fishing. Boys stop, talk to him, and then run off.

Boys pass through ripe rice fields where woman is harvesting rice with a sickle.

Boys walk along on paved road with motor traffic. They pass sign saying: Mashid Tanah English School (Primary). CU of signboard.

Boys arrive in school just in time to join lineup. Entering three-story, modern school building.

Interior classroom: Chinese-Malay teacher (lady) at blackboard says: "[in Malay] Repeat after me: [in English] My father works in the field with the water buffalo. It is hard work." Children repeating in English.

Father harrowing with buffalo in water-soaked field. Modern road and car traffic in back. Man on bicycle also on road.

(Sound on the picture: "My mother taps the rubber trees and collects the latex which she makes into rubber sheets.") We see; Mother tapping rubber tree. She cuts a fine layer off the bark and the tree starts bleeding. Latex drips into cup, in this case, half a coconut, fastened to tree.

Mother collects latex into buckets. She carries buckets with yoke over shoulders, leaving field.

With yoke and two empty buckets, older daughter leaves house. Pan with her past shed where women are coagulating the latex.

CU mother pouring acetic acid into form with latex and stirring same, which then coagulates.

Girl takes bucket with water from well next to shed. She brings water to shed. Mother pours it on concrete floor to clean floor and prevent latex from sticking.

CU mother squeezing thick square form of coagulated latex into thinner sheet.

Girl winds wringer, and mother puts the latex through the wringer, which is thereby squeezed into quarter-inch sheet of rubber.

Mother walks to yard between houses, hangs up rubber on a bamboo pole to dry.

Father arrives with buffalo. Kids run to meet him. Father puts Aslan on back of buffalo. They walk past shed to well, where boys help wash buffalo. (Sound on film: "This cools off the buffalo and prevents the skin from drying and cracking. It is done daily.")

CU boys throw water over their feet to clean them.

They leave and mother arrives to wash clothes. Another daily task. Here we see the two wells. Mother washing clothes on cement around well. (Sound: "Each family has two wells. One for washing and one for drinking and cooking.")

Father on bicycle asks mother something in Malay.

Kids playing hockey, in yard.

Father in market. He buys vegetables and fish. (Cucumbers, eggplants, onions, sprouted beans, and celery are on display.)

CU fish being weighed. (Hand scale.)

Father leaves with fish and vegetables on bike.

Mother cutting bananas from tree with large knife. Then walks to other tree and picks papaya. Walks into house.

Father comes out, picks two bananas from mother's bunch, walks over to monkey tied to pole in yard. Girl brings big ball of heavy string. Father ties one end to monkey's collar. Monkey climbs up coconut palm and picks nuts while kids watch. (Sound on film: "This monkey is kept and trained to pick coconuts. Only two families in the village have a monkey.")

The two daughters pick up coconuts and go to kitchen, while the boys return to hockey game.

Kitchen. Girl picks over sprouted beans. Other girl grates coconut. Mother cooks rice and frys fish. CU fish frying.

Yard with boys playing hockey. Mother comes out and calls in Malay: "Come in and eat."

Interior. Father and girls seated on mats on floor. Mother arrives with food from kitchen. Aslan enters and sits down. They all eat with their hands. Rice, fried fish, curry, eggs, bean sprouts, and cucumbers. Before and after eating they wash their hands in a glass bowl filled with water.

Father gets up and switches on radio. Then sits down and reads paper. Half of each page is set in English letters; the other half in Arabic.

CU radio, which plays Malay music then changes to voice.

Father, two girls and boy sit on floor reading Koran. Father and boy wear hats, and girls wearing scarfs.

Mother prepares beds. She moves pillows on parents' bed into other room.

Kids at table in nightgowns and pajamas. The big girl closes book — her homework is finished — while boy and little sister play dice game.

CU of game.

Bigger girl passes, telling them to go to bed. They pack up and follow girl to other room, where girls get into thin cotton bag and lay down on floor covered with reed mats. Aslan lays down on bed. (Wooden frame covered with similar mat, no matress.) He sleeps with a pillow.

CU of girls and CU of boy's face.

End superimposed over last frame: THE END.

Credits

Sound of frogs croaking starts under kids going to bed and continues over end and credits.

Only natural background sounds and people talking used in the film. No music used.

THE FILM GUIDE

There are three basic elements in a guide to the use of a film. The guide should give the teacher an abstract of the content of the film. The guide should specify the objectives that might be achieved through use of the film. The guide should provide a set of suggested activities for introducing the film and another set of suggestions for activities for after the film has been shown. The teacher can then select, adopt, and expand on this information about content, objectives, and activities.

The content abstract must include a certain amount of "hidden" background information, so the teacher won't have to do a world of research to answer, or to help pupils answer, questions that are certain to be asked.

For example, you will remember that the two boys walked through a field and came to a bridge where a slightly older boy was fishing. The likely pupil question, of course, is Why isn't that boy going to school? In the guide, I added this statement:

> The older boy isn't playing hooky; his classes are in the afternoon session. Many schools in Malaysia are so crowded that pupils can go only a half day.

Another characteristic of the film is the prevalence of green vegetation. But even if that isn't noted, someone is bound to ask: "What's the weather like there?"

> The reason the fields and other vegetation are so green is that it rains, and the sun shines, nearly every day; the temperature is about 86°F all year long.

In the closing scene, the boy goes to bed. He has a pillow, but the viewer sees no blanket. I added this:

> Aslan has a bed and pillow, but it is so warm that no covering is needed.

These bits of information are useful to the teacher, particularly when a question would be difficult to research. There is no reason a teacher should know about double-shifts in Malaysian schools, and it is doubtful that any standard reference would contain this information. The question on vegetation and rainfall, on the other hand, is easily researched; however, a teacher might not consider the answer to be worth a pupil's effort in this instance. These types of comments in a guide are helpful, especially if you want your pupils to develop their powers of observation.

The adviser usually circulates his objectives for a film—his ideas of what he hopes to see in the various scenes—on a memo. If you look back at the first memo, you will note the nine basic human activities I wanted the film crew to consider. The nine categories of behavior are particularly useful, for research has shown that every known society engages in these activities to meet their needs. The universality of the activities, in turn, provides opportunities for comparing and contrasting life in the filmed society with the life pupils know.

With these general categories as a guide, a teacher can pull specific objectives out of the content of a film. For example, the coconut-picking monkey touches on three activities—production, education, and recreation. The monkey helps get food (production) that would otherwise be difficult to reach. The monkey had to be trained and rewarded with bananas (education). And the monkey provides a certain amount of fun for the watchers (recreation). Consider how easy it is to ask questions related to these facts.

What are animals used for in the United States? How did you train your dog? Why do you like to visit the zoo? In fact, the use of muscle power—human and animal—in Malaysia is in sharp contrast to our lives. As categories for goals, the basic human activities have a particular value—if you manage to get at least one question from each category, your pupils get a more comprehensive view of other people's lives than if you concentrated only on production and transportation.

I always hesitate to tell others exactly what goals they should strive for in using a specific film. The Malaysian film could be used as a study of rubber gathering and processing. It could also be used to demonstrate how girls are discriminated against in this society. The matter of goals (or objectives, if you wish) rests with a teacher's insights into what her class needs at a given moment.

The activities you use before showing a film should combine motivation and information. They should also be mercifully brief. Where is Malaysia located? What do we know about it? What do you think you will see? Let's watch and see if your hunches were right.

The activities following a film are critical if you have in mind any goal other than amusement. How are the lives of these people different from ours? How are they the same? How are their lives like and different from the lives of other people we have seen in films? What do you think you would like most about living with the Kasims for a year? What would be hard for you to get used to? What would the Kasim children like or dislike if they were to live in our town for a year? There may be questions your pupils want to research after seeing the film. The pupils may want to role-play certain scenes. They may want to run the film again with the sound off so they can make up their own dialogue and narration.

To give you some general ideas about goals, content, and activities, the next section deals with a social science particularly suited to films and their interpretation.

ANTHROPOLOGY

Anthropology, like history, draws ideas and data from each of the social sciences. But anthropology, unlike history, tends to create a number of analytical ideas useful in examining the behavior of people. Further, the anthropologist has more confidence in the use of comparison and contrast than the historian does.

In teaching anthropology, the era and area under study often is quite remote from the pupil in time and space. Almost from its beginning, popular anthropology has used pictures or film as part of its record of man's activities. The photograph has been used to convince the unbelieving and to provide visual detail. A photograph of a spear thrower, a series of photographs of flint chipping, or a movie of Masai youngsters moving a village herd across the Rift Valley provides accurate detail difficult to equal with either the written or spoken word. Film brings past eras and far areas into the classroom experiences of children.

Today, as never before, the elementary teacher has a range of audio-visual aids, in type of material and nature of subject, sufficient for almost any purpose. Further, the teacher can adapt them to inquiry or to exposition.

The anthropologist deals with *biocultural evolution,* the study of the emergence of common humanity. The term *evolution,* of course, is a red flag to fundamentalists in many communities. There are a great many Americans who believe that Genesis treats the question of man's beginnings quite adequately. Each teacher must answer for herself how she will deal with this problem. My answer was to distinguish carefully between what I asked pupils to know and what I asked them to believe. On the matter of the evolution of man, I never asked a pupil to *believe* either the Biblical or the evolutionary version. I did ask pupils to *know* that some people believe one version and some the other, and I asked that they know both versions. Further, I asked that they know that all societies have some version of how man and woman (or society) was created. Every society has been concerned with who they were and how they began.

Culture and *civilization* are two other key anthropological terms. In a way, each is a "ghost" term, for the anthropologist often is reluctant to define either in a single, neat sentence.

Culture is a technical term referring to the artificial extensions people have created to permit them ever greater control over their natural environment, their social system, and themselves. The human being is a generally nonspecialized creature. Humans aren't particularly fleet; they can't camouflage themselves naturally; they don't have fighting teeth or horns. What each does have is a highly specialized brain and central nervous system that permits thinking, a vocal system that permits complex communication, and two hands that permit the use of a wide range of complicated tools. Humans have one more great advantage—they have specialized in the creation of a complex culture. Humans create ideas and things to serve their purposes.

Culture combines all the material and nonmaterial things people have created. Each human being is born into a society with its own culture and its own history. Because we all are human, we all have had to meet some common needs. Because we all have some common needs, we all have some common activities; we all need food, so all people have ways of producing food. Because of common needs and common activities, all cultures share some characteristics. Because of variations in leadership, environment, beliefs, and customs, each culture differs in some ways from other cultures. All people must eat, but what people eat depends on such factors as environment and technology.

Because of this commonality of culture and of the variations among and within cultures, anthropological data are rich with possibilities for comparison and contrast. Two other terms, *ethnocentrism* and *culture shock,* help explain comparison and contrast. Ethnocentrism refers to the exaggeration of the worth of one's own customs and values. Ethnocentrism is not just believing our ways are best for us, but extending the belief to say our ways are best for others. To fail to acknowledge that other cultures have contributed to our culture also shows a person to be ethnocentric.

Culture shock is what a people suffer as a reaction to the sudden impact of another culture on one's own culture. When one people borrow cultural elements from another people, there may be little cultural shock. For example, our borrowing English common law was not a matter of cultural shock for us. But if one culture thrusts tractors, plows, hybrid seeds, fertilizers, and pesticides on another culture, there may be considerable cultural shock in discarding old farming customs and adapting to the new ones.

Civilization is a term describing a state of culture with certain characteristics. There must be a fairly large population, a certain amount of urban concentration, the production of food surpluses, written records, a knowledge of mathematics, a division of labor, and a system of government. Paul Bohannan, in "Beyond Civilization" (*Natural History,* February, 1971, pp. 50–69), lists these culture traits as necessary to civilization: writing, calendars and mathematics, food production, trade, government, and stratification. A reading of this article will give you the details about each trait; for example, under government, he discusses administrators, armies, contracts, police, and bureaucracies. Professor Bohannan then goes on to deal with the present problems of civilizations: computers; poverty; specialization of tasks; government, bureaucracy, and tyranny; status; garbage and urban blight; and, population control and room to live.

Anthropologists also deal with prehistory and with ancient history. They examine how people learned to make tools, use of fire, communicate, and hunt in teams. They examine the beginning of agriculture and animal husbandry, of villages and cities, of wealth and power. When dealing with these topics, teachers are on somewhat safer ground than when dealing with evolution, for even though we do not know all we want to know about early man or ancient civilizations, we do know something about those times and cultures.

Educators argue, often fruitlessly, about the worth of teaching some of these anthropological ideas to children. I have no hard-and-fast advice for you, but I must point out that children are fascinated with early man. Yet, I have seldom seen comparisons and contrasts made between early man and people today. The child learns that paleolithic man had fire, and sometimes he can tell you fire was used for warmth, cooking, and keeping animals away. Seldom can he guess at what it meant to keep a fire buring— who gathered the wood, who fed the fire, and who was yelled at if it went out. Seldom can he talk about the fire as a social center—a place where people gathered and talked and remembered. And seldom can the child discuss what people had to invent to take the place of *a* fire in our own times.

Many teachers fear the intrusion of anthropology into the elementary classroom. Their fears are reasonable, for they are based on limited coursework in anthropology. In another sense, their fears are unfounded, for if they ask the same categories of questions about others as they ask about Americans, they are on the right track. Some anthropologists will think my comment inelegant, but what an anthropologist really wants to know are answers to three questions. What makes this society tick? What can we learn about ourselves by studying this society? How do we get along with them on their turf and in our international relations?

How are their families composed? Why? To what effect? Who has what power in the family? Who plays which roles? How are conflicts resolved within the family? Outside the family? What allegiances are there to others outside the family? How do these allegiances benefit both parties? These are questions we can ask of any society.

Why teach anthropological content in schools? The simplest answer I know is Bohannan's: the culture that was adequate for yesterday is inadequate for today and disastrous for tomorrow.

OTHER VISUAL AIDS

There is a significant difference between the verb forms *to see* and *to look at*. *To see* implies perception, to be aware of something. *To look at* implies some sort of search or close examination. Except for the blind, all of us see. When we look at something, we do it because we are interested or because we intend to find out something. There are at least three visual aids that can be looked at, discovered, rather than merely seen.

The Filmstrip

Filmstrips are easier to preview and run than films. They are cheaper than films, and they can be stored in your building. Often, however, they are cluttered up with captions filled with difficult words. Even when they are captionless and used with records, the narration may be abstract and pedantic. For these two reasons alone, filmstrips need to be previewed.

The advantage of the filmstrip is obvious. You can vary the amount of time spent on each frame, depending on the amount of detail in the photograph. Control of time also permits you to let questions be raised and answers be proposed before the filmstrip is turned to the next frame.

Filmstrips have been written on almost every conceivable topic in the social studies. There are filmstrips on the school, on pickup truck assembly, on corn growing, on sewer systems, on court cases, on value dilemmas, and on interpersonal conflicts. You name it—and the chances are you can find it. The basic sources are:

Film Catalog for Classroom Use. Modern Talking Picture Service, 2323 New
   Hyde Park Road, New Hyde Park, Long Island, NY 11040.
Educators Guide to Free Films.
Educators Guide to Free Filmstrips.
Educators Guide to Free Tapes, Scripts, and Transcriptions.
Educators Guide to Free Social Studies Materials.
Elementary Teachers Guide to Free Curriculum Materials.
   All from Educators Progress Service, Inc., Randolph, WI 53956. (Each
   costs $10 or so, and should be part of your school or district library.)

It is now possible for you and your pupils to make your own filmstrip
or series of 2-×-2-inch slide mounts. All you need, other than regular classroom materials, is a product called *Rite on 35,* made by the Bro-Dart
Company (see your local art-supply store).

There are a number of ways to make a filmstrip, but the most efficient
is to approximate the procedure used by professionals. You start with an
idea of what you want to get across to viewers. Next, you draft a script,
numbering each frame as you go. For example:

6. Caption: Which of these ways takes the most muscle power?

7. Art: Show a woman washing clothes with a washboard and tub.

8. Art: Show a woman using a modern automatic washer.

After the script is edited, you make a storyboard. On construction
paper, rule off the frames needed until you have the number of frames
needed (40–80). Number each frame and put the artist's name after it.
Cut the storyboard into strips. (If Janie were doing frames 6 through 13,
she would get a strip with eight frames. She then prints in her captions and
draws in her artwork.)

Figure 24.

6. Janie	7. Janie	8. Janie
Which of these ways of washing takes the most muscle power?	Janie's drawing of woman, tub, and washboard.	

An easy-to-use guide comes with the *Rite on 35 kit* and its use assures that spaces and alignments will be accurate, no matter how many pupils work on a filmstrip. After Janie finishes her artwork and captions, and has them edited, she traces them onto the *Rite on 35* material and puts in whatever colors she wishes. When all pupils working on the project are done, the filmstrip is ready to show.

Making a filmstrip is usually a group project and can involve a division of labor. Each group can include an editor, researchers, writers, artists, and caption printers. Or, one person can do all these jobs for a few frames. In either case, the product will be one of the most carefully observed visual aids you will ever find used in a classroom.

The Study Print

The successful historian knows the value of verisimilitude. Of all visual aids, the study print offers clear and extensive detail to the viewer. The print focuses on a part of an object, an object, or a small set of related objects. The print is a magnification of detail for the purpose of creating opportunities to observe the nature of the object. For example, I have seen youngsters pore over a study print of a mature corn plant. Before they began, they knew about corn flakes, but they knew nothing about growing corn. By the time they were done, they had excellent visual images of the stalk, leaves, ears, and tassels. The viewing, in turn, led the pupil to research the function and uses of each of these parts of the corn plant.

There are more good study prints for use in science classes than there are for social studies. If you are good with a camera, you can take closeup shots of things that interest you and have them made into slides. Almost every filmstrip projector has a slide attachment, and you can use your slides as study prints.

Magazines are sometimes excellent sources of study prints. If you are studying the characteristics of high plateaus, *Arizona Highways* will meet your needs. *Natural History* and *The National Geographic* are old standbys. *Petroleum Today* and other industrial or business journals are great for some purposes. *Scientific American* has some of the best graphs, line drawings, and flow charts you could ask for.

You can combine pictures to make a studyboard—a display concentrating on a single concept. See Figure 25.

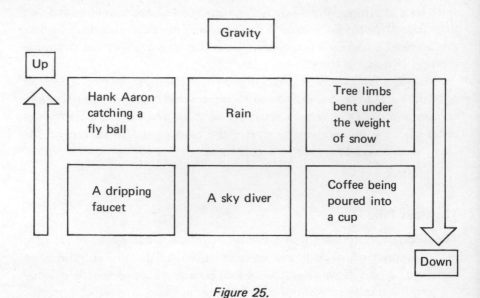

Figure 25.

I always try to use 10 or 12 pictures. I leave the caption slips blank for a day or so. Then I ask, "What one word should we print in here? In here? In here? Thus, we get at the meaning of gravity visually and we arrive at these conclusions: Down is toward the center of the earth (or toward a center of gravity). Up is away from the center of the earth (or away from a center of gravity).

Similar studyboards can focus on homes around the United States, pets around the world, signs and signals, level land, sloping land, and so on. Groups of pupils can choose their own topics, do their own research, construct their own studyboards, and see if the rest of the class can discover the meaning the group tried to convey visually.

Art Exemplars

Painters' canvases are mirrors of their time. They reflect the artists' beliefs, events, culture, fears, values and manners. But the painter goes beyond just recording the events of his time: he also gives the world a view of the past.

Giotto raised the curtain of the Dark Ages and brought to viewers glimpses of angels from heaven. Leonardo da Vinci pioneered inventions way beyond his time and Michelangelo gave us an image of God. Rembrandt, with his lights and shadows, gave the world insights into the culture of his time, and David helped start a revolution. Rubens played the dual role of artist-diplomat.

Paintings of great artists have influenced the thoughts and actions of men throughout the ages. Studying a work of art motivates pupils into further study of a country and its culture. A painting is not merely an arrangement of colors, lines, and shapes to give pleasure to the eyes, but also an historical document, like the Bill of Rights, or the letters of Napoleon, which can tell about a subject, a period, a country, or an artist.

The use of works of art and their creators in stimulating the learning of social-studies concepts is as unlimited as the number of works of art and the number of classroom teachers. There are two criteria you should consider in choosing art for interpretation in social studies. The painting must have a direct relationship to the social-studies topic. The time and event should correlate with the social-studies topic.

What kinds of games were played by children in the 1600's? Students can study Pieter Bruegel's *Children's Games* and try to count how many games and what types are depicted in the painting. There is only one adult in the picture, a woman at the side window throwing water on two boys who are fighting. You could divide the class into groups and have each group see how many games they can count (over 70) and how many children are in the picture (about 200). With this close observation, pupils become aware of the dress and customs, as well as of other aspects, of the seventeenth century Low Countries.

In many of his portraits Joshua Reynolds used the "dress up theme." Contrasting Reynolds' work on this theme with that of other artists makes interesting study both of famous works of art and in the dress and culture contrasting. Reynolds painted *Master Crewe as Henry VIII* in the middle 1700's. Crewe's stance, his look, his dress, all imitated a Henry VIII portrait which Hans Holbein had painted over 200 years before. By looking at *Master Crewe as Henry VIII* closely one can see a half smile painted on Master Crewe's face. He is almost laughing at the stance in which Sir Joshua Reynolds is painting him. Another Holbein painting shows Henry VIII confirming a charter to the company of barber-surgeons. Compare all three paintings. Notice the arrogant outlook Henry VIII has toward his subjects. Were the people, 300 years later, still impressed by him? Or were they mocking him by having a small boy imitate him?

It is not always necessary to use a particular artist with a particular work of art. At times it is better to contrast and compare times in history with the artists' style and subjects.

Pieter De Hooch (1629–1684) and Jan Vermeer (1623–1675) were both artists of the middle-class people. They were called the "squared away" artists, because they loved to paint pictures of interiors with doors that opened up into courtyards. The people who lived in these houses were good, solid people. This can be seen in De Hooch's painting, *Interior With Cardplayers*. Examination of the painting reveals emphasis on squares and rectangles, repeated over and over again. The rooms are blocks opening up from room to room. One room is dark, the next light, and so on. Examine the painting carefully. Do you notice anything that isn't squared off? Pictures from the Old World tell students many things about their own heritage. These are the houses and the people that the Pilgrims knew when they stopped in Holland on their way to the New World. From such homes came the emigrants who founded old New Amsterdam, where one can imagine steep-roofed houses like the ones in both Vermeer's and De Hooch's paintings.

George Catlin's *A Bird's Eye View of the Mandan Village* (1832) depicts the life in an Indian Village located north of St. Louis, Missouri. It shows how the Indian chiefs dressed. Inquiry and examination of this painting can lead to research on other painters whose works depicted the life of the early pioneers, the landscapes, and the wealth of the natural resources which abounded in the New World in the 1800's.

Winslow Homer's *The Pioneer* (1900) gives the viewer the feeling of the loneliness the first settlers must have felt on their way west. Much can be learned about the territory by studying this painting and other works by Homer. His *New England Country School* visually represents the style, dress, and type of schools in the late 1800's. It is a picture of a small schoolroom flooded with afternoon sunlight. The scene, with its warm colors, gives the viewer the first impression of a pleasant, informal air. Upon closer observation, however, you can see the rigidity of the students' postures, the stern look of the teacher and the sterile atmosphere.

Frederick Remington's *The Sentinel* (1890) shows the rugged appearance of the people who pioneered the Far West. Determination is written on every line of the sentinel's face; with his gun ready, he stands guard over his few possessions in the covered wagon.

John Mix Stanley made many trips into Indian country to paint the life-style of various Indian tribes. The oil, *Prairie Indian Encampment,* is extremely useful for inquiry and discussion about different cultures, the needs and wants of people, and how within each culture these needs and wants are satisfied in different ways.

The *Self Portrait* of Captain Thomas Smith is one of the few seventeenth century paintings about "Americans" for which the artist is known. Smith was both a mariner and a painter by profession. In the painting his hand rests on a death skull and on a poem, in the latter he bids farewell to the world. Everyone likes a mystery. Why was he bidding farewell to the world? Was the hand on the skull symbolic of his farewell, or was he a pirate at heart? In the left hand corner of the painting is a picture on the wall showing ships burning in the harbor. Why? Was he confessing something or was he prophecying? Such pictures as Smith's motivate pupils to ask questions and engage in research.

John Singleton Copley's *Portrait of Paul Revere* depicts Paul as a plain, hard-working man. But even after just a casual glance at the picture, the viewer can observe that Revere's profession was that of a silversmith. The details of the painting show that Revere was a gifted artisan, and also shows the types of tools a silversmith used in the 1700's. Discussion and research into Revere's life also reveals that not only was he known for his famous ride and his talent as a silversmith but also as an engraver. Revere became interested in the movement for independence and engraved a number of political cartoons. *The Boston Massacre* is an example of Revere's engraving. Even though Revere was not a professional engraver, his forceful rendering of contemporary issues earned him recognition. An art activity that could correlate with Copley's portrait and Paul Revere's life would be *Etching Made Easy* (see Chapter 15).

What did George Washington really look like? Many pupils ask this question, and the answer is that no one really knows. Using art exemplars of George Washington makes this an interesting social-studies topic. The most famous painting, by Gilbert Stuart, probably hangs in most schools in the United States. No one really knows, however, whether it is true to life or an idealized portrait, for in Stuart's day the artist's custom was to idealize his subjects, especially the important ones. When Washington was 25, Charles Wilson Peal painted his portrait. When Washington was 40, Peal painted another portrait of him. John Trumbull painted Washington at 48. The contrast between the Peal and the Trumbull is great. They do not look like the same person. Not too long ago an almost unknown portrait of

Washington by Archibald Robertson was returned to this country from France. Robertson had come to the United States to do a portrait of Washington for the Earl of Buchan, and while here he did one for himself. Referring to the miniature, Washington wrote: "The manner of its execution gives no discredit to the artist I am told." Robertson's work was done when Washington was 60, four years before the Stuart portrait, yet it looks remarkably different. A picture of Washington in "advancing age" by William Williams was considered an excellent likeness by persons who knew Washington well. What did Washington look like? Why are there no pictures of him smiling? Mystery again—a motivating force for learning social studies.

SUMMARY

Although film can be abused as a means to learning, it also may be used as a most effective avenue for getting at any type of goal a teacher has in mind. Over the past few years commercial producers have turned out films and filmstrips of high quality on almost every topic that might be included in the social studies. This combination of subject matter makes the use of film in the classroom a positive delight.

Films are not made in a vacuum. Someone—adviser, editor, producer —had an idea. That idea, in turn, gets translated into a series of visual scenes, with or without dialogue or narration, that presents the original idea in a form youngsters should be able to interpret. Out of their discussion of what they saw, out of their reasoning about what they knew before and what they observed, out of their emotional reactions to their observations come the learnings the film producer and the teacher hoped to achieve.

One of the limitations on elementary social studies is the children's lack of prior experience in dealing with past times and distant places. The first can be recreated on film, the second can be reproduced on film. Each of the social sciences has something to contribute to film, but anthropology has particularly pertinent insights to offer when other peoples and other places are the subjects of study. The language of anthropology is a useful one for comparing and contrasting life in a variety of societies and cultures.

Filmstrips, study prints, and art exemplars are other effective visual aids for use in social studies. Most particularly, they are useful because you can freeze time with them. That is, you can stop and concentrate on one view for as long as you or your pupils wish. Again, these visual aids may be used as means for achieving any type of goals you have in mind.

The award-winning film discussed earlier in this chapter is *Family Life in Malaysia: We Live in a Kampong.* (Code 618203-7–13 minutes–Color) It is published by McGraw-Hill Films, 330 West 42nd Street, New York, N.Y. 10036, and is one of 12 films on family life around the world.

SUGGESTED READINGS

Gerlach, Vernon S. and Donald P. Ely, *Teaching and Media: A Systematic Approach.* Englewood Cliffs, N.J.: Prentice-Hall, 1971. (A sound basic book of use to elementary teachers.)

Muessig, Raymond H., "Using Projective Pictures." *Social Education,* vol. 22, May, 1958, pp. 250–52. (An interesting article on the subjectivity of what we see when we view visual aids.)

Nichols, Arthur S., "Photographs as Sources of Information." *California Council for the Social Studies Review,* vol. 11, Fall, 1971, pp. 13–14. (An article you can adopt if you use a camera.)

EXERCISES

1. Locate and preview a film with a title that appeals to you. Take brief notes as you view it. Then list the activities you would use before and after showing the film to youngsters. What goals would you have in mind for using this film? (This is a good small group activity.)

2. Pick a concept you would like to develop meanings for, and then construct a studyboard for display to your classmates. Leave the caption slips blank for them to fill in. Ask them to critique your project.

3. Write a script and create a storyboard for a filmstrip you would like to see used in elementary social studies. If you can get some Rite on 35 materials, turn out the filmstrip for your class. (This is a good small group activity.)

4. Choose an art exemplar and work up a brief lesson plan (use the back of an envelope as discipline in brevity) for a particular grade. Ask a few of your classmates to role-play pupils and teach them the lesson.

Pot Pourri

For an author, ending a book is like dying a little death. For the reader —an author hopes—the ending is like a little birth. Your view is a little clearer; your head is a bit more together; your hopes are higher. Why not? The world of social studies no longer belongs to me or to my peers. It belongs to you, because you occupy the classrooms.

When you, in your near future, walk into your classroom, close the door, and choose to direct the attention of your pupils to certain ideas and values, then you are defining the social studies. I know this, and in a way I resent it. I'm no longer one of your operational definers; I'm an observer and a critic confined to the sidelines of my own choosing.

This last chapter is not a bang or a whimper but a measure of what you choose that social studies shall become. If I have planted a few ideas, stimulated your imagination, or made you reflect on what your social studies might become, then I thank you for letting this book influence you a bit.

RANDOM THOUGHTS

If you can get pupils to ask you the questions you usually ask them, you don't have to worry much about extrinsic motivation.

If a class is eagerly working to solve a problem they want to solve, you don't have to worry much about discipline.

If a class has stated its own rules and set its own standards for judging the usefulness of those rules, then you don't have to worry much about juvenile outlaws.

If every pupil in a class loves, respects, or admires you, then you don't have to worry about anything except living up to their expectations.

The worst punishment is to ignore a kid all the time; the second worst punishment is to humiliate a kid at any time. Never punish a child when he is mad; you can't get him to reason out a situation if he is deep in emotion. Never punish a child when you are mad; you can't be reasonable when you are emotional.

When you go into your first classroom, you have a great illusion of competence in what you know. After a time you lose that illusion and you know children know a great deal. You know more of what is in the books, but you don't know more about what makes up the life of a seven- or nine- or eleven-year-old. When you find out children know a great deal about life, you can have a bad time until you figure out that nothing can happen to you that has not happened to other teachers.

In school, a child lives in three worlds. He lives in the world of the classroom—a real world peopled with other children and an adult. He lives in the world of his memory of the immediate outside community—a real world he will return to at the end of the school day. He lives in a world of books and films and other materials—the world of other people in other places and other times.

In each of his worlds the child deals with other people and other things. Some of his dealings are pleasant; some are not. In dealing with others, the child makes choices. He chooses to please himself or his friends. He chooses to join a gang or avoid it. He chooses to believe that all people are human or that only some have value.

The job of the teacher is to use whatever she can from the worlds of the child, so he will make the wisest possible choices. To do this, the teacher must help a child clarify the values that influence his behavior. To do this, the teacher must help a child develop the intellectual tools he uses to reason effectively and humanely. To do this, the teacher must help the child build the research skills he needs to locate and interpret information about the human species and its environments.

The sagas or folklore of all peoples in all places in all known times have one central persisting theme: We are a people with a beginning and a tradition, with our hopes and aspirations; and our culture must be transmitted if we are to survive.

The transmission of a culture should not be modeled on the mechanics of industry but on the agriculture of nature. Provide a rich soil, a healthy climate, proper nourishment, and let children grow. The teacher's role is to fertilize, but remember that no grain grows in pure manure.

EQUALLY RANDOM CONCLUSIONS

Over my 25 years of teaching, I have seen a set of ideas come nearly full circle for the third time. Since Sputnik the pattern has been:

1. the full-throated cry for a return to *subject matter,*
2. which turned into a reasoned argument by each of the *social sciences* for stress on its questions, content, and mode of inquiry,
3. followed immediately by the identification of *generalizations* from the social sciences,
4. and then by a stress on *concepts* as necessary building blocks for generalizing.
5. Then comes a renewed concern for *values* and *attitudes* as antidotes for overintellectualization.
6. This shift to values requires more attention to firsthand *childhood experiences,*
7. and this introspection brings the *humanities* into the picture,
8. followed, for no apparent reason, by a return to *skills,*
9. which brings up *subject matter* again.

The sequence isn't always exactly the same, but my approximation is reasonably correct. Around the fringes of the mainstream flow two other warm currents.

One of the warm, gulflike streams has to do with reasoning, valuing, conceptualizing, generalizing, and the like. They usually crop up after we suffer a bad attack of subject matter in which the approaches are memorizing and reciting. Unfortunately, an emphasis on thinking calls for a great deal of thought by teachers and a tolerance for differences of opinion. This strain is too much for some of us, so we mouth the mighty slogans of rational thought and clarified values, while falling back into our old ways by asking questions whose answers are in the book. Fortunately for children and society, enough of us do believe in thinking to keep the process alive beyond the early years, when thought is a natural process.

The other warm stream spawns means of organizing materials and activities beyond the basics of books and lessons. Units, cases, sources, role playing, dramatic play, and audio-visual approaches find their ways into our classrooms now and again, and we all benefit from them.

What I have never been able to understand about this razzle-dazzle of shifting, repeating, spiraling emphases is why we, as teachers, simply do not *constantly* acknowledge our need for each of these elements in social studies. What is the point in a program without subject matter? Aren't two of the sources of subject matter always the social sciences and the life of the child? Aren't concepts and generalizations, both factual in nature, the economical distillations of subject matter? Don't we have valuational reactions to most things we learn? Don't we always have to balance our emotions with our intellect? And how do any of us benefit if a rational, humane person lacks the will or skill to act on what he knows and feels? My position on these questions and their elements is that social studies must blend all of them into a coherent set of experiences productive to children and to the society in which they live.

If there is one sound bit of advice I have for you on *methods,* it is this: variety is both the meat and the spice of learning social studies. Vary your methods! Use a text, shift to role playing, show a film, make a map, use dramatic play, shift to cases, hold a mock trial, simulate running a business, and so on, and so on. Any of these can become old hat if it is used day after eternal day. My favorites are dramatic play, simulation, and cases. They are my favorites because I'm good at them; I know it, the pupils know it, and observers know it. For some reason, I'm weak with role playing, so I don't use it too often. The point is painful, but a teacher should use the methods (note the plural) that work for *her* and with *her* pupils. But, you have to try the full range and give each a fair trial before you settle for the four or five staples in your teaching diet.

If your pupils haven't used the type of materials and activities you want to use, then they have to learn the new ways. They learned early to recite from a text, but they had to learn that approach. Beginning teachers often miss this point, thinking the pupil only has to learn the content of an activity. Wrong! The pupil also has to learn the form of the activity. Lawyers neatly talk about substantive and procedural questions. We social-studies teachers should borrow from them and remember always to plan for procedural, as well as for substantive, learning.

The first 20 chapters emphasized, directly or indirectly, the unity of thinking, feeling, and acting. Wise decisions are based on solid reasoning and self-acknowledged values. If I haven't made it clear before that by wise decision I mean *a wise decision to act* in a particular way, then let me be clear now. There are few instances in which we do not blend perceiving, feeling, thinking, and acting in the freedom of our own lives. A school assignment or a teacher's question may call for far less—can you list the states in the Northeast region, or who shot Hamilton, or what was the color of Jackson's kitchen cabinet? These call for low-level intellectual responses, but the pupil responds to them as a whole human being. He views the question about Hamilton as trivia. He feels cruddy about the task, because the only thinking he has to do is to remember and the only doing he has to do is to open his mouth and blab out the answer. You may not recognize the levels of perception, thought, emotion, and action, but they are there. The products of low-level responses are crippling—inattention, resentment, dulling of curiosity, the belief that memorizing is thinking, and that quiz-kid answers are really worth learning.

I've tried to keep this book reasonably free from jargon and cant, but I haven't tried to keep it free from bias. I am biased toward a social-studies program that focuses on reflective thinking, freedom of expression, and the subject matters of a child's life and the social sciences. I am biased toward a social-studies program that is accurate, learnable, and useful. To the extent that a program reflects the academic disciplines, it is accurate. To the extent that it follows principles of psychology, it is learnable. To the extent that it develops thinking and valuing through concentration on the problems and successes of society, it is useful. I am biased toward a social-studies program that grounds itself in concrete learning situations of such variety that every pupil has opportunities for success.

NORTON PEARL

I began this book with my recollection of three teachers; I end it with a fourth example.

As a beginning teacher, I had been sent to the big city—Dee-troit—to observe in a few elementary schools with a high proportion of black pupils. I had visited two schools and found they were traditional in a bad sense. The classrooms were silent. The pupils were sullen. The teachers carried thick maple yardsticks with one end drilled out and filled with lead. The yards were torn up; windows and lights were broken; toilets were clogged;

walls were covered with uninspired graffiti. These two schools were institutions in the worst sense of the word.

When I walked up to Washington School, I noticed grass and flowers in
front of the building. The kids on the playground were having a great time.
Inside, the walls and floor were clean; pupils were moving freely but quietly
in the halls; and I could hear the buzz of activity in the classrooms.

I checked in at the principal's office. A clerk glanced at me, but I was
greeted by a pupil sitting behind the principal's desk. The principal was
down in a third-grade room, the pupil said, and then he gave me clear
directions on how to find the room. I strolled down the hall and looked in
the boy's toilet. No broken glass, no lights out, no dirty toilets, no dirty
words on the walls. I went on down the hall, nodding to boys and girls who
examined me silently and gave me shy little smiles.

I found the third-grade room, tapped on the door, opened it, and
stepped inside. The class was gathered in a semicircle, some sat on chairs,
some sprawled on the floor. If anyone noticed my entrance, they gave no
sign. In the center of the half-moon, on a third grader's chair, sat a man
of 60-odd years with a head of thick, wavy, white hair. Although he barely
moved his head to look from pupil to pupil, I got a clear impression of
catlike, rippling power. I found a chair.

"Tell me a story," the old man said, "about how people first made
laws."

I had never heard a group tell a story; one pupil began and others
broke in to add their ideas.

"There was this caveman, see. He lived in a cave and hunted for food.
The lady of the cave kept the fire going. The kids picked berries and nuts.

"Sometimes the caveman took his oldest boy hunting for rabbits. That's
the way kids learned, see? They got to go along and see how their old man
did it. Back then, people had to catch rabbits with their hands, and that's
hard to do.

"One day a rabbit ran into a hollow log. The dad got at one end, and
the boy got at the other, and the rabbit sat in the middle of the log. The
caveman and the caveboy waited and waited. The rabbit waited, too.

"Then the caveman saw a stick. He picked it up and stuck it in the log.
He poked the rabbit and it ran and tried to get past the caveboy. But the
boy grabbed it. He carried the rabbit home and his dad carried the stick.

"The mother cooked the rabbit. They had fire. I saw a picture of it in a
book. The guy in the next cave smelled the rabbit and came over for a bite.

They were all sitting around the fire when the new guy saw the stick and wondered what it was.

"He picked it up and the man—you know, the man who found the stick—he went 'Raarrr' at the new guy. They didn't have any words in those early cave days, but *Raarrr* meant 'Keep your cotton-pickin' hands off my stick!' "

For the next 30 minutes or so, I listened as those third graders talked about law and why people made laws. Then the old man said, "What do you want to talk about tomorrow?" And the pupils shouted a bit but finally decided on brotherly love.

I followed Norton Pearl from class to class for three days and I never bothered to visit any other schools. He asked the damnedest questions of kids. "Why was money invented?" "Why do people live in groups?" "What do you have to *have* to make a car?" "What do you have to *know* to make a car?" "What do you need to stay alive?" "How do people learn?" "What does it take to make you happy?" "Who do you admire the most?" "How do you make your momma love you?" "Why do we grow cherries instead of lemons in Michigan?" And in every case the pupils came up with their answers. That old man never told anyone anything, he just asked and asked and asked.

I found out the pupils pretty much ran the school. Teachers were guides, not commanders. The sixth-grade teacher said to her pupils, "How do we get the morning milk to the kindergartens? You solve the problem and then tell me how you did it." The fifth-grade teacher said to her pupils, "The second graders want to look for bugs on the playground. Will you plan out a set of experiences for them?" The third graders told me, "We're being trained to run the school. You start in here and when you're a sixth grader, you've got it right."

"Progress can only be measured by the overt behavior of individuals," Mr. Pearl told me. "And the value of a school subject can be measured only when children have opportunities to apply what they know and how they feel to the life they live. A school is a community and the conduct of life in any form of community requires overt behavior. It is a teacher's job to see that her pupils have a chance to solve the day-by-day problems of living together, as well as to understand the persisting problems of living in societies."

That's good social studies.

Good luck!

Index